BUSINESS ECONOMICS IN A RAPIDLY-CHANGING WORLD

LABOR MARKETS

DYNAMICS, TRENDS AND ECONOMIC IMPACT

BUSINESS ECONOMICS IN A RAPIDLY-CHANGING WORLD

Additional books in this series can be found on Nova's website under the Series tab.

Additional e-books in this series can be found on Nova's website under the e-book tab.

BUSINESS ECONOMICS IN A RAPIDLY-CHANGING WORLD

LABOR MARKETS

DYNAMICS, TRENDS AND ECONOMIC IMPACT

SAMIR AMINE
EDITOR

Nova Science Publishers, Inc.
New York

For permission to use material from this book please contact us:
Telephone 631-231-7269; Fax 631-231-8175
Web Site: http://www.novapublishers.com

Additional color graphics may be available in the e-book version of this book.

Library of Congress Cataloging-in-Publication Data

Labor markets : dynamics, trends and economic impact / editor, Samir Amine.
p. cm.
Includes index.
ISBN 978-1-61470-825-4 (hbk.)
1. Labor market. 2. Unemployment. I. Amine, Samir.
HD5706.L2185 2011
331.1--dc23
2012010406

Published by Nova Science Publishers, Inc. † New York

CONTENTS

Preface

This book focuses on the views of the NAIRU (Non-Accelerating Inflation Rate of Unemployment) concept. It introduces unemployment in economic growth models. It presents empirical studies which analyze and discuss the labor market evolution in several countries and regions such as the European Union and the United States. The unemployment benefits and its effects on unemployment in the United States is also evaluated. An empirical study is presented which analyzes the evolution of regional labor market dynamics in Taiwan.

LIST OF FIGURES

LIST OF TABLES

INTRODUCTION

The first chapter entitled *Unemployment and Macroeconomics* discusses the views of the NAIRU (Non-Accelerating Inflation Rate of Unemployment) concept. By analyzing the Phillips curve and its rearrangements, the authors demonstrate that, especially in the economic crisis context, more attention should be paid on unemployment and income inequalities. In the same macroeconomic approach and using the nonlinear modeling of the Phillips curve, the second chapter entitled *Nonlinear Phillips Curve and Growth Cycles* introduces unemployment in economic growth models. According to authors, "the resulting dynamics of the model show that unemployment rate and *per capita* income fluctuate in between a sequence of stable points". In a theoretical study, the third chapter *Productivity and duration of employment in a Matching Model* suggests a matching model where firms face a trade-off between the productivity and the expected duration of jobs. Financing the unemployment costs by lay-off taxes lead the firms to internalize the budgetary consequences of their technological choices, reducing at the same time unemployment.

The second part of this book presents empirical studies which analyze and discuss the labor market evolution in several countries and regions such as the European Union and the United States. Indeed, the fourth chapter entitled *A Single European Labor Market? How Differences in Skills, Competitiveness, and Productivity Are Shaping the 'New' Map of Europe* attempts to answer the question "Why the European labor market is unable to allocate resources on an intra-EU basis?" Through a comparative study of European Union countries, the author indicates that "the competitiveness requires a highly skilled and adaptable workforce, along with efficient labor markets and an innovation-conducive environment and a sophisticated business culture." Remaining in the European Union, the fifth chapter, *Spanish Unemployment and Beveridge Curve shifts,* analyzes the unemployment rate evolution in Spain from 1977-2003. By using a Beveridge curve, the authors illustrate that "structural unemployment seems to be one important explanation for unemployment, in particular for the period where it's observed unemployment-vacancy curve shifts". In another European Union country and according to a dynamic model estimated by the GMM (General Method of Moments) methodology, the sixth chapter *Regional Unemployment and Spatial Interactions in Greece* studies the factors responsible for the evolution of regional unemployment in Greece during 1981-2006. The empirical results point to the "existence of significant spillover among regional labor markets that are responsible for the asymmetric behavior of regional unemployment in Greece".

The seventh chapter, *The Relationship Among Unemployment, Unemployment Duration, and Unemployment Benefits Revisited,* evaluates the unemployment benefits and its effects on unemployment in the United States. Using time series techniques on deseasonalized monthly data from 1959 to 2010, this study concludes that "changes in unemployment benefits have no appreciable effect on the unemployment rate, *ceteris paribus*".

Another empirical study is presented in the eighth chapter *Regional Labor Market Dynamics in Taiwan* which analyzes the evolution of regional labor market dynamics in Taiwan. In this contribution, the authors demonstrates that "interregional migration plays more roles in adjustment mechanisms than any other nation and this implies that labor markets in Taiwan are more flexible and hence lead to low unemployment rates". The ninth chapter, *Strong and weak labor market regions in Australia: Implications for individual employment outcomes,* asks the question of uneven performance across Australia's labor market regions. The study concludes that "the employment outcomes are associated with individual characteristics and circumstances plus regional labor market differentials".

In the framework of a psychological approach, the last chapter, *The Vocational Interests and Values of Secondary School Students: A Three-Decade Evolution in France,* analyzes the evolution of representations about vocational choices of high-school students in France from the 1970s to the 2000s. The author shows that "youth internalize very broadly social change in their vocational interests, in the general values that guide them, and in daily activities they want to do".

Samir Amine

In: Labor Markets: Dynamics, Trends and Economic Impact ISBN: 978-1-61470-825-4
Editor: Samir Amine

Chapter 1

UNEMPLOYMENT AND MACROECONOMICS

***Bozani Vasiliki*[1,*] *and Drydakis Nick*[2,†]**

[1] Department of Economics, University of Crete, Greece

[2] Department of Economics, University of Patras, Greece

ABSTRACT

This chapter is an attempt to review the existing literature and raise questions about the appropriateness of the way that employment policies are set. The current macroeconomic and labor policy is built on the adoption of the Non-Accelerating Inflation Rate of Unemployment (NAIRU). This simplifies the relation between unemployment and inflation, and determines the long-run equilibrium level of unemployment at which there is neither upward nor downward inflation pressures, while any unemployment level below the predetermined NAIRU level itself should be followed by inflation reductions and vice versa. The recognition of NAIRU as the guide for policy decision and its concentration on inflation targeting, is believed to have significantly affect in the shaping the broader macroeconomic conditions, within which the spectacular macroeconomic imbalanced could build up and eventually lead to collapse of economies and the presence of current economic crisis. As a result, the interest in this concept has been resurgent, indicating the need for a basic evaluation of its origins and a brief explanation of some of the claims surrounding it.

This study focuses on the Phillips curve and its rearrangements, discusses the views of the NAIRU concept, evaluates that the necessity that arises from empirical evidence, concerns the appropriateness of mix labor market institutions and laws that will actually protect employment, and concludes that attention should be paid on the unemployment level itself and income inequalities in order economic growth to be raised. Actually, the dynamic economic system can be only balanced by achieving its general reconstruction, which should be represented on the adoption of a full employment target and the regulation of the financial sector in the sense that this sector affects essentially economic process.

---

* E-mail address: bozanivaso@gmail.com.

† ** E-mail address: ndrydakis@econ.soc.uoc.gr.

INTRODUCTION

It is beyond any doubt that the reference point for current macroeconomic and labor policies is the adoption of the Non-Accelerating Inflation Rate of Unemployment (; NAIRU hereafter). This simplifies the relation between unemployment and inflation, and determines the long-run equilibrium level of unemployment at which there is neither upward nor downward inflation pressures, while any unemployment level below the predetermined NAIRU level itself should be followed by inflation reductions and vice versa. Moreover, by considering the consistency of new Keynesian NAIRU concept with supply side economics, the presence of any unemployment gap (except for the case where actual unemployment is close to NAIRU) is assumed to be limited by changes in labor market; the adoption of this framework implies the direct dependence of unemployment on a broad variety of labor market issues and setting policies relative to their treatment. In these conditions, the variable of unemployment is being treated as a structural factor, which actual levels are allowed to be fluctuated around its long-run equilibrium.

However, the recognition of NAIRU as the guide for policy decision and its concentration on inflation targeting is believed to have significantly affect in the shaping the broader macroeconomic conditions, within which the spectacular macroeconomic imbalanced could build up and eventually lead to collapse of economies and the presence of current economic crisis. The reasons for which the NAIRU concept and its policy implications have implicated in the current crisis are reflected on the huge social inequalities, unemployment expansions and low growth levels. As a consequence, the interest in this concept has been resurgent, indicating the need for a basic evaluation of its origins and a brief explanation of some of the claims surrounding it.

Although this study focuses on the problem of unemployment, the fact that NAIRU is set at the center of making labor policy decisions, we examine the theoretical background of this concept. As a result, the first part of this study focuses on the Phillips curve and its rearrangements, since the Phillips curve is the key element about the relation between inflation and unemployment. Hence, in section 2, the study provides a brief representation of the theoretical developments that took place until the introduction of NAIRU in macroeconomic theory. Although, for many economists the concept of the NAIRU is a useful piece of business cycle theory, for a number of economists the NAIRU concept is being of a limited use for predicting inflation, understanding its causes and therefore making employment policies.

Thus, in section 3 we discuss several critical views about the way that NAIRU level is being estimated and determined, while in section 4, we evaluate that the necessity that arises from empirical evidence, concerns the appropriateness of mix labor market institutions and laws that is supposed to protect employment and not constrain economic expansion. The last section of this study concludes that attention should be paid on the unemployment level itself and income inequalities in order economic growth to be raised.

The dynamic economic system can be only balanced by achieving its general reconstruction, which should be represented on the adoption of a full employment target and the regulation of the financial sector in the sense that this sector affects essentially economic process.

THE THEORETICAL FRAMEWORK OF NAIRU

The last few decades, significant developments have taken place within macroeconomic theory in relation to the analysis of unemployment. The most significant among them is the replacement of the orthodox Keynesian Phillips curve, as a framework to examine unemployment, with the supply side framework of NAIRU. This development signifies theoretical changes as well as crucial policy implications. Despite the central role of NAIRU in taking policy decisions, contemporary macroeconomic analysis rarely focuses on their assumptions and their changes in theoretical frameworks, which to a great extent determine their realism and applicability in the analysis of real world economies. Considering all these, we examine the process of Phillips curve form and implications until its connection with the NAIRU concept.

I. The Orthodox Keynesian Phillips Curve: The Basis for Macroeconomic Evaluation

Starting our analysis with the change of the economic scene with the introduction of "General Theory" by Keynes (1936), that led to the development of Keynesian economics, we intent to examine the developments that took place until the introduction of NAIRU in economic theory. The choice of this point is explained by the fact that at its center is set the problem of unemployment.

Besides, Keynes' main intention was to explain at the best possible way and solve adequately, the high unemployment levels that were characterized economies during the Great Depression; this was the outset for a number of changes in economic thought. To be more specific, although until then unemployment was characterized as involuntary and could be faced, in accordance with the "Invisible Hand", through markets' coordination and clearing so as capitalist economies operate efficiently, in Keynesian grounds the assumption about the presence of the positive relation between unemployment and wage gap was rejected. In Keynesian grounds, aggregate demand was recognized to be essential about the behavior of economic activity, while its shortages due to the high volatility of investment were regarded as the driving source of unemployment and economic stagnation in general. In these conditions, unemployment turned out to be involuntary[1]. As a result, in Keynesian demand-constrained economies attention is paid on the appropriate treatment of demand management policies (fiscal policies) in order for economic activity to be upward shifted; suggestions that are enriched with the assumption about the presence of involuntary unemployment even at the equilibrium level (Mankiw, 1990)[2]. In other words, a Keynesian type economic expansion is related with the adoption of policies that provide adequate ways so that the behavior of investment and government expenditures shifts aggregate demand upward and fuel economic activity. This is the main reason for why economic destabilization is usually attributed to the possible negative effects of demand shocks on marginal efficiency

[1] For more informative analysis see, Snowdon and Vane (2005).

[2] Although in Keynesian grounds only demand policies can cause permanent price stability and full employment conditions, the adoption of other policies or their combination with fiscal policies is not rejected as long as they aim at economic expansion (Snowdon and Vane, 2005; Mankiw, 1990).

of investment and thereby on the level of investment confidence, as reflected on Keynes's "*animal spirits*" (Romer, 1993; Mankiw, 1990).

In particular the Keynesian approach is believed to be reflected on the IS-LM model which defines the intersection between product and money markets as the necessary condition for determining equilibrium levels of interest and income rates consistent with both of these markets and the assumptions about wage and price stickiness[3]. In these conditions, money wages and interest rate rigidities cause under unemployment levels in terms of IS-LM. Furthermore, under the assumption about consistency of fixed money wage and price levels with their money market equilibrium, unemployment is attributed to excess labor supply without the equilibrium price affecting money wages (Snowdon and Vane, 2005; Solow, 1979).

Despite the importance of the Keynesian IS-LM system, its implications were characterized as incomplete due to the absence of any reference to price level. Such incompleteness was filled with the development of the Phillips curve that introduced the variable of wage (and later price) inflation rates and provided supporting empirical evidence on Keynes's beliefs about the downward stickiness of nominal wage rates. Phillips (1958) by using data about the British economy during the period 1861-1957[4], examined the hypothesis of whether rates of changes in money wages could be explained through unemployment levels or the rate of its changes[5]. The fundamental characteristic of the adopted sample period was the association of low unemployment rates with rapid wage increases and respectively in cases of high unemployment rates. It is also believed that the provided results, were essentially affected by the specific characteristics of each of the distinguished sub-periods and mainly by changes in import prices on retail prices and thus on the cost of living of workers in terms of real wages. In any case the strength of unemployment rate in relation to wage changes seemed to depend on the unemployment rate itself.

In particular the Keynesian Phillips curve implied an inverse but non-linear relation between the rates of changes of money wages (growth level of money wages) and unemployment levels (rates of changes of unemployment level). Both the structure and the direction of this relation are determined by the intersection between demand and supply for labor and thereby the actual levels of employment and unemployment. Thus, in cases where labor demand exceeds its supply there are increases in money wages that in turn raise firms' willingness to hire more employees, given the higher level of nominal and thereby lower real wages. It is thereby suggested a distinction between demand and supply for labor, which determines the power of employers and employees in labor market (Phillips, 1958).

---

[3] The determination of equilibrium through the IS-LM system is affected by the factors that determine the slope and the elasticity of each curve (respectively to whether economies are closed or open). The significance of the slopes of IS-LM curves is reflected on the fact that their responsiveness to fiscal and monetary policies determines the final impacts from the adopted policies on economic activity (Snowdon and Vane, 2005; Romer, 1993).

[4] Although Phillips (1958) is regarded as the generator of Phillips curve, it is believed that Irving Fischer (1926) initially provided evidences about an inverse relation between prices and employment by using data for the American economy during the period 1915-1925.

[5] The time period that was adopted for empirical investigation did not include the years that were in the wake of periods of rapid rise in import prices and their consequences on the cost of living. Furthermore, the introduction of the variable of cost living allowed Phillips (1958) to reach an inverse relation between levels of unemployment and inflation rates, though the use of this variable is believed to contribute a close relation between its levels and the behavior of money wages (Espinosa-Vega and Russell, 1997).

Indeed, according to Phillips curve implications and the specific characteristics of each period used for estimation the dependence of unemployment relative to wage changes on unemployment rate itself can be suggested (Phillips, 1958). All these implications are reflected on Phillips curve equation:

$$\dot{W} = -0.9 + 9.638(U)^{-1.394} \quad (1)$$

where, $\dot{W}$: the variables of changes in the wage rates.

U : the variable of unemployment rate.

The strength of Phillips curve implications is proved by the compatibility of results that cover the period during 1948-1957 with those of the early period of 1816-1913. But the well fitted data and Phillips curve outcomes are regarded as being responsible for forcing many Keynesians to consider the possibility, in both theoretical and empirical grounds, for long-run stability of the relation between changes in wage rates or changes in wage inflation and unemployment levels. This thought was reflected on a stable long-run relation between unemployment and wage inflation on relatively low levels (Espinosa-Vega and Russell, 1997; Snowdon and Vane, 2005). However, the co-existence of a stable long-run Phillips curve and the Keynesian IS-LM system suggested that price stability would arise in cases where economies lay at levels below full employment so that real income and employment would be affected by shifts in aggregate demand. Such a policy suggestion would be inappropriate in cases where the economy was found at levels above its full employment, since fixed money wages could not respond to aggregate demand shifts. In these conditions it was implied a relation between the Keynesian theory of output and employment with a theory of wage (and later price) inflation (Dixon, 1995).

Although the assumed long-run stability of downward Phillips curve "allowed" policymakers to control both inflation and unemployment levels via the appropriate use of "aggressive" demand management policies and governmental intervention, its adoption raised a number of questions about the labor market characteristics that had affected Phillips' estimations (Espinosa-Vega and Russell, 1997). Questions were also raised about the inability of Phillips curve's to reflect conditions of other economies, apart from the British economy (see Friedman, 1968). According to Samuelson and Solow (1960), this inability was resulted by the differences in institutional and structural characteristics, included in variables and transmission mechanisms of each of these economies that were employed. Furthermore, the fact that Phillips curve estimations included nominal, instead of real, wages, in the sense that workers determine their decisions between working and leisure with respect to the former, raised additional doubts about Keynesian Phillips curve's appropriateness (Friedman, 1968). Considering however, Phillips' (1958) Keynesian beliefs about the determination of the power and social position of each worker as well as the determination of labor costs and thereby firms' labor demand through demand and not real wages, the choice of nominal wages is directly explained. Besides, in Keynesian theory the determination of money wages, contrary to that of real wages, is assumed to be affected by labor and not by product market conditions (Snowdon and Vane, 2005; Romer, 1993)[6].

Another relative question concerns the preference on the use of money wage instead of price inflation in the determination of Phillips curve relation (Friedman, 1968). The dilemma between these two forms of inflation is explained by the concentration of Keynesian economics on aggregate demand mainly and secondly on the supply side, without distinguishing the costs that arise from each side. According to Lipsey (1960), however, the variable of inflation in Phillips curve does not include any supply side elements, while Samuelson and Solow (1960) distinguished between the cost push and the demand pull inflation, which effects on wage and price levels are independent of whether economy lies on its full employment level or below it[7]. As a result of this distinction, Samuelson and Solow (1960) redefined the Phillips curve relation in terms of unemployment and price inflation rates.

All these questions about the Phillips curve and the assumptions, upon which its estimation was based, provided unanswerable evidences about its use as the most representative instrument for stabilizing economies through demand side policies. Additionally, the inability of long-run stable Phillips curve in facing stagnation conditions and reflecting the dynamic form of economy, led to the abandonment of Keynesian thought and the tendency to use monetary policies during 1970s.

II. Phillips Curve and Microeconomic Foundations

Given the inappropriateness of the purely Keynesian Phillips curve in reflecting the dynamic character of economies due to the assumption about anticipated inflation (zero inflationary expectations) its rearrangement was required. Such rearrangement was implied by the relatively high cost in terms of inflation that was needed for unemployment to be settled down, as well as by the harmful constraints that were imposed against economic expansion because of the assumed Phillips curve stability even in the long-run (Phelps, 1967, 1968). In order a more dynamic form of economies to be captured, Phillip's curve rejuvenation took place into new classical and monetarism grounds with the introduction of unanticipated and unexpected inflation rate, the use of inflation and unemployment steady state paths, the constraints against capacity utilization and investment levels as well as the

[6] The concentration of classical and new classical economics on real wages stems from the assumption that the negotiations about the determination of employment levels between employees and employers take place in terms of real wages. As a result, it is considered an inverse relation between real wages and unemployment as well as between fully flexible wages and prices; assumptions that are opposed to Phillips curve assumption about price rigidity (Friedman, 1977).

[7] Considering policymakers' inability in distinguishing inflation sources and thereby explaining satisfactorily the behavior of each of the effects with respect to time that are being examined, as well as the inappropriate explanation about the way that inflation should be treated, Samuelson and Solow (1960) distinguished between demand (demand pull) and supply side (cost push) inflation. In general cost push inflation stands when money wages rise faster than price levels, though in accordance with the proper view wages rise faster than productivity in the presence of excess demand inflation. The importance of distinguishing between demand pull and cost push inflation, proves the overcoming of problems such as the presence of a specific standard from which the price level can be measured or the presence of identification problem that characterises data or even more the independency in a closed economy among the markets.

mechanisms for price behavior for equilibrium to be determined (Phelps, 1967, 1968; Friedman, 1968). Alternatively, Phillips curve was enriched with the introduction of microeconomic foundations.

According to these changes, a downward sloping Phillips curve would lie on a specific unemployment level on the horizontal axis of unemployment at which the equality between expected and actual inflation was ensured so as the former to be unchanged. Thus, when actual unemployment rate was below its equilibrium level, inflation would be accelerated and thereby further employment expansions would take place and adequately for the other side of the inequality. In this case, the implied relation between unemployment levels and inflation rates sets the behavior of the former a good approximation for the behavior of wages (Phelps, 1967, 1968). But the extension of Phillips curve with microeconomic foundations into monetarism grounds was completed with the determination of long-run equilibrium level of unemployment, which according to Friedman (1968) would result from the intersection of the vertical, due to the fulfillment of expectations, long-run Phillips curve with the horizontal axis of unemployment. This long-run equilibrium level of unemployment is well known as the "*natural rate of unemployment*", according to which: "*it would be ground out by the Walrasian system of general equilibrium equations, provided there is imbedded in them the actual structural characteristics of the labor and commodity markets, including market imperfections, stochastic variability in demands and supplies, the cost of gathering information about job vacancies and labor availabilities, the cost of mobility and so on*", (Friedman, 1968, p. 8).

The definition of the natural unemployment rate suggests, in accordance with the Wicksellian definition of the natural interest rate[8], that any decision to keep unemployment below its natural levels is consistent with the adoption of inflationary policies (Friedman, 1968)[9]. Furthermore, due to the dependence of the "*natural unemployment rate*" on specific characteristics, rigidities and imperfections of labor and commodity markets in conjunction with the introduction of price and wage expectations, the constancy of natural rate is no constrained as long as it is assumed to be affected by real factors.

According to Friedman' (1968) and Phelps' (1967, 1968) implications about the introduction of price expectations, the *augmented adaptive-expectational Phillips curve equation* is therefore defined as:

$$\dot{W} = f(U) + \beta \dot{P}^{e} \tag{2}$$

where, $\dot{W}$: the rate of money wages

$f(U)$: a component determined by the state of excess demand and simply a proxy for the level of unemployment.

---

[8] According to Wicksellian approach the natural interest rate, which depends on the actual inflation level, is defined as the distinction between its market and natural levels. Moreover, when interest rate rests on its natural level, the equality of interest rate in capital markets with the return on physical capital as well as the equality between actual and natural unemployment rate is implied; besides, at equilibrium money is neutral and both labor and capital markets are balanced with respect to 'real' market conditions. Hence, in case where natural level of interest rate is above its market level, economy is characterised by inflation and respectively for the other side of the inequality (Snowdon and Vane, 2005).

[9] In this case, inflation arises once its anticipations become known.

$\dot{P}^e$: the expected rate of inflation.

that requires $\beta = 1$, so that no trade-off to characterize the long-run. For the case where $0 \prec \beta \prec 1$, the presence of a long-run trade-off that is less favorable compared to short-run, is implied, whereas for estimations where $\beta = 0$ the Keynesian suggestion for a stable trade-off is ensured.

Obviously, the implications about the presence of microeconomic foundations on Phillips curve are summarized by Friedman (1977) into a relation between real wages and unexpected inflation[10]. But the introduction of expected inflation as the variable that determines excess demand and thereby the levels of changes in nominal wage rates, a "family" of Phillips curves that are determined relative to the expected inflation and its consequences on the other two variables, is suggested. This is explained by the fact that individuals and policymakers form their expectations and behavior, after the choice of optimal Phillips curve with respect to actual conditions (Phelps, 1967). Besides, in the face of unanticipated inflationary expansions the Phillips curve is shifted to new equilibrium points that stand until individuals adjust their behavior and expectations to these conditions[11]. In this case, only temporarily can monetary authorities achieve their targets, since equilibrium comes up at the time when individuals become aware of them and respond to these changes.

In particular, once actual inflation is fully anticipated in the long-run, there is no trade-off between inflation and unemployment, while in the absence of excess demand any shift in money wage, mainly upward, equals to the level of expected inflation rate. However the assumption about the consistency of the natural unemployment rate itself with stable inflation, declares that only unanticipated monetary expansion can push actual unemployment below it. In these conditions, economies will be characterized by inflationary pressures. So, there is no long-run stable trade-off between inflation and unemployment because of the distinction is caused between the short and long-run effects of unanticipated changes in nominal aggregate demand. Moreover, the presence of a vertical Phillips curve requires money neutrality, whereas the procedure behind the possibility of reducing unemployment below its natural unemployment rate is defined as "*accelerationist hypothesis*"[12].

The introduction of microeconomic foundations in Phillips curve was notwithstanding followed by a number of difficulties in making policy decisions, which according to Lucas (1975) could be successfully solved by distinguishing between real and money economy. It was believed that their presence would be figured out by combining the rational expectations with the natural unemployment rate within a Walrasian framework, where continuous market clearing and fully flexible price and wages prevail. Besides, in Lucas' (1975) view the impact of Keynesian business circle approach on equilibrium is determined by considering GDP fluctuations as a disequilibrium phenomenon due to market rigidities. Lucas also notes the possibility for a positive serial correlation between movements of trend and actual output level, which cannot be explained through changes in the production function during the

[10] Due to Friedman's (1968) concentration on quantity theory of money, inflation is attributed to money supply expansions.

[11] As a result, workers do not suffer from complete money illusion, which duration, according to Friedman (1968), is determined by the persistence of unanticipated inflation.

[12] According to accelerating hypothesis any attempt to push unemployment below its natural level is followed by permanent inflation acceleration that is possible to lead to hyperinflation; respectively for cases where unemployment is above its natural rate (Phelps, 1967).

business circle. Considering all these, he (Lucas) claimed that only unanticipated changes in money supply, which in turn lead to unanticipated demand shocks, could be defined as competitive equilibria that affect the economic system and cause errors in rational expectations about prices. Clearly, the combination of unanticipated shocks and incorrect expectations, due to incomplete information, is considered to be responsible for the distinction between actual employment and output levels from their long-run equilibrium (natural) and thereby from full employment levels.

Hence, in Lucas' (1973) view the introduction of the natural output rate implied the dependence of the distinction between actual and natural output level on the deviation between actual and inflation rate. Also the introduction of Okun's Law (see Okun, 1962) that suggests a stable inverse relation between unemployment and GDP allowed him (Lucas) for redefining the equation of aggregate supply and expressing unemployment relative to surprise price change. As a consequence, the *rational-expectations augmented Phillips curve* equation is written as:

$$U_t = U_{N_t} - 1/\phi\left[\dot{P}_t - E\left(\dot{P}_t / \Omega_{t-1}\right)\right],\ \phi \succ 0 \qquad (3)$$

where, U_t: actual unemployment rate

U_N : natural unemployment rate.

$E\left(\dot{P}_t / \Omega_{t-1}\right)$:rational expected inflation that is based on the available information set from preceding period.

$\dot{P}_t^e$: expected inflation rate.

Equation (3) signals that the introduction of rational expectations is consistent with a temporary reduction of unemployment below its natural level that results only from 'unanticipated' or surprise inflation changes[13]. The coexistence of both real and nominal variables in equation (3) breaks down the classical dichotomy between real and nominal variables, since the introduction of rational expectations in Phillips curve allows only for unanticipated changes of money growth. Besides the relation between unemployment levels and inflation rates stands in the absence of any form of "*money illusion*", in the sense that prices clear markets and allow agents to form their expectations optimally (Lucas, 1972, 1973, 1975).

Nevertheless, the adoption of new classical view and its implications about natural unemployment rate implies the appropriate response of nominal interest rate to unexpected inflation shocks. Thus, in cases where inflation changes are once and for all, long-run interest rate remains unchanged since in the short-run interest rates level falls and causes output increases. All these do not concern the case of vertical Phillips curve, since any unexpected inflation shift (usually upward) does instantaneously affect the nominal interest rate (Sargent, 1972; Sargent et al., 1973). Only if interest rate changes are fixed can real economic

[13] The randomly and unpredictability of the short-run trade-off is explained by the fact that the serially correlation of predictable and unpredictable components of unemployment with the unpredictable part of the error term, is explained by indirectly observed variables (Lucas, 1972; Sargent, 1972).

magnitudes influence the behavior of Phillips curve and therefore real economic conditions (Sargent, 1972; Sargent et al., 1973). Hence, the final outcome of rational-augmented Phillips curve depends on the form of expectations and the size of interest rates elasticities, while the natural unemployment rate can be shifted only by random disturbances.

Despite the differences that are raised between Friedman-Phelps' and Lucas' approaches about the factors that prevent the achievement of equilibrium levels, it is clear that in both of these approaches Phillips curve's verticality determines the natural unemployment rate. However, the importance of these differences and especially the way that each of the variables of unemployment and inflation is being treated; in making policy decisions should be considered. For instance, for both monetarism and new classical school where inflation is being treated as a purely monetary phenomenon, the possibility that workers' price expectations can be fooled by inflation surprises is consistent with the presence of persistent prices increases. In these conditions, an unemployment reduction can be achieved when the curve of workers' labor supply is located to the right of its non-surprises position. On the other hand, in orthodox Keynesian grounds the assumption about shifts in fixed rates of inflation allows policymakers to attribute unemployment to the attempt for inflation reduction (Friedman, 1968; Phelps, 1967, 1968). As a matter of fact, the Keynesian Phillips curve is assumed to be flat so as high unemployment rates to be solved through small increases in inflation, contrary to Monetarist Phillips curve that is assumed to be steep enough in order to prove that expansionary demand policies cannot reduce unemployment levels through increases of inflation rates (Espinosa-Vega and Russell, 1997).

Evidently the introduction of inflationary expectations, regardless their form, sets the dependence of inflation on unemployment and expected inflation levels. Moreover, the distinction between short and long-run period implies that only during the short-run can the distinction between actual and natural unemployment rate (unemployment gap) affect economic activity, whereas in the long-run inflation behavior allows these magnitudes to be equal. Besides, only during the short-run trade-off, activist demand policies are proved to be appropriate since an upward demand shift, according to the usual slope of Phillips curve, pushes actual unemployment below its predetermined natural level. In these conditions, the short-run Phillips curve would be shifted up by taking the equality between expected and actual inflation rate for granted. But as long as the natural unemployment rate is affected by labor markets' structural characteristics but not by the aggregate demand level, the whole process of trade-off cannot be affected by fiscal policy. All these resulted in viewing the long-run Phillips curve to be vertical and stable at the natural unemployment rate.

III. From Natural Unemployment Rate to Nairu

Despite the success of augmented with expectations Phillips curve in solving the problems that economies faced, the severe recession in the mid 1970s in conjunction with the high levels of both unemployment and inflation rates, persuaded many economists that the return to Keynesianism was the only resolution. Considering this, some Keynesian economists reinterpreted the Phillips curve within a framework that combined the natural unemployment rate and the accelerating hypothesis with the adoption of demand management policies; this synthesis of orthodox Keynesianism with the new classical economics is reflected on the development of the new Keynesian economics.

The adoption of new Keynesian framework imposed constraints against the use of augmented expectational Philips curve, which concentrated on squeezing unemployment at levels below its threshold natural unemployment rate, in the presence of accelerating inflation. In addition, according to Modigliani and Papademos: "*...the existence of NIRU, the non inflationary rate of unemployment, is implied by both the "vertical" and "non vertical" schools of Phillips curve*" (1975, p. 242).

More precisely, Modigliani and Papademos (1975) viewed the use of NIRU as the representation of the relationship between inflation and unemployment, implied by the intersection of the downward Keynesian Phillips curve with the vertical Friedman's natural unemployment rate. In these conditions, the NIRU (Non- Inflationary Rate of Unemployment), is included in the horizontal axis of unemployment level and the vertical axis of inflation rate. In other words, there is a level of unemployment for which inflation is expected to remain constant; this is the NIRU level. As for the intermediate positions of Phillips curve, it was suggested a relatively flat Phillips curve for high unemployment rates and an approximately vertical for low unemployment levels were assumed (Espinosa-Vega and Russell, 1997). Given this distinction Modigliani and Papademos (1975) interpreted NIRU as a constraint in policymakers' ability to exploit the trade-off between unemployment and inflation in the long-run but as an ability to be used during the short-run.

Although in the view of some economists, NIRU is an alternative expression for the natural unemployment rate, it can easily be understood the contradiction of this concept to monetarists' and new classicals' rejection of a possible trade-off between unemployment and inflation. As a consequence the stagnation problem of that period could be solved by attempting to reach a specific unemployment level consistent with a steady inflation level. The incorrectness of this thought is also proved by considering that in accordance with the adopted definitions a gradual unemployment reduction in a specific time period is implied so that economy to rest upon its predetermined natural unemployment rate, which was re-defined as the non inflationary unemployment rate or simply NIRU. Moreover, the long-run equilibrium level rests upon the assumptions about money neutrality and requires the absence of any trade-off in the long-run and a linear relation between unemployment and inflation. However, the required conditions for Phillips curve verticality and its achievement are determined by the implications of the adopted approach. Hence, for monetarist and new classical schools a vertical Phillips curve implies that unexpected changes in price levels reduce real unemployment rates that are above NIRU regardless of their initial level. On the other hand, a change in the Keynesian downward sloping Phillips curve pushes economy towards a new Phillips curve with respect to the distinction between current and initial inflation levels. In general the philosophy of this new Keynesian concept suggests that any unemployment level below the predetermined NIRU should be followed by inflation reductions and *vice versa*.

Evidently the transformation of the natural unemployment rate to NIRU changed the form of monetary policies, in the sense that current stance of monetary policy can be determined by observing unemployment directly and comparing it with its predetermined natural rate. Additionally actual unemployment level is being used as a good approximate for the behavior of future inflation, as long as low levels of current unemployment are related with future inflation rises in the short-run and inflation acceleration in the long-run. Thus, as Tobin mentions: "*according to the standard augmented Phillips curve' view, rates of price and wage increase depend partly on their recent trends, partly on expectations of their future movements and partly on the tightness...of markets for products and labor. Variations in aggregate monetary demand whether the consequences of policies or other events, affect the course of prices and output and wages and employment, by altering the tightness of labor and product markets and in no other way";* he additionally observes that: "*inflation accelerates at high employment rates because tight markets systematically and repeatedly generate wage and price increases... At the Phelps-Friedman natural rate of unemployment, the degrees of resource utilization and market tightness generate no net wage and price pressure up or down and are consistent with accustomed and expected paths, whether stable process or any other inflation rate. The consensus viewed accepted the notion of a non-accelerating inflation rate of unemployment (NAIRU)*[14] *as a practical constraint on policy*" (1980, p. 23).

There is no doubt, that the way that NAIRU is defined and used in the relevant literature rarely differs from Tobin's (1980) implications. For example, according to Tobin (1980) the comparison of actual unemployment levels with their natural rates reflects monetary policies' conditions during the short-run and the structure of future inflation. Furthermore, the adoption of the new Keynesian NAIRU concept implies that for cases where unemployment is below its natural rate, inflation acceleration in the future is possible.

Nevertheless, the use of the NAIRU concept is regarded as the most useful instrument for making monetary policy decisions. Although its use seems to be simple, it requires policymakers' knowledge of the mechanisms that are behind it so that its policy implications are easily explained. Hence, as long as the use of NAIRU concept assumes the adjustment of real wages on both prices and wages, it is implied that in cases where unemployment is below the determined (via intersection between wages and prices) NAIRU level, wages rise faster than the level of expected prices in the wage equation, whereas in the price equation the level of price grows faster than expected wages (Sawyer, 2001). Both of these cases are characterized by upward inflation shifts, the effects of which are reflected on the level of real wages. But the magnitude of these effects depends on the relative size of wage and price inflation and possibly on the responsiveness of wages and prices to unemployment and capacity utilization respectively and on the expectational form.

The requirement about policymakers' knowledge about the theory and the mechanisms, upon which NAIRU concept rests, becomes urgent because of the doubts that are raised about the correctness of NAIRU's implications that will be presented in the following section[15]. These doubts stem from the fact that labor market's imperfections cancel out the assumption about neutrality, so as any attempt to test the natural unemployment rate to require a tight specification for the determination of unemployment's equilibrium (Perasan and Smithin, 1995; Osberg, 1996).

In particular, the general form of Phillips curve equation that is being used in current literature for estimating NAIRU is the *augmented Phillips curve* equation that equals to:

$$\pi_t = \pi_t^e + \beta(L)(u_t - \bar{u}_t) + \delta' z_t + \varepsilon_t \tag{4}$$

[14] Tobin (1980) instead of using the term NIRU, he used the widely known nowadays term of NAIRU (Non-Accelerating Inflation Rate of Unemployment), without changing its core assumptions.

[15] These are related with the absence of any constraints about the adopted methodologies, variables, data and models for its estimations.

where, π_t : inflation rate from $t-1$ to t

π_t^e : inflation rate expected at $t-1$

u_t : unemployment rate at time t

$\bar{u}_t$: natural rate of unemployment at time t, which could be a constant but could shift with structural changes in the economy.

z_t : a vector of variables such as supply shocks, which have zero ex ante expectations[16]

ε_t : an unspecified disturbance term.

In empirical grounds the above equation is estimated under the assumption that inflation is measured as a distributed lag on past inflation and other variables, while it is additionally assumed that the variable of inflation rate is integrated of order one, in order the difference between actual and expected inflation to be stationary. Equation (4) can be therefore equally rewritten as:

$$\Delta\pi_t = \beta(L)(u_t - \bar{u}_t) + \gamma(L)\Delta\pi_{t-1} + \delta' z_t + \varepsilon_t \qquad (5)$$

where, $\Delta\pi_t$: denotes the differences between inflation rates of current and past period.

In this case NAIRU is represented by the term $\bar{u}_t$ that can be represented either as a constant, a random walk, a linear transformation of some step function or spline process (Staiger et al., 1997b). But since NAIRU is the guidepost for monetary policy, the adopted policies should be determined relative to the unemployment gap between actual unemployment and NAIRU levels[17]; besides, such a distinction is being used as an indicator for future inflation[18]. In any case, the form of augmented Phillips curve that is being used for policy decisions includes the "*accelerationist hypothesis*" since unemployment can be below NAIRU level only in the presence of a price acceleration without any limit.

The argument that NAIRU is determined by supply side factors suggests that its level can be affected only through them, while according to new Keynesian literature the unemployment gap can be eliminated (except in the case where actual unemployment is close to NAIRU) by changes in labor market; some of these are represented by softening minimum wage restrictions, taxes on labor and restrictions on hiring and discriminatory or other impediments to hire either by reducing or eliminating unemployment benefits by upgrading

---

[16] The introduction of the vector Z_t of the supply side variables is attributed to new classical since until then Keynesians concentrated their attention on aggregate demand side and recognized only a limited role for supply side effects on economic activity.

[17] According to Ball and Mankiw (2002), the level of output gap is the key determinant of inflation behavior under the assumption that all the factors that impress inflation are reflected on lagged values of inflation and variables of the Z_t vector.

[18] McDonald (1995) claims that the natural rate theory prevents the use of the size of inflation as an indicator for whether economy lays on its equilibrium level or not, whereas the relation between actual and natural unemployment is generally used as an indicator for future inflation behavior.

education and training of workers and perhaps by offering subsidies to new hiring that will be examined below.

IV. Similarities and Differences between the Natural Unemployment Rate and Nairu

Although among economists either the synonymy of natural unemployment rate and NAIRU terms or the treatment of the new Keynesian NAIRU theory as the reformulation of monetarist natural unemployment theory is prevalently argued, in practice a comparison between their basic characteristics makes clear their distinction. The importance of signifying their main characteristics and pointing out their differences provides evidence about the differences in their policy implications.

First of all, the fact that the Phillips curve is common for both natural unemployment theory and NAIRU does not imply community in their implications. In this manner, the usefulness of the Phillips curve as a guide to monetary policy is implied, while the use of natural unemployment rate as a reference point for policy decision requires the absence of any variation in the long-run stability as well as the absence of expectational errors about wages and prices (Espinosa-Vega and Russel, 1997; Karanassou and Snower, 1997). In addition, the fact that the NAIRU level itself is the long-run equilibrium that determines an unemployment level consistent with a constant inflation rate, suggests that at the equilibrium there is equality between actual and expected inflation rate and thereby between actual and natural unemployment levels so as the behavior between wage and price setters to be competitive (Solow, 1986).

But the most crucial difference between natural rate theory and NAIRU concept, according to Snowden et al. (1994), is that Friedman's natural rate is a market clearing concept, while according to implications of NAIRU concept the long-run equilibrium level is determined by the balance of power between workers and firms thus theories of imperfect competition in the labor and production markets are related. This difference stems from the fact in the natural unemployment rate economies are assumed to operate according to a Walrasian process that refers to perfect competitive conditions, whereas in NAIRU grounds imperfect competitive conditions are recognized (Jekinson, 1987). As a result, the adoption of the natural unemployment hypothesis implies that economy always returns to its natural rate without any inflationary pressure, whereas in accordance with NAIRU concept the presence of persistently unemployment levels above the predetermined NAIRU stands as a result of markets' failure to be cleared (Tobin, 1995, 1998; Galbraith, 1996). Besides, in the new Keynesian interpretation the NAIRU concept depends on labor market institutions that determine wage claims and on the market power of firms that set the price level.

All these are closely related with the way that unemployment is being treated in each of these two concepts. Hence, the treatment of unemployment as a search (voluntary) in terms of natural hypothesis unemployment implies the absence of any equality between actual unemployment level with its natural and reflects people's decisions about the way they decide to spend their time between leisure and working hours. On the other hand, the magnitude of unemployment in NAIRU framework is defined as involuntary, while at the equilibrium is level is assumed to be determined by the characteristics of labor market and its level is being used for holding inflation under control (Layard et al., 1991). It is thereby clear that the

Monetarist natural rate of unemployment is not a NAIRU theory in the strong sense, even though the policy recommendations based on the NAIRU coincide with Monetarist policies. Further, in accordance with the implications of NAIRU concept, the equilibrium unemployment level intents to control inflation. As a result, in terms of NAIRU concept, labor market reform is needed to combat unemployment. Thus, the belief that NAIRU and natural unemployment rates are just synonyms requires either the presence of a vertical long-run Phillips curve or the inclusion in NAIRU definitions of the lagged inflation coefficients (Solow, 1986).

It should be also mentioned that the natural unemployment rate can be explained as a microeconomic phenomenon since it can be thought to lie implicitly onto individual's decisions and behavior is also of vital importance. On the other hand, NAIRU includes both macroeconomic and microeconomic foundations that concern price and wage behavior so as inflation to be constant. This difference is attributed to the fact that the natural unemployment rate in monetarism grounds rests on the assumption about the competitiveness of labor and product markets, so that high unemployment levels are faced by setting inflation under control and markets are cleared. Contrary to this, in imperfect competitive new Keynesian markets the presence of persistently high unemployment is attributed to markets' failure (Tobin, 1995).

In particular we should always consider that Friedman's and Phelps' natural unemployment rate is defined as the equilibrium level whose value is determined by the characteristics of labor market, whereas NAIRU is simply an empirical rather than an equilibrium value. It however cannot be ignored that the natural unemployment rate is a theoretical magnitude toward which actual unemployment is assumed to move, though it cannot be estimated, whereas NAIRU is assumed to be indirectly determined and easily estimated under specific assumptions (Karanassou and Snower, 1997). Thus, despite similarities in policy implications in the sense that Friedman (1968) and Phelps (1968) laid the cornerstone for the later discussions of the NAIRU by proposing the long-run vertical Phillips curve, the Monetarist natural rate theory should be considered a distinct theory and not a variant of the NAIRU theory. In any case, both the natural and NAIRU magnitudes can be only indirectly observed and estimated. Considering thereby all these differences between the two definitions it is evident that the choice of any of these is related with alternative policy implications.

Critical Views of NAIRU[19]

As we have already mentioned in the previous section, the general acceptance of NAIRU as the policy guide is coincided with a long and intensive debate about the ups and the downs that the concept has experienced. Thus, although some economists (e.g. Stiglitz, 1997; Blanchard and Katz, 1997; Ball and Mankiw, 2002) view the concept of the NAIRU as a useful piece of business cycle theory, for others such as Chang (1997) the NAIRU concept is being of a limited use for predicting inflation, understanding its causes and therefore making

[19] It should be mentioned that in this section we will attempt to point out the questions that are raised about the methodological issues about NAIRU estimations; this criticism takes place within the new Keynesian grounds.

employment policies. Moreover, the possibility for the whole idea of the NAIRU to be harmed if inflation, wages and unemployment do not behave together or even more in times of low inflation the Phillips Curve not to be vertical as used for the NAIRU derivation, raise additional questions about the appropriateness of using NAIRU (Franz, 2003). In particular, the criticisms about NAIRU arise from the fact that a theoretical argument is based upon a non-theoretical foundation.

The cornerstone about NAIRU criticism is that NAIRU level itself can only indirectly be observed through estimations about the long-run unemployment equilibrium point. This implies the absence of any constraint in methodologies, variables and approaches that are being used for NAIRU estimations. For that reason, it is widely argued that NAIRU estimations are sensitive not only to the assumptions of the adopted framework but also to the employed specifications, the sample period and data as well as the included variables and estimation method. In this manner, it is believed that the number of included lags is essential, since it reflects the degree and form of included information; the lower their number the closer to actual economic conditions NAIRU estimations turn out to be (Galbraith, 1997; Gordon, 1997). Hence when lags refer to the variable of inflation or economies are characterised by favorable supply side shocks, inflation deceleration is possible to come up; in both cases inflation decelerates even when actual unemployment is below its natural level. On the other hand when lags concern the variable of unemployment, the presence of more complicated dynamics that ensure the association of a current unemployment reduction with decelerating inflation is implied (Estrella and Minshkin, 1999). For that reason, there are many new Keynesian economists such as Staiger et al. (1997b), Stiglitz (1997), Rogerson (1997) who recognize the direct effects of the included number of lags on the variable of unemployment as well as the presence or not of contemporaneous unemployment values on NAIRU estimations, although they are not preferable because of their exogenous character. In any case the number of lags for included variables reduces the degree of standard errors and affects the estimated coefficients importantly (Fair, 1997).

Moreover, the form of included expectations in the augmented-expectational Phillips curve affects NAIRU estimations as well as the degree of policymakers' confidence about the adopted targets definitely. The fact that new Keynesians have no unique view of the form of included expectations[20], allows expectations to have an outstanding role in determining policy decisions, though in recent literature there is a preference on adaptive expectations in the sense that they perform sufficiently and their implications are similar to those of rational expectations (Ball and Mankiw, 2002). Although, the introduction of adaptive expectations in Phillips curve seems to be adequate in providing a perfect fit for the stylized facts of monetary macroeconomics so as monetary shocks to affect unemployment, it is also possible for the effects of these shocks to be reflected on inflation with some delay (Mankiw, 2001). It is therefore obvious that expectations affect the assessment of future inflationary pressures, though it is argued that the NAIRU concept loses its simplicity if inflation expectations are taken into account, since inflation level itself might change due to inflation expectations which are unrelated to deviations of unemployment from the NAIRU (Chang, 1997). Thus, in

[20] Their thought rests somewhere between the adaptive and rational expectations, since in Keynes's (1936) view expectations are essentially affected by social conventions, whereas according to Lucas (1972) rational expectations provide the opportunity to workers to decide upon their working hours. In general both the inflation and unemployment policies are directly determined by the way that expectations are formed.

cases of more forward looking expectations, NAIRU estimations are determined by backward looking (adaptive) expectations in the sense that their presence is anchored by the experience of lower and more stable inflation. Under these suggestions, it is possible for estimations to be misleading and biased[21].In any case this form of expectations in Phillips curve equation requires the introduction of lagged inflation term, whereas in the presence of rational expectations inflation is represented as a random walk process (Ball and Mankiw, 2002)[22]. It can generally be said that despite the 'dilemma' about the included form of expectations in NAIRU estimations, there are still doubts about the effectiveness of this concept; its solution arises from the economic regime that characterizes each economy.

But NAIRU estimations are also affected by the adopted method of inflation and unemployment measurement (Staiger et al., 1997b; Ball and Mankiw, 2002). Apart from the unemployment and output gap that are widely used as indicators of future inflation, there is a range of alternative and possibly more appropriate measures (Nickell, 1990; Estrella and Minshkin, 1999). For example after examining alternative ways of inflation forecasting, Stock and Watchon (1999) concluded that inflation estimates with respect to Phillips curve are more accurate relative to others. Additionally, Stock and Watchon (1996) signified the presence of, at least, sixty nine alternative indicators that can be used for inflation prediction, such as output and sales, labor markets and so forth, which are expressed in either nominal or real terms and provide different information and thus inflation predictions. Further, it has been found that the use of unemployment as an indicator of inflation predictions is characterized about its impropriety, while the alternative ways of measuring it reduce the degree of uncertainty in forecasts (Gordon, 1988). The absence of any proper inflation measure is verified by the fact that in Phillips curve literature gross domestic product is widely used as an indicator of 'core inflation' by excluding prices of foods and energy goods (Staiger et al., 1997a). In practice, there is no qualitative information about both inflation and unemployment across economies, while the measurement of a number of variables assumes arbitrariness that in fact influences the NAIRU estimations.

In particular the way that NAIRU is defined, the form of included variables, the degree of information and the included form of expectations are directly determined by each researcher's intention; a suggestion that casts doubts on the appropriateness of the concept of NAIRU itself as well as the correctness of its policy suggestions. In these grounds, the way that unemployment is being treated is also essential. Thus in recent literature, NAIRU is considered to be the macroeconomic outcome of labor market that distinguished excess demand markets and inflation decreasing pressures from excess supply markets (Perasan and Smithin, 1995; Tobin, 1998). However, the fact that in practice NAIRU suggestions are not always consistent with non accelerating inflation rate, cannot dispute the dominance of NAIRU concept in theoretical models. Despite the presence of this inconsistency, there are some economists i.e. Solow (1998), Taylor (1998), Collignton, (2003), Gordon (1997), Karanassou and Snower, (1997), who are in favor of the NAIRU concept and its

[21] This is explained by the high degree of included inertia, which slows down NAIRU adjustment towards new conditions of economy.

[22] The advantage of adaptive expectations is the ability to treat the natural unemployment rate as the NAIRU level so that both the stability of inflation between two period and the absent of supply shocks to be ensured (Ball and Mankiw, 2002).

disinflationary implications in the sense that continuous unemployment expansions cannot be attributed to expectational errors or incorrect adjustment dynamics for reaching equilibrium.

Generally, the way that unemployment and its long-run equilibrium are approached in new Keynesian grounds, is explained by their adherence to Say's Law and supply side factors. The fact that Say's Law allows economy to correspond to its full employment and capacity utilization, provides the opportunity to contemplate the way that supply can be compared with demand[23]. Besides, the use of models of bargaining power efficiency wages and insiders-outsiders and the implied rigidities and imperfections in labor markets for explaining unemployment, turn out to be incorrect[24]. Nevertheless the assumed uniqueness of supply side NAIRU and neutrality conditions set the dominance of new classical implications despite its incorrectness[25].

Another issue that sets the use of NAIRU as a policy guide inappropriate, concerns its treatment as constant or time varying. In general, recent literature implies the treatment of NAIRU as a time variant. For example, although the American NAIRU level was believed to be constant around the level of 6%, it is now admitted that its levels can be considered as time varying. Thus in a number of estimations, NAIRU ranged around 3.5% in mid-1960s, reached its peak during 1980s at the level of 7.25% and fell at the level of 5.75%, while in the recession of 1990s NAIRU estimations set it around 6% (Staiger et al., 1997a, 1997b; Rogerson, 1997; Gordon, 1997; Stiglitz, 1997; Galbraith, 1997). Nowadays, both American and European time varying NAIRU levels are set close to 5.5-6% or even lower, despite the incorrectness that is included in NAIRU forecasts even under its time variance (Staiger et al., 1997a)[26]. In general, Staiger et al. (1997b), imply that NAIRU can be presented as a constant or spline or even as a break procedure or as being determined simply by its previous levels[27].

But the presence of constant or time varying NAIRU has some consequences in terms of economic policies, the most essential of which is the degree of their correctness. Thus, the treatment of NAIRU as constant or time-variant raises additional difficulties for monetary authorities, in the sense that policy decisions are made with respect to its predetermined level (Collignton, 2003). On the other hand, the assumption of a time variant NAIRU, although raise the difficulty for making policy decisions, it contemporaneously raise the degree of their correctness; besides the correctness of policy suggestions is highly depended on the length of the period to which observed data and estimations are referred (Galbraith, 1997; Gordon, 1997). Furthermore, the adoption of a time variant NAIRU is supposed to provide the adequate conditions for the adoption of techniques and reduce the degree of uncertainty

---

[23] A possible way to do this is to consider the value of marginal propensity to spend that requires its equality to unity in order for Say's Law to hold without the presence of any problem (Sawyer, 2001).

[24] The common characteristic of these models is the implied positive relation between unemployment and wage levels that is being used as the determinant of unemployment levels (Blanchard and Katz, 1997).

[25] Usually this equality is accepted regardless of whether or not economists are aware of the factors that determine the marginal product or the differences between theoretical and empirical grounds (Sawyer, 1998).

[26] According to Friedman (1968) a shift of NAIRU level itself is determined by changes either in demographic compositions or in technological and hence changes in productivity levels; suggestions that are adopted even nowadays. In recent literature however, such as Ball and Mankiw (2002) and Gordon and Stock (1998), the introduction of 'new technology' that is referred to speedy development of new technologies, openness of the competition and trade among countries as well as the increase of the productivity growth rate, turns to be the most significant reason for shifting NAIRU levels.

[27] In recent literature the time variance of constancy of the NAIRU level can be examined by employimg Gordon's (1997) "triangle model".

(Clark and Laxton, 1997). In no case, should the adoption of a time varying NAIRU and its shifts be considered as changes in actual unemployment level (Blinder, 1997).

Due to the absence of any guidance on NAIRU behavior and the incomplete knowledge of its implications, in mainstream grounds it is possible to assume the slow adjustment of NAIRU to changes (Staiger et al., 1997a, 1997b). Besides, policy decisions rest upon NAIRU constancy and its equality with actual unemployment level so as policy decisions about inflation to provide the expected results. In any case, in the process of policy determination monetary authorities should consider whether the average rate of unemployment, that is usually adopted, is being affected by monetary policies. If this stands, the natural rate cannot be posited as completely exogenous and the neutrality hypothesis would not apply even in the long-run (Collignton, 2003). In other words, the essence of any monetary policies suggestions is cancelled out.

Closely related with the tendency to treat NAIRU as a time varying, is the assumption about its uniqueness; an issue that concerns the degree of NAIRU correctness in new Keynesian grounds. More specifically, the information that is provided by the NAIRU variance over time is cancelled out by assuming its long-run uniqueness (Staiger et al., 1997a). However, in new Keynesian theory there is no reference about the possibility of NAIRU concept to be characterized by multiple equilibria, although this is directly implied by considering the 'usual' phenomenon of hysteresis (Ball, 1997). The assumption about NAIRU uniqueness stems from the suggested consistence of natural unemployment rate with market clearing and the inverse relation between unemployment and real wages. However, the consistency of new Keynesian economics with a range of models and thereby theoretical implications, makes the existence of multiple rather than unique equilibrium more convincing (Sawyer, 1998, 2001). Besides, it is exactly the combination of the assumptions about multiple equilibria and hysteresis that distinguishes new classical from new Keynesian economics, although the latter rest upon a range of new classical assumptions (Sawyer, 2001). Indeed, the assumption about a unique employment and output equilibrium level is relatively strict, while such equilibrium is possible to be biased because of the specific assumptions upon which it lies (Dixon, 1995).

Additionally, the determination of natural unemployment level in accordance with Wicksellian natural interest rate, so as equilibrium to be simultaneously determined in both labor and capital markets, enriches the dynamic adjustment that raises the possibility of multiple natural equilibria (Dixon, 1995). As a consequence, the suggestions against NAIRU uniqueness cast doubts on its use as a benchmark for monetary policy and as the appropriate instrument for achieving price stability. Regardless of the uniqueness or not of NAIRU, it should be considered that the implied equilibrium is neither competitive nor Pareto optimal and thereby cannot reflect real abilities of economy (Dixon, 1995). Besides, its presence becomes inconsistent at high unemployment rates for which multiple equilibria are highly possible (McDonald, 1995). Obviously, the way that unemployment is defined as well as the suggestion about whether its estimations include a whole set of unemployment levels each of which is associated with different values, affects the presence or the absence of unique equilibrium definitely (Bean, 1994).

All these are essential for the conduct of monetary policies, given that in new Keynesian grounds policy decisions are determined with respect to interest rate rules and implicitly by the acceleration model (NAIRU). Further, the inability to separate among the structural characteristics of unemployment and simply treat NAIRU as the magnitude that reflects actual unemployment makes the absence of any policy solution about the unemployment problems reasonable. Thus, by regarding a specific value for NAIRU, it is certain that the achievement of policy targets will affect economies mischievously, regardless of the uncertainty about the correctness of these policies.

The implied uncertainty and doubts that characterize NAIRU concept and its estimating process enforce the thought of solving high unemployment and inflation levels by using short-run Phillips curve (Demertzis and Hallett, 1995; Dixon, 1995). Besides, historically there is no explicit NAIRU level that characterizes economies, whereas the dependence on labor market conditions and specifications is widely accepted, although there are few empirical studies that prove its existence in real economies (Tobin, 1980). Moreover, the use of short instead of long-run Phillips curve to make policy decisions seems to reflect actual economic conditions perfectly, while its implications raise the possibility of improving economy's performance and providing Pareto optimal results. Such a consideration is enriched by the possibility many economies not being characterized by an explicit long-run relation between inflation and unemployment. In addition, the fact that the concentration on long-run equilibrium level and the use of unemployment gap can provide limited useful policy suggestions should be also considered (Estrella and Minshkin, 1999).

In any case policymakers are called to be well aware of the mechanisms that characterize NAIRU, namely the adopted methods for its estimations as well as the included variables in order for policy suggestions to reflect real economies (Solow, 1998). Thus, the thought that NAIRU sets the consistency between inflation reductions and economic growth suggests that unemployment reductions can be achieved through changes in structural and cyclical characteristics of labor market due to changes in the participation level and the required skills that should characterise workers or even demand weaknesses (Summers et al., 1986). Nevertheless, the achievement of full employment cannot be ensured by considering the equality of real wages at their natural levels (Hall, 1975).

Despite the criticism about the correctness of NAIRU supply side framework that mainly concerns its inability to reflect real economies, this framework is still considered by economists and policymakers as the theoretical benchmark for stabilizing monetary policies. However the questions raised above, concern not only the correctness of NAIRU estimations but also the correctness of policies that stem from its use, which are proved to provide only sub-optimal suggestions. The problem of these policies is not to persuade the public about their advantages but to provide evidence against its imprudent consequences on economic activity. Besides, what is really required is the adoption of policies that reflect actual necessities of economies so as the targets of price stability and full employment to be reached without harmful consequences in economic activity. It thereby seems accurate to adopt an alternative and more realistic framework which would be recognized an active role for aggregate demand. In other words, the adoption of a framework that would account for all the problems stemming from NAIRU concept in order for promoting employment and economic expansion, seems to be reasonable. In any case, the adoption of an alternative NAIRU framework should be easily understood and widely accepted.

NAIRU AND UNEMPLOYMENT

The dependence of NAIRU implications about unemployment policies on the trade-off between unemployment and inflation that is reflected upon the Phillips curve is implicitly implied from the above analysis. However, by treating the new Keynesian supply side NAIRU concept as the policy reference point, any attempt for expanding economic activity can be achieved only by balancing the dangers of inflation (Solow 1998; Ball and Mankiw, 2002). In this manner, the common characteristic of economies is their adherence on inflation targeting regimes and the treatment of unemployment as an indicator of future inflation[28].

More specifically, inflation targeting has been proposed as the necessary monetary policy regime to tame inflation and inflationary expectations and to keep economies at the natural rate of unemployment. Usually these regimes are reflected on the adoption of feedback rules[29] that intent to push economies towards the adopted inflation target; this target is assumed to be the optimal one and to aim at a lower inflation level than the existent (Taylor, 1998; Clarida et al. 1999). Discipline, accountability, transparency, credibility, flexibility and legitimacy are the most often proposed advantages of this monetary strategy[30] (McCallum, 1984; Bernanke and Minshkin, 1997; Debelle, 1997). In general, the key advantage of inflation targeting regime is believed to be the compatibility of the achieved inflation target with high growth levels, even during the expansionary phase of the economic cycle (Debelle, 1997)[31].

In practice, the achievement of inflation targets is related with the appropriate treatment of short-run nominal interest rates[32] (Solow, 1998; Galbraith, 1997). According to Friedman's (1968) definition of natural unemployment rate, the distinction between nominal and real interest rates equals the inflation level, whereas upward shifts of short term interest rates intend to provoke economic slowdown and feed inflation reductions through tight money policies. Further, it is widely recognized that short interest rate reductions cause recessions that are expected to be temporary and stem either from short-run nominal wage or price rigidity or even from inertia of inflationary expectations. But in a longer time horizon, the achievement of equilibrium levels of wages and expectations and thereby of full employment would be consistent with a lower inflation level (Smithin, 1996). It is generally argued that

[28] Considering new Keynesians' adherence on inflation as the main source for accelerating economic activity within NAIRU framework, it is proved their consistency with Friedman's (1968) suggestion about the treatment of inflation as a purely monetary phenomenon towards which output levels can be adjusted. Further, the treatment of monetary policy as the most appropriate in stabilizing economic activity stems from the time lag and the time sluggishness with which the effects from fiscal policy come up (Solow, 1998; Ball and Mankiw, 2002).

[29] These rules suggest the absence of any long-run trade-off between unemployment and inflation within the NAIRU concept (Taylor, 1998; Clarida et al., 1999).

[30] The consistence of monetary authorities' characteristics with new classical implications becomes clear in Kydland and Prescott (1972); Barro and Sargent (1983).

[31] Despite the constraints that are raised from the downward rigidities of either wages or prices and thereby further price adjustment, policy targets can refer to both low inflation and high stabilized output levels (Debelle, 1997).

[32] The most widely used and known mechanism through which interest rate affects inflation and economic activity is the known as Taylor's (1993) rule. This is an interest rate rule which employs the short-run nominal interest rate in order to stabilize inflation via its relation with the behavior of real GDP and money growth. In particular, the use of Taylor's rule reflects economic activity of many economies from 1987 onwards (Clarida et al. 2000).

policymakers' intentions about disinflationary policies are not always confirmed by the final results and impacts on economic activity (Blinder, 1997).

Considering the globalized environment into which economies are called to operate, unemployment is essentially affected by the behavior of interest rates and mainly by upward shocks of international real interest rate that increase the natural unemployment rate and at the same time affect employment level and capital markets negatively[33] (Phelps, 1995). In addition to this, the high degrees of uncertainty that characterizes the effects from the adoption of interest rate policies, suggest that monetary authorities should regard their decisions by taking into account counter-inflation action, in the sense that it is preferable to follow policies that aim at educing high inflation levels before the presence of accelerating inflation levels. This form of policy is known as "*long-lag response*". The second policy form, known as "*genie and-the-bottle response*", suggests the adoption of policies whose results are unexpected because of their inability to control the non linear relation between inflation and unemployment levels, when the former is relatively high. As a result, it is believed that policymakers should have the ability to limit their uncertainty and their actions be characterized by freedom if their intervention is required (Solow, 1998). In any case we should take into account that the behavior of interest rate policy rules depends on the adopted monetary regime (Taylor, 1995, 1999; McCallum, 1984)[34].

Generally the consequences of disinflation policies are determined in relation to the equilibrium natural unemployment rate as well as the degree of validity and uncertainty included in the behavior of inflation. Nevertheless, new Keynesians' concentration on inflation targeting rules is possible to lead economies to a transitory period, during which current inflation rates move towards targeted inflation and thereby output stabilization (Bernaske and Mishkin, 1997). Although, it is possible for inflation itself to be affected by unemployment shocks (Mankiw, 2001)[35], policy targets can be achieved without causing additional problems by regarding the uniqueness of inflation targeting framework (Taylor, 1993; Clarida et al., 1999). Further, the assumptions about money neutrality and Phillips curve verticality in the long-run, increase the degree of independency of the adopted NAIRU level from inflation behavior (Solow, 1998; Tobin, 1995). Thus, attention should be concentrated on possible unanticipated shocks that can be settled and at the same time provide forecasts about price level at long horizons that will vary under inflation targeting regime (Bernaske and Mishkin, 1997). In practice monetary authorities tend partially to compensate for missed targets, particularly in shorter time horizons, although there is a reduction in the role of intermediate targets such as money growth and exchange rate (Tobin, 1995).

But the concentration on inflation targeting regimes in conjunction with the high degree of uncertainty that characterizes the results of monetary policies, instead of expanding

---

[33] It seems reasonable to attribute unemployment persistency to investment reductions, after considering the relation between interest rates and unemployment (Nickell, 1998; Bean, 1994).

[34] Even in the case where exchange rates are being used as a key instrument for stabilizing economy, the specific characteristics of each monetary regime should be considered. Hence with respect to real economic conditions, satisfactory results about economic performance can be reached by using either exchange rates or money stock as instruments as long as these variables satisfy all the required conditions for the adoption of a policy rule (McCallum, 1984). But in current economies there is no dependency between exchange and interest rates, so as economic activity to be constrained by them (Taylor, 1999).

[35] This refers to long-run term during which unemployment shocks are raised by monetary authorities' attempt to refrain from being forward looking and responding to inflationary pressures even before inflation arises (Mankiw, 2001).

economic activity, pushes economies to a circle of continuous recessions and unemployment expansions (Solow, 1998; Taylor, 1998). For instance, Fitoussi et al. (2000), Phelps and Zoera (1998) and Bean et al. (1986), characterize the use of real interest rates as the most representative monetary instrument, though sets monetary policies only partially responsible for the persistent high levels of unemployment across economies. Moreover, Fischer (1993) provides evidence for a positive correlation between price stability and economic growth, while Romer and Romer (1999) prove that the American economy in the long-run has been characterized by low inflation levels and macroeconomic stability as well as with high degrees of income inequality. According to Easterly and Fischer (2001) however, the effects of inflation are harmful for poor societies, while Ball and Sheridan (2003) suggest that the uncertainty of disinflationary policies rises in both low and high inflationary economies. In the view of Shiller (2000) and Schettkat (2010) however, deflationary policies slowed recoveries and led to high and persisting unemployment in Europe, while the enormous employment growth in the USA was mainly the result of strong recoveries.

Contrary to these suggestions, Fortin (1996) proves the absence of any correlation between inflation and unemployment or of their growth rates to the heterogeneity of characteristics across sample economies. According to Ball (1997) however, the possibility a fully credible disinflation to be related with an economic boom cannot be rejected. In this case by suggesting that disinflation booms are announced and credible, firms respond by reducing their prices, while a rise in money balance that will cause a rise in output but an unemployment reduction is possible (Mankiw, 2001). Even if the consequences of disinflation policies are ex ante recognized, attention should be paid on the qualitative characteristics of economies in order to provide evidence about their significant impact on economic performance (Fortin, 1996). Evidently, there are many other constraints except for inflation that prevent economies from improving their performance in terms of employment, while it is always possible an incorrect policy choice since the adopted disinflationary policy can be different from real necessities and therefore affect economic activity in terms of employment incorrectly (Solow, 1998).

Notwithstanding, the negative consequences on unemployment from the adoption of disinflationary policies are mainly raised by the way that unemployment is being treated. The fact that in recent literature NAIRU is defined in accordance with Friedman's (1968) definition of natural unemployment rate, which is determined by both market and non market factors and by the labor market factors, implies that employment policies should be based on labor market that distinguish excess demand markets and inflation decreasing pressures from excess supply markets. As a result, in the majority of current literature the persistently high unemployment levels are not associated with the effects of contractionary demand policies, neither is believed that the productivity slowdown with workers' aspirations[36], changes in tax[37] and import price nor higher commodity prices, especially of oil[38], explain

[36] It is believed that across European economies the combination of adopted labor market policies and supply side shocks during 1970s, led to the creation of a positive wage gap and disproportional shifts between wages and productivity (Bean, 1994; Blanchard and Wolfers, 2000; Solow, 1998).

[37] In new Keynesian grounds, it is argued the negative relation between tax policies and unemployment, since the introduction of these policies increases the level of labor costs for firms (Nickell, 1997, 1998; Blanchard and Wolfers, 2000). Despite the doubts about the effects of taxation policies on consumption in the long-run, the presence of European unemployment during 1980s and 1990s is satisfactorily explained (Elmeskov, 1993; Baker et al., 2004; Glyn et al., 2004; Nickell, 1997).

unemployment adequately. On the contrary, the last few years the persistent unemployment is usually attributed to institutional characteristics of labor markets and the power of factors, the differences of conditions across economies as well as macroeconomic shocks that create an unfriendly employment environment, although there are some institutions that lead to employment expansion (Blanchard and Wolfers, 2000; Blanchard and Katz, 1997; Baker et al., 2004; Glyn et al., 2004; Nickell, 1997, 1998). The division of labor market implied by the natural rate theory assigned monetary policy the sole task of maintaining low inflation and thereby reaping its benefits in terms of economic performance (Issing, 2000). However, neutrality of monetary policy with regard to real economic activity is a theoretical construct based on strong but implausible assumption. Institutions designed according to natural rate theory neglected the impact of restrictive macroeconomic policy.

As a result, the policies that are employed for facing unemployment are associated with labor market rigidities namely increases in the union power, the mismatching between the demand and supply of labor, the effects of increasingly generous unemployment benefits, rising the reservation wages as well as increases in the mark up that stem from the especially high interest rates and demographic developments. In practice, it is argued that the levels of minimum wages and unemployment benefits are those that directly determine workers' intention to work or not as well as labor's mobility, especially in European economies during 1970s and 1980s. Although these usually take the form of employment protection, they ultimately opposed to employment expansion and turn out to be responsible for unemployment expansions and increases in unemployment duration (Nickell, 1997, 1998; Siebert, 1997).

In a number of empirical studies, (i.e. Nickell, 1997, 1998; Fitoussi et al., 2000; Siebert, 1997; Phelps and Zoera, 1998; Baker et al., 2004; Glyn et al., 2004; Bean, 1994; Layard et al., 1991), it is proved that unemployment persistence is determined by minimum wage, unemployment benefit system, relatively high firing and hiring restrictions, welfare system, unemployment protection system, directly. But the uniqueness of the insurance system across heterogeneous economies should not be considered, in the sense that the comparison and convergence of unemployment benefits across countries will become complicated. Further, each economy is characterized by its own labor market laws and institutions that determine the actual unemployment levels and their forms. For example, it is believed that the European insurance systems are more protective relative to the American (Bean, 1994), although there is evidence that during 1980s the Canadian economy was characterised by the coexistence of the high unemployment levels along with the relative and comparatively high levels of insurance benefits (Ossama et al., 2005). But it is exactly the existence of these differences in macroeconomic institutions that diverges the employment trends across economies (Schettkat, 2010). Generally European institutions are believed to have been designed in the heyday of NAIRU are overly restrictive and geared towards price stability and low public budgets in order European Economies to be prevented from inflation heating, but without effective instruments to prevent the underutilization of capacity. As such, the European framework lacks effective instruments to stimulate economic activity. Indeed it is clear that supply side factors and differences in institutions and social characteristics of each market have played an

[38] According to Phelps and Zoera's (1998) suggestions, the unemployment levels during 1970s were essentially affected by energy prices.

important role. In general, it is argued that labor market policies set an unfriendly environment for workers regardless of whether there is an unemployment protection system or not.

To the contrary, the significance of labor market rigidities on economic activity is determined by whether economies face macroeconomic shocks as well as whether these are observable or not. Thus, when shocks in labor markets are unobservable then all rigidities are significant, whereas in cases of observable shocks that concern the total productivity growth rate, only real interest rate and labor demand shifts, affect economic activity essentially (Blanchard and Wolfers, 2000). Generally the difference in the degree of significance of labor market rigidities in explaining unemployment are attributed to differences in the form and the structure of domestic shocks that characterize each economy and thereby its response to them (Phelps and Zoera, 1998) as well as to regional unemployment disparities (Bande and Karanassou, 2007).

Among unfriendly employment market institutions there are also 'good' institutions (i.e. coordination variable, active labor market policy) that reduce unemployment and create the appropriate conditions for employment and economic expansion, although the level of the coefficients of these variables is not always plausible. Besides, the thought that labor market deregulation is possibly the best route to raise employment rates is prevailing.

The quite mixed evidence that concern not only the impact of labor market institutions on unemployment, which is generally argued to exist, or the sign of the impact, but also the degree of their significance in explaining them can be attributed to the fact that researchers use different measurement and estimation methods as well as different data about the used variables. Although there is no direct linkage among labor market institutions and macroeconomic shocks with actual unemployment levels, with respect to heterogeneity of each economy their presence appears to explain the persistently high unemployment levels across economies adequately. It can therefore be said that the explanation of persistently high unemployment levels is in many cases problematic. Consequently the necessity that arises, concerns the appropriateness of mix labor market institutions and laws that will actually protect employment and not constrain economic expansion. The inconsistency between theoretical implications of NAIRU and economic reality as is represented by growth and employment rates in conjunction with the inability of the implied policies to control unemployment, especially after the expansion of financial crisis, set the appropriateness of NAIRU under question. Besides, the supposed correct mix of labor policies might not be the same for all economies but should be determined with respect to their actual needs and conditions or eve more consider other sources for facing unemployment.

Financial Crisis[39], NAIRU and Unemployment: Conclusive Remarks

The burst of the current worldwide economic crisis and the ensuing drop in economic activity came to most economists as a big surprise. Despite the provided signals through the high degrees of economic system's instability and its consequences on imbalanced accounts

[39] In this Section, we examine the financial crisis from the Post Keynesian perspective.

and income inequalities, policymakers' and economists' inability or denial to understand and solve them, created the appropriate conditions for the expansion of the current crisis.

In addition to all these, the tendency for deregulating the financial sector and the introduction of new financial instruments in economic activity as well as the relation between the financial and real sector, implied the dominance of finance-led regime (Onaran et al., 2010; Stockhammer, 2004c; van Treck 2008). All these are reflected upon the notion of financialization, which in particular presents a wide range of facts but it is assumed to concern: "*the increasing importance of financial markets, financial motives, financial institutions, and financial elites in the operation of the economy and its governing institutions, both at the national and international level*" (Epstein, 2002, p.1).

What it is of high interests is that the adoption of the financialization term in our daily glossary is not coincided with a unique explanation[40]. Hence in mainstream grounds, given the recognition of the endogenous growth theory and the new informative economies, it is argued that the concentration on the behavior of independent monetary authorities (central banks) and financial markets can ensure the assumed positive relation between financialization and long-run growth (Hein, 2009). The fact that in mainstream perspectives financial markets, which are being treated as an "individual" part of the economic system, are assumed to operate in terms of economic efficiency given income distribution and a passive role for aggregate demand, raise the degree of inappropriateness of the adopted policies. On the other hand, Post Keynesians (e.g. Hein, 2009; Hein and Truger, 2010, Onaran et al. 2010; Stockhammer, 2008) provide a more realistic approach about financialization, which is adopted in this study, by examining the financial market orientation and financialization and considering its effects on aggregate demand, income inequality, employment levels and instability of the economic system. In this manner, the current crisis turns to be more a crisis of real economy that can be solved only by facing the core of financial instability and economic stagnancy.

Besides, the increasing degrees of globalization and the coherence on inflation targeting regime in the sense that low inflation is the driving force for restoring high levels of economic activity[41], changes the structure of macroeconomic behavior and strengthens the degree of financialization in economic activity. Furthermore the neoliberalism implications in favor of liberalizing, flexibilizing and deregulating the labor and the financial markets in both internal and international levels, encourage economies to encounter sustain budget deficits in the sense that financial markets were willing to provide to them the corresponding capital inflows (Stockhammer, 2010; Palley, 2007)[42]. In these conditions, the recognition of a limited role for governmental intervention in conjunction with the preference on privatization could prevent neither the collapse of interdependent financial markers, nor the power transfer from labor to capital (Hein, 2006; Stockhammer, 2008, 2010). On the contrary, economies were expected to be characterized by economic growth, but the dependence of capital accumulation on finance-led regime did only negatively affect aggregate demand.

[40] Analytical surveys are provided by Arestis and Sawyer (2005).

[41] According to Eipstein (2002) and Palley (1996), the concentration of independent monetary authorities on low inflation is directly supported by financial interests.

[42] The international form of this crisis is explained by considering that in liberalized international market exchange arrangements turned to be responsible for uunderstanding the accumulation and growth dynamics in the finance-dominated accumulation regime (Stockhammer, 2008, 2010).

More precisely by considering the case of a closed private economy, the behaviour of aggregate demand is explain by considering the behaviour of investment and consumption expenditures. On the one hand, the recent Post Keynesian literature (e.g. Hein and van Treeck, 2008; Crotty, 1990) argues that the depression of investment profitability due to the increasing degrees of globalization and financialization, has changed the structure of investment by raising the necessity for external finance[43] in order for the materialization of investment plans. The presence of this necessity becomes consistent with the possibility for the development of a third income class that is well known as rentiers[44]. According to Dutt (1992) and Palley (2007) the main characteristic of this income class is the fact that their incomes derive mainly from interest payments, while their presence entails an income distribution from real to financial sector and thereby squeeze wage. Reasonable therefore can be argued that higher interest rates are likely to distribute income in favor of profits (Smithin, 1996), though different regimes of accumulation are proved to range from the expected adverse effects of interest rate variations on capital accumulation, profit rates and therefore economic activity to positive effects (e.g. Lavoie, 1992, 1995; Hein, 1999; Hein and Oschen, 2003). In particular, the increasing power of rentiers and the low propensity to consume, that is assumed to characterize them, has resulted to a reconstruction of their priorities and their concentration on short term profitability that in turn is responsible for a slowdown in capital accumulation (Stockhammer, 2004c; van Treeck, 2008; Orhangazi, 2008).

However we should keep in mind that the higher level of interest rates induces a gradual increase in the debt-to-capital ratio of firms accompanied by higher rates of accumulation, until its new long-run equilibrium is reached. Hence, opposing to the expectations that higher interest rates lead to higher debt-to-capital ratios, a shift leading to higher accumulation rates is not expected. But the stability or instability of the economic system, determines the level of debt that will be accompanied with the level of capital accumulation and thereby the levels of the general economic activity[45]. Nevertheless, the degree of external finance and therefore the degree of sensitivity of economy to financial fragility depends on the level of capacity utilization that determines investment and capitalists' internal funds regarding the actual profit levels. External finance might therefore increase the possibility of macroeconomic instability and financial fragility, which depends on the stability or instability of the financial sector.

As a consequence of this financial instability and its implied uncertainty, additional constraints[46] are raised against the undertaken of investment plans (Carruth et al., 2000),

[43] Alternative sources of finance are usually considered to be: retained profits, bank borrowing and the creation of new shares and bonds.

[44] Considering that this chapter is an attempt to review the existing literature and raise questions about the appropriateness of the way that employment policies are set, for simplicity we do not make any explicit distinction between creditors receiving interest income and shareholders receiving dividend income. For that reason we assume that external finance is represented by rentiers. Besides, there is a growing empirical literature (i.e. Epstein and Power, 2003; Palley, 2007) that provides evidence on the consistency between dramatic growth of rentiers' income class and dramatic relaxation of constraints for external finance and thereby changes in the propensities and priorities of each income class, since 1970s.

[45] This indicates that the roots of the financial crisis are on Minsky's "financial instability hypothesis" (Minsky, 1975).

[46] These constraints are attributed to monetary authorities' concentration on interest rate policies so as inflation to be controlled and not on creating the adequate conditions for higher investment (Dutt, 2006; Hein, 2009; Hein and van Treeck, 2007).

while the presence of rentiers profit earners and their intention to maximize their short-run profits without paying attention in the long-run growth impoverishes investment expenditures further (Hein, 2009). It can be thereby said that financialization not only affects negatively investment but it also distributes income at the expense of labor (Crotty, 1990; Stockhammer, 2004c; Orhangazi, 2008; Stockhammer and Graft, 2010).

From a Kaleckian point of view, such income distribution has dampen effects on aggregate demand as long as wage earners are supposed to have the higher consumption propensity relative to profit earners[47] (Palley, 1994, 1996). But in highly flexible financial markets, the lowered credit standards and the ease households' access to credibility raise the possibility consumption to remain unaffected and being characterized as debt-driven (Cynamon and Fazzari, 2009). In these conditions, though initially rising debt stimulates the levels of aggregate demand, because of the transfer of purchasing power towards low income households that are supposed to have relatively high consumption propensity, finally the levels of debt interest payments burden aggregate demand (Palley, 1994, 1996; Dutt, 2006; Bhaduri et al, 2006). Evidently, the deterioration of income distribution puts downward pressure on the income class with the higher propensity to consume, while financialization stabilizes consumption expenditures by increasing the access of household to credit.

Hence, in finance-led economies the appropriate conditions for economic growth can be created unless investment plans are taken on and consumption expenditures are set as the driving force of growth, so as workers improve their gains and their credit positions (Stockhammer, 2008). Besides, the majority of post Keynesian literature (e.g. Hein, 2006) treats finance-led regime as the fundamental source of capital decumulation and economic instability. This comes to be added to the presence of wage or profit-led regimes that are determined by whether economic activity is expanding through private consumption or private investment (Bhaduri and Marglin, 1990, 1991). Clearly, both of these regimes are related with workers' and capitalists' income shares or rates (wage and profit respectively). According to Post Keynesian literature the period during 1960s and 1980s economic growth was fuelling by wage growth was fuelling economic activity (e.g. Hein and Kramer, 1997; Naastepard and Storm, 2006; Palley, 2007), while the increasing globalization in conjunction with the integrated markets and income distribution in favor of profits, allowed them to determine the whole economic process, though in conditions international competitiveness and rising net exports is supposed to encourage the development of aggregate demand[48] (e.g. Bowles and Boyer, 1995; Gordon, 1995a,1995b; Naastepad and Storm, 2006). In particular, the effects of financialization on aggregate demand and therefore unemployment depend on the sensitivity of economic activity on changes in aggregate demand and profit and wage shares as well as on the impact of interest payments on consumption and investment

---

[47] Stockhammer et al. (2009) provide significant evidence about the way that changes in wage shares are related with changes in consumption expenditures in the euro area.

[48] According to Stockhammer (2004a,2004b) profit-led economies are inconsistent with NAIRU in the sense that unemployment can be reduced through increasing flexibility of wages and reductions in workers' bargaining power, although the equilibrium level of unemployment rate depends on aggregate demand. On the other hand wage-led demand conditions in conjunction with the inverse real balance effects imply an unstable equilibrium, since increases in wage and employment growth improve workers' labor position so that the possible deviation from equilibrium is self fulfilling. As a result, Kalecki's view that the long-run is only a recession of short-run equilibrium is proved.

expenditures and the degree of financial stability (Lavoie, 1995; Lavoie and Goldley, 2001-2; Hein, 2006, 2007; van Treck, 2008; Palley, 2007).

Evidently the debt-driven consumption in conjunction with the weak investment performance and the liberalization of capital flows has relaxed domestic constraints, raised the degree of exchange rates' volatility and created international imbalances (Stockhammer, 2008, 2010). Moreover, the distribution in favor of capital and the implied wage stagnation relative to the limited governmental intervention are proved to be the main sources that underlie current economic crisis, which is proved to be a real economy crisis that is amalgamated with systematic financial fragility[49] (Power et al. 2003; Boyer, 2000; Hein and van Treeck, 2007, 2008; Palley, 2007). Bearing in mind all these, we can easily understand the inappropriateness of the policies of massive liquidity credit and massive governmental intervention through expenditures, though opposing to implications of neoliberalibism, which were adopted in the face of this crisis; the only the achieved was to reassure the credibility of financial institutions and to prevent their collapse (Hein, 2009).

Contrary to expectations, only superficially were the problems resolved; income inequalities were extended, unemployment levels and production slowdown did not overcome, while budget deficits and systematic instability became the major characteristic of economic activity (Palma, 2009; Storm and Naastepad, 2011). This is because on one hand, the increase inequality depressed aggregate demand and prompted monetary policy to react by maintaining low interest rates, which itself allowed private debt to increase beyond sustainable levels. On the other hand, the search for high-return investments led to a process of virtual wealth creation on an unprecedented scale, based on financial innovations which could go on and on in effectively unregulated financial markets. Net wealth became overvalued and house prices gave the false impression that high level of debt was sustainable. Besides, the crisis revealed itself when the financial weapons of mass destruction exposed (Storm and Naastepad, 2010). But in conditions of increasing globalization and financialization there is no room for policy experiments or errors; on the contrary, attention is required to be paid on the actual conditions and the core of the problems.

Thus, the dynamic economic system can be balanced only by achieving its general reconstruction, which should be represented on the adoption of a full employment target and the regulation of the financial sector in the sense that this sector affects essentially economic process (Hein and Truger, 2010). All these in conjunction a reduction in income inequalities and current imbalances, it is possible to push economies away from economic stagnation. Notably, a comparison between the current financial crisis and the period of Great Depression signifies that attention should be concentrate on welfare policies so as unemployment and income inequality to be limited. This means the adoption of a full employment target, which in conjunction with a more active governmental sector can regulate the financial system and push economies away from recession and stagnation conditions. Further, a more active governmental intervention and thereby a more competitive and productive government sector is required to perform as the administrator of any situation in economic system so as to ensure the demand levels that should characterize economies in order to perform efficiently (Palley, 2007; Hein, 2009).

---

[49] This fragility stems either from international (foreign exchange rate) or domestic financial markets (Stockhammer, 2008, 2010).

Nowadays, what it is really required is the deregulation of the financial sector that dominates and determines the whole economic procedure. It must be followed the appropriate policies in order the levels of uncertainty and instability that characterize the financial sector to be reduced, so as attention to be paid on the long rather the short-run growth; only in this way an income distribution will be on favor of actual investment so as to fuel real economic growth (hein and Truger, 2010). For that reason, the use of short-run interest rates as the main instrument for financial and macroeconomic policies should be reconsidered and be used so as to protect rentiers' economic activity from unpredicted behavior of inflation and at the same time to ensure an income distribution in favor of the productive sector of economies so as long-run economic growth to be achieved (Hein, 2009; Hein and Truger, 2010).

In this manner, there is no space for the use of NAIRU as a policy guide unless positive contributions by labor market regulations are taken into account. Therefore in order economies to face unemployment even in the presence of financial fragility it is required the assumptions about ex ante equality between NAIRU level and full employment and full capacity levels, as well as the consideration about long-run money and productivity neutrality that implied the constancy of income distribution, to be rejected (Sawyer, 1998, 2001, 2002; Setterfield, 1996). It is time to understand that economies have the ability to be expanded. For that reason, wages should not be regarded as a cost to firms as the NAIRU model assumes, since higher wages also provide macro benefits in terms of higher demand and faster productivity growth. Higher wages mean higher demand, higher capacity utilization for firms, and hence higher profits. Capital accumulation, in turn, will increase in response to the growth in demand and profit and this will result in higher productivity because investments in new equipment embodies the most advanced technologies and also due to more rapid learning-by-doing in firms. Thus, higher wages and labor market regulations will motivate workers to commit to firms through higher productivity. In accordance, higher wages and pro-worker regulation will also motivate firms to step up investment in labor-saving technological process, thus raising productivity growth (Storm and Naastepad, 2011).

In any aspect of the above analysis, it is proved that economic activity can be fuelled and employment be expanded unless attention is paid on the demand side of economy. This simply means the adoption of Post Keynesian economics, which consider the main reason for persistent unemployment levels the low degree of realism that characterizes mainstream employment policies as well as the shortage of demand that is caused by them, In conditions of general economic stagnation, only income and fiscal policies seem to be the most appropriate for limiting financial instability, regulating economic process and achieving sustained and maintained economic growth. Besides, what it is actually required is the understanding of the core of the problem and the introduction of a new era for economic activity without the perpetuation of current economic problems. This seems to be able only by regarding the actual and not ideal conditions of economy, alongside with the possibility for stable or unstable (mainly) economic activity.

REFERENCES

Arestis, P., Sawyer, M. (2005). Financial liberalization and the finance-led nexus: what have we learned?, in Arestis, P., Sawyer, M., (eds.):*Financial Liberalization. Beyond Orthodox Concerns,* Palgrave Macmillan, Basingtone.

Baker, D., Glyn, A., Howell, D., Schmitt, J. (2004). Unemployment and Labor Market Institutions: The Failure of the Empirical Case for Deregulation, New School CEPA papers, September 2004, Available at: http://www.newschool.edu/cepa/papers/archive/ cepa200404.pdf.

Ball, L. (1997). Disinflation and the NAIRU, in *Reducing Inflation: Motivation and Strategy,* pp. 167-194, edited by Christina Romer and David Romer, University of Chicago Press, also available at: http://www.nber.org/chapters/c8884.pdf.

Ball, L., Mankiw, G.N. (2002). The NAIRU in Theory and Practice. *Journal of Economic Perspectives, 16(4),* 115-36.

Ball, L., Sheridan, N. (2003). Does Inflation targeting Matter?. *NBER Working Paper Series,* No.9577, National Bureau of Economic Research: Cambridge, MA, also available at: http://imf.org/external/pubs/ft/wp/2003/wp03129.pdf.

Bande, R., Karanassou, M. (2007). Labor Market Flexibility and Regional Unemployment Rate Dynamics: Spain 1980-1995. *Institute for the Study of Labor (IZA),* Discussing Papers Series, No.2593, 1-26.

Barro, R. J., Gordon, D. B. (1983). Rules, Discretion and Reputation in a Model of Monetary Policy. *Journal of Monetary Economics, 12(1983),* 101-121.

Bean, C. R. (1994). European Unemployment: A Survey. *Journal of Economic Literature, 32(2),* 573-619.

Bean, C., Layard, R., Nickell, S. (1986). The Rise in Unemployment: A Multi-Country Study. *Economica, 53(210),* Supplement: Unemployment, 1-22.

Bernaske, B.S., Mishkin, F.S. (1997). Inflation Targeting: A New Framework for Monetary Policy. *Journal of Economic Perspectives, 11(2),* 97-116.

Bhaduri, A., Laski, K., Riese, M. (2006). A model of interaction between the virtual and the real economy. *Metroeconomica, 57(3),* 412-427.

Bhaduri, A., Marglin, S.A. (1991). Profit squeeze and Keynesian theory, in Neil, E. J., Semmler, W., (eds), *Nicholas Kaldor and Mainstream Economics,* Basingstoke, London: Macmillan, 123-163.

Bhaduri, A., Marglin, S.A. (1990). Unemployment and the Real Wage: the economic basis for contesting political ideologies. *Cambridge Journal of Economics, 14(4),* 43-39.

Blanchard, O.J., Wolfers, J. (2000). The Role of Shocks and Institution in the Rise of European Unemployment: The Aggregate Evidences. *Economic Journal, 110(462),* Conference Papers, 1-33.

Blanchard, O. J., Katz, F. L. (1997). What We Know and Do Not Know About the Natural Rate of Unemployment. *Journal of Economic Perspective, 11(1),* 51-72.

Blinder, A. S., (1997). Is there a core of Practical Macroeconomics That We Should All Believe?. *American Economic Review, 87(2),* 240-243.

Bowles, S., Boyer, R. (1995). Wages, Aggregate Demand and employment in an open economy: an empirical investigation, in G., Epstein, and H., Gintis, (eds.),

Macroeconomic Policy after a Conservative Era: Studies in Investment, Savings and Finance, Cambridge University Press, 143-171.

Boyer, R. (2000). Is a finance-led growth regime a viable alternative to Fordism? A preliminary analysis. *Economy and Society, 29(1),* 111-145.

Carruth, A., Dickerson, A., Henley, A. (2000). What do we know about investment under uncertainty? , *Journal of Economic Surveys, 24(2),* 119-153.

Chang, R. (1997). Is low unemployment inflationary?. Economic Review, Federal Reserve Bank of Atlanta, Issue Q I, 4-13.

Clarida, E., Gali, J., Gertlet, M. (2000). Monetary Policy Rules and Macroeconomic Stability: Evidence and Some Theory. *Quarterly Journal of Economics, 115(1),* 147-180.

Clarida, E., Gali, J., Gertlet, M. (1999). The Science of Monetary Policy - A New Keynesian Perspective. *Journal of Economic Literature, 37(4),* 1661-1707.

Clark, P., Laxton, D. (1997). Phillips Curves, Phillips Lines and the Unemployment Costs of Overheating, *IMF Working Paper* 97/17.

Collignton, S. (2003). The Role of Monetary Policy in Setting the Natural Rate of Unemployment, paper prepared to be presented at *Workshop Quantitative Prognosen realwirtschaftlicher Effekte der Gelpolitik*, 1-38.

Crotty, J. (1990). Owner-management conflict and financial theories of investment instability: a critical assessment of Keynes. Tobin, and Minsky. *Journal of Post Keynesian Economics, 12(4),* 519-542.

Cynamon, B., Fazzari, S. (2009). Household debt in the consumer age: source of growth-risk of collapse, *Capitalism and Society, 3(2),* Article 3.

Debelle, G. (1997). Discussion of Design Inflation Targets. *Reserve Bank of Australia*, 1-12, available at: http://www.rba.gov.au/PublicationsAndResearch/Conferences/1997/BrashDebelleDisc.pdf.

Demertzis, M., Hallet, A.H. (1995). Is the natural rate of unemployment a useful concept?, in R. Cross (ed.), *The Natural Rate of Unemployment,* Cambridge: Cambridge University Press,315-345.

Dixon, H. (1995). Of coconuts, decomposition and a jackass: the genealogy of the natural rate in R. Cross (ed.), *The Natural Rate of Unemployment,* Cambridge: Cambridge University Press, 57-74.

Dutt, A.K. (2006). Maturity, stagnation and consumer debt: a Steindlian approach. *Metroeconomica, 57(3),* 339-364.

Dutt, A.K. (1992). Rentiers in Post Keynesian Models, in P. Arestis and V. Chick (eds), *Recent Developments in Post Keynesian Economics,* Aldershot: Edward Elgar, 95-122.

Easterly, W., Fischer, S. (2001). Inflation and the Poor. *Journal of Money and Credit and Banking, 33(3),* 160-178.

Elmeskov, J. (1993). High and Persistent Unemployment: Assessment of the Problem and Its Causes. *OECD Economics Department Working Papers,* No. 132, OECD Publishing.

Epstein, G.A. (2002). Financialization, Rentier Interests, and Central Bank Policy, Paper prepared for PERI (Department of Economics and Political Economy Research Institute) Conference on "Financialization of the World Economy", December 7-8, 2001, University of Massachusetts, pp. 1-43, available at: http://www.peri.umass.edu/fileadmin/pdf/financial/fin_Epstein.pdf.

Epstein, G., Power, D. (2003). Rentier incomes and financial crises: an empirical examination of trends and cycles in some OECD countries. *Political Economy Research Institute,* Working paper No. 57, 1-23.

Estrella, A., Mishkin, F. S. (1999). Rethinking the Role of NAIRU in Monetary Policy: Implications of Model Formulation and Uncertainty, in "*Monetary Policy Rules*", edited by Taylor, J.B, NBER- Business circles Series, *31*, 405-435.

Espinosa-Vega, M.A. and Russell, S. (1997). History and Theory of the NAIRU: A Critical Review. *Economic Review, Federal Reserve Bank of Atlanta*, 4-25.

Fair, R. C. (1997). Testing the NAIRU model for 27 Countries. Cowles Foundation, Yale University, March, 1-32.

Issing, O. (2000). The Monetary Policy of the European Central Bank: Strategy and Implementation. Institute for Economic Research, Munich.

Fischer, I. (1926). A Statistical Relation between Unemployment and Price Changes. *International Labor Review, 13(6)*, 785-792.

Fischer, S. (1993). The Role of Macroeconomic Factors in Growth", *Journal of Monetary Economics, 32(1993),* 485-512**.**

Fitoussi, J.-P., Jestaz, D., Phelps, E., Zoega, G. (2000). Roots of the Recent Recoveries: Labor Reforms or Private Sector Forces?. *Brookings Papers on Economic Activity, 2000(1),* 237-331.

Fortin, P. (1996). The Unbearable Lightness of Zero Inflation Oprimisism, in MacLead, B. K., and Osberg, L., (eds) *The Unemployment Crisis,* 14-38.

Franz, W. (2003). Will the (German) NAIRU Please Stand up? Zentrum für Europäische Wirtschaftsforschung, Discussion Paper No. 03-35, Mannheim.

Friedman, M. (1968). The Role of Monetary Policy. *American Economic Review, 58 (1)*, 1-17.

Friedman M. (1977). Nobel Lecture: Inflation and Unemployment. *Journal of Political Economy, 85(3),* 451-472.

Galbraith, J. K. (1997). Time to Ditch the NAIRU. *Journal of Economic Perspectives, 11(1)*, 93-108.

Galbraith, J.K., (1996). Inflation, Unemployment and the Job Structure. *Jerome Levy Economics Institute,* Working paper No. 154, 1-31.

Glyn, A., Baker, D., David, H., Schmitt, J. (2004). Labor Market Institutions and Unemployment: A critical Assessment of the Cross-country Evidence, *University of Oxford, Department of Economics Discussion Paper Series*, No, 168, Available at: http://www.economics.ox.ac.uk/Research/wp/pdf/paper168.pdf.

Gordon, D.M. (1995a). Putting the Horse (back) before the cart: disentangling the macro relationship between investment and saving, in G. Epstein and H. Gintis (eds.), *Macroeconomic Policy after a Conservative Era: Studies in Investment, Savings and Finance,* Cambridge University Press, 57-108.

Gordon, D.M. (1995b). Growth, distribution and the rules of the game: social structuralist macro foundations for a democratic economic policy, in G. Epstein and H. Gintis (eds.), *Macroeconomic Policy after a Conservative Era: Studies in Investment, Savings and Finance,* Cambridge University Press, pp. 384-407.

Gordon, D.M. (1988). The Un-Natural Rate of Unemployment: An Econometric Critique of the NAIRU Hypothesis. *American Economic Review, 78(2)*, 117- 123.

Gordon, R.J. (1997). The Time-Varying NAIRU and its implications for economic policy. Journal of Economic Perspective. *11(1)*, 11-32.

Gordon, R.J., Stock, J. H. (1998). Foundations of the Goldilocks Economy: Supply Shocks and the Time-Varying NAIRU. *Brookings Papers on Economic Activity, 1998(2)*, 297-346.

Hall, R.E. (1975). The Rigidity of Wages and the Persistence of Unemployment. *Brookings Papers on Economic Activity, 1975(2)*, 301-349.

Hein, E. (2009). A (Post-) Keynesian perspective on 'financialisation'. IMK Working Paper 1/2009, Macroeconomic Policy Institute (IMK) at Hans Boeckler Foundation, Duesseldorf.

Hein, E. (2007). Interest rate, Debt, distribution and capital accumulation in a post Kaleckian model. *Metroeconomica,* 58(2), 310-339.

Hein E. (2006). Interest, debt and capital accumulation- a Kaleckian approach. *International Review of Applied Economics, 20(3)*, 337-352.

Hein, E. (1999). Interest rates, income shares and investment in a Kaleckian model. *Review of Political Economy and Social Sciences, 5*, 5-22.

Hein, E., Kramer, H. (1997). Income shares and capital formation: patterns of recent developments. Journal *of Income Distribution, 7(1),* 5-28.

Hein, E., Oschen, C. (2003). Regimes of interest rates, income shares, savings and investment: A Kaleckian model and empirical estimation for some advanced OECD-economies. *Metroeconomica, 54(4)*, 404-433.

Hein, E., Truger, A. (2010). Finance-dominated capitalism in crisis- the case for a Keynesian New Deal at the European and the global level. Institute for International Political Economy Working Paper No. 06/2010, Berlin.

Hein, E., van Treeck, T. (2008). "Financialisation' in Post-Keynesian models of distribution and growth- a systematic review. IMK Working Paper 10/2008, Macroeconomic Policy Institute (IMK) at Hands Boeckler Foundation, Duesseldorf.

Hein, E., van Treeck, T. (2007). 'Financialisation' in Kaleckian/Post Keynesian models of distribution and growth. IMK Working Paper 7/2007, Macroeconomic Policy Institute (IMK) at Hands Boeckler Foundation, Duesseldorf.

Jekinson, T. (1987). The natural rate of unemployment: Does it Exist?". *Oxford Review of Economic Policy, 3(3),* 20-26.

Karanassou, M., Snower, D.J. (1997). Is the natural rate a reference point?. *European Economic Review, 41(3-5),* 559-569.

Kydland, F.E., Prescott, E.C. (1977). Rules Rather than Discretion: The Inconsistency of Optimal Plans. *Journal of Political Economy, 85(3),* 473-492.

Lavoie, M., Godley, W. (2001-2). Kaleckian models of growth in a coherent stock-flow monetary framework: a Kaldorian view. *Journal of Post Keynesian Economics,22,* 277-311

Lavoie, M. (1995). Interest rates in post-Keynesian models of growth and distribution. *Metroeconomica, 46(2)*, 146-177.

Lavoie, M. (1992). *Foundations of Post Keynesian Economic Analysis,* Edward Elgar, Aldershot

Layard, R., Nickell, S., Jackman, R. (1991), Unemployment, Macroeconomic Performance and the Labor Market. Oxford: Oxford University Press.

Lipsey, R.G. (1960). The Relation between Unemployment and the Rate of Change of Money Wage Rates in the United Kingdom, 1862-1957: A Further Analysis. *Economica, 27(105)*, 1-31.

Lucas, R.E. (1975). An Equilibrium Model of the Business Circle. *Journal of Political Economy, 83(6)*, 1113-1144.

Lucas, R.E. (1973). Some International Evidence on Output-Inflation Trade-offs. *American Economic Review, 63(3),* pp. 326-334.

Lucas, R.E. (1972). Expectations and the Neutrality of Money, *Journal of Economic Theory, 4(2),* 103-124.

Mankiw, G.N. (2001). The Inexorable and Mysterious Trade-off between Inflation and Unemployment. *Economic Journal, 111 (471)*, 45-61.

Mankiw, G.N. (1990). A Quick Refresher Course in Macroeconomics. *Journal of Economic Literature, 28 (4)*, 1645-1660.

McCallum B.T. (1984). Monetarist Rules in the Light of Recent Experience. *American Economic Review, 74(2)*, 388-391.

McDonald, I.M. (1995). Models of the range equilibria, in R. Cross (ed.), *The Natural Rate of Unemployment,* Cambridge: Cambridge University Press, 101-152.

Modigliani, F., Papademos, L. (1975). Targets for Monetary Policy in the Coming Year. *Brooking Papers on Economic Activity, 1975(1)*, 141-165.

Naastepad, R., Storm, S. (2006). OECD Demand Regimes (1960-2000). *Post Keynesian Journal of Economics, 29(2),* 213-248.

Nickell, S. (1997). Unemployment and Labor Market Rigidities: Europe Versus North America. *Journal of Economic Perspectives, 11(3)*, 55-74.

Nickell, S. (1998). Unemployment: Questions and Some Answers. *Economic Journal, 108(448)*, 802-16.

Nickell, S. (1990). Unemployment: A Survey. *Economic Journal, 100(401)*, 391-439.

Onaran, O., Stockhammer, E., Graft. L. (2010). Financialisation, income distribution and aggeregate demand in the USA. *Cambridge Journal of Economics,* Forthcoming, doi: 10.1093/cje/beq045.

Orhangazi, O. (2008). Financailisation and capital accumulation the non-financial corporate sector a theoretical and empirical investigation on the US economy: 1973-2003. *Cambridge Journal of Economics, 32(6),* 836-886.

Osbeg, L. (1996). Digging a Hole or Laying the Foundations? The Objectives of Macroeconomic Policy in Canada, in *The Unemployment Crisis,* edited by MacLead Brian K. and Osberg Lars (eds), 14-38.

Ossama, M., Curtis, E., Jagdish, H. (2005). On the Evidence of Non-Linear Structure in Canadian Unemployment. *Applied Economics Letters, 12(2)*, 101-104.

Palley, T. I. (2007). Financialization: What it is and Why it Matters?. Working Papers Series, No, 153, *Political Economy Research Institute*, 1-37.

Palley T.I (1996). Inside Debt, Aggregate Demand and the Cambridge Theory of Distribution. *Cambridge Journal of Economics, 20(2),* 465-474.

Palley T.I (1994). Debt, Aggregate Demand and the Business Cycle: An Analysis in the Spirit of Kaldor and Minsky. *Journal of Post Keynesian Economics, 16(3).* 371-390.

Palma, G. (2009). The Revenge of the Market on the Rentiers. Why Neo-Liberal Reports of the End of History Turned Out to be Premature. *Cambridge Journal of Economics, 33(5)*, 531-38.

Perasan, H., Smith, R. (1995). The natural rate hypothesis and its testable implications, in R. Cross (ed.), *The Natural Rate of Unemployment,* Cambridge: Cambridge University Press, 203-230.

Phelps, E.S. (1995). The origins and further developments of the natural rate of unemployment in R. Cross (ed.), *The Natural Rate of Unemployment,* Cambridge: Cambridge University Press, 15-31.

Phelps, E. (1968). Money-Wage Dynamics and Labor Market Dynamics. *Journal of Political Economy, 78(4)*, 678-711.

Phelps, E. (1967). Phillips Curves, Expectations of Inflation and Optimal Unemployment over Time. *Economica, 34(135)*, 254-281

Phelps, E., Zoera, G. (1998). Natural-Rate Theory and OECD Unemployment, *Economic Journal, 108(448)*, 782-801.

Phillips, W.A. (1958). The Relationship between Unemployment and the Rate of Change of Money Wage Rates in the United Kingdom, 1861-1957. *Economica, 25(100)*, 283-299.

Power, D., Epstein, G., Abrena, M. (2003). Trends in the Rentier Income Share in OECD Countries, 1960-2000. PERI Working Paper Series No. 58, Political Economy Research Institute (PERI), University of Massachussetts Amherst.

Rogerson, R. (1997). Theory Ahead of Language in the Economics of unemployment. *Journal of Economic Perspective, 11(1)*, 73-92.

Romer, D. (1993). The New Keynesian Synthesis. *Journal of Economic Perspectives, 7 (1)*, 5-22.

Romer, C.D., Romer, D.H. (1999). Monetary Policy and the well being of the poor. *Economic Review, Federal Reserve of Kansas City,* Q1, 21-49.

Samuelson, P.A., Solow, R.M. (1960). Analytical Aspects of Anti-Inflation Policy. *American Economic Review, 50 (2),* 177-194.

Sargent, T.J. (1972). Anticipated Inflation and the Nominal Interest Rate. *Quarterly Journal of Economics, 86(2)*, 212-225.

Sargent, T.J. Fand, D., Goldfeld, S. (1973). Recent Expectations, the Real Rate of Interest, and the Natural Rate of Unemployment. *Brookings Papers on Economic Activity, 1973(2),* 429-480.

Sawyer, M.C. (2002). The NAIRU, Aggregate Demand and Investment. *Metroeconomica, 53(1),* 66-94.

Sawyer, M.C. (2001). The NAIRU: a critical appraisal, in P. Arestis and M. Sawyer (eds): "*Money, Finance and Capitalist development",* Northampton Mass Edward Elgar Publishing, 220-254.

Sawyer, M.C. (1998). New Keynesian Macroeconomics and the Determination of Employment and Wages, in *"New Keynesian Economics/Post Keynesian Alternatives,* eds by Rotherm Roy J., 118-133.

Schettkat, R. (2010). Something Unforeseeable Happened? Natural Rate Theory and Economic Crisis. *Intereconomics, 45 (5)*, 297-304.

Setterfield, M.A. (1996). Using the NAIRU as a Basis for Macroeconomic Policy: An Evaluation, MacLead Brian K. and Osberg Lars (eds) *The Unemployment Crisis,* 56-72.

Shiller, R. (2000). *Irrational Exuberance.* Princeton: Princeton University Press.

Siebert, H. (1997). Labor Market Rigidities: At the Root of Unemployment in Europe. *Journal of Economic Perspectives, 11(3),* 37-54.

Smithin, J. (1996). Real Interest Rates, Inflation and Unemployment, MacLead Brian K. and Osberg Lars (eds) *The Unemployment Crisis,* 39-55.

Solow, R.M. (1998). How Cautious Must the Fed Be?. in Solow M. Robert and Taylor B. John (eds.), *Inflation, Unemployment and Monetary Policy*, MIT Press, 1-28.

Solow, R.M. (1986). Unemployment: Getting the Questions Right. *Economica, 53(210),* 23-34.

Solow, R.M. (1979). Alternatively Approaches to Macroeconomic Theory: A Partial View. *Canadian Journal of Economics, 12 (3)*, 339-354.

Snowdon, B., Vane, H.R. (2005), *Modern Macroeconomics: Its Origins, Development and Current State.* Edward Elgar: Cheltenham, UK, Northampton, MA, USA.

Snowden, B., Vane, H., Wynarczyk, P. (1994). A Modern Guide to Macroeconomics: An Introduction to Competing Schools of Thoughts. UK: Edward Elgar.

Staiger, D., Stock, J. H., Watson, M. W. (1997a). The NAIRU, Unemployment and Monetary Policy. *The Journal of Economic Perspectives, 11(1),* 33-49.

Staiger, D., Stock, J.H., Watchon, M.W. (1997b). How Precise Are Estimates of the Natural Rate of Unemployment, in Romer Christina D. and Romer David H. (eds) *Reducing Inflation: Motivation and Strategy,* 195-246.

Stiglitz, J. (1997). Reflections on the Natural Rate Hypothesis. *Journal of Economic Perspectives, 11 (1),* 3-10.

Stock, J. H., Watchon, M.W. (1999). Forecasting Inflation. *Journal of Monetary Economics, 44(2),* 293-335.

Stock, J.H., Watchon, M.W. (1996). Evidence on Structura*l Instability in Macroeconomic Time Series Relations. Journal of Business and Economic Statistics, 14,* 11-29.

Stockhammer, E. (2010). Neoliberalism, Income Distribution and the Causes of Crisis. Research on Money and Finance Discussion Paper No. 19, Kingston University.

Stockhammer, E. (2008). Stylized facts on the finance-dominated accumulation regime. *Competition and Change. 12(2),* 189-207.

Stockhammer, E. (2004a). Explaining European Unemployment: testing the NAIRU hypothesis and a Keynesian approach. *International Review of Applied Economics, 18(1),* 3-24.

Stockhammer, E. (2004b). Is there an equilibrium rate of unemployment in the long-run?. *Review of Political Economy. 16(1)*, 59-77.

Stockhammer, E. (2004c). Financialization and the slowdown of accumulation. *Cambridge Journal of Economics, 25(5)*, 719-741.

Stockhammer, E., Graft, L. (2010). Financial uncertainty and business investment. *Review of Political Economy, 22(4),* 551-568.

Stockhammer, E., Onaran, O., Ederer, S. (2009). Functional income distribution and aggregate demand in the Euro area, *Cambridge Journal of Economics., 33(1),* 139-159.

Storm, S., Naastepad, C.W.M. (2010). Paying for Inequality: The Costs of NAIRU-Based Macroeconomics. Global Labor Column, Corporate Strategy and Industrial Development, University of the Witwatersrand.

Storm, S., Naastepad, C.W.M. (2011). Macroeconomics Without the NAIRU. Cambridge, Massachusetts: Harvard University Press.

Summers, L.H., Abraham, K.G., Watchter, M.L. (1986). Why Is the Unemployment Rate So Very new Full Employment?. *Brookings Papers on Economic Activity, 1986(2),* 339-396.

Taylor, J.B. (1999). A Historical Analysis of monetary Policy Rules, in "*Monetary Policy Rules*", edited by Taylor John B, NBER- Business circles Series, 31, 319-347.

Taylor, J.B. (1998). Monetary Policy Guideness for Employment and Inflation, in Solow M. Robert and Taylor B. John (eds.), Inflation, Unemployment and Monetary Policy, MIT Press, 29

Taylor, J.B. (1995). The Monetary Transmission Mechanisms: An Empirical Framework, *Journal of Economic Perspective, 9(4)*, 11-26.

Taylor, J.B. (1993). Discretion versus policy rules in practice. *Carnegie- Rochester Conference Series on Public Policy, Vol. 39(1993)*, 195-214.

Tobin, J. (1998). Monetary Policy: Recent Theory and Practice. *Cowles Foundation Paper, No. 75*, 1-10, available at: http://cowles.econ.yale.edu/P/cp/p09b/p0975.pdf.

Tobin, J. (1995). The natural rate as new classical macroeconomics, in R., Cross (ed.), *The Natural Rate of Unemployment,* Cambridge: Cambridge University Press, 32-42.

Tobin, J. (1980). Stabilization Policy Ten Years After. *Broking Papers on Economic Activity, 1980 (1)*, 19-89.

Van Treeck, T. (2008). Reconsidering the investment-profit nexus in finance-led economies: an ARDL-based approach. *Metroeconomica, 5(3)*, 371- 404.

In: Labor Markets: Dynamics, Trends and Economic Impact ISBN: 978-1-61470-825-4
Editor: Samir Amine

Chapter 2

NONLINEAR PHILLIPS CURVE AND GROWTH CYCLES

María J. Roa,[1]* Dulce Saura[2] and Francisco J. Vázquez[3]
[1]Centro de Investigación y Docencia Económicas, CIDE A.C., México
[2]Universidad de Zaragoza, Spain
[3]Universidad Autónoma de Madrid, Spain

ABSTRACT

In this chapter, we begin by discussing the literature on economic growth models with unemployment. In particular, we analyze how unemployment is introduced in economic growth models through nonlinear modeling of the Phillips curve, and the dynamics that emerge as a result. We show how an appropriate nonlinear modeling allows an analysis of global dynamics, and adjusts to what the economic theory of labor markets dictates. In the second section of the chapter we develop an economic growth model that includes unemployment and exogenous population growth. Labor market disequilibrium is introduced through a non-market real wage clearing modeled by a nonlinear Phillips curve. The resulting dynamics of the model show that unemployment rate and per capita income fluctuate between a sequence of stable points. They may even follow chaotic paths, exhibiting an unpredictable, completely aperiodic evolution. The resulting dynamics reveal that the emergence of irregular sustained oscillations is related to the lack of sensitivity in wage growth to changes in the employment rate. In the third section, we discuss how introducing unemployment in models of endogenous population growth results in new insights regarding the interaction of economic and demographic variables. Labor force growth is endogenized through micro-founded individual fertility choices. The results show the contribution of considering the following three areas of the literature jointly: unemployment, neoclassical economic growth and demography.

* E-mail address: mariajose.roa@cide.edu.

Introduction

In this chapter, we begin by discussing the literature on economic growth models with unemployment. In particular, we analyze how unemployment is introduced in economic growth models through nonlinear modeling of the Phillips curve, and the dynamics that emerge as a result. Most of this literature introduces a linear approximation of the Phillips curve, following Goodwin [1]. This linear approach is suitable for the study of dynamics very near to full employment. We show how an appropriate nonlinear modeling allows an analysis of global dynamics, and adjusts to what the economic theory of labor markets dictates. Since the work of pioneering authors such as [2], [3], [4], the nonlinearity of the Phillips curve has been used to model the non-responsiveness of wages to unemployment. Near full employment, firms raise their wage rates in order to attract the most suitable workers. However, when unemployment is high, workers are unwilling to accept wage reductions. These non-linear Phillips curve models introduce several key concepts associated with New Keynesian Economics: efficiency wage, insiders-outsiders, and wage bargaining between employers and unions [5]. The labor market disequilibrium is justified by imperfections that explain wage dynamics based on the optimizing behavior of individuals.

In the second section of the chapter we develop an economic growth model that includes unemployment and exogenous population growth. Labor market disequilibrium is introduced through a non-market real wage clearing modeled by a nonlinear Phillips curve. The resulting dynamics of the model show that unemployment rate and per capita income fluctuate between a sequence of stable points. They may even follow chaotic paths, exhibiting an unpredictable, completely aperiodic evolution. The resulting dynamics reveal that the emergence of irregular sustained oscillations is related to the lack of sensitivity in wage growth to changes in the employment rate.

In the third section, we discuss how introducing unemployment in models of endogenous population growth [6], [7], [8], [9] results in new insights regarding the interaction of economic and demographic variables. Labor force growth is endogenized through micro-founded individual fertility choices. The results show the contribution of considering the following three areas of the literature jointly: unemployment, neoclassical economic growth and demography. The concluding section summarizes the results of the chapter. The main conclusions are that the introduction of both a) unemployment in economic growth models (through an appropriate nonlinear modeling of the Phillips curve) and b) endogenous population growth, allows a deeper understanding of the origin and irregular nature of long-run oscillations from an endogenous perspective.

1. Labor Market Disequilibrium Models: Background

The traditional literature on economic growth has assumed that the labor market is in equilibrium [10], [11], [12], [13], [14], [15], [16]. These models of economic growth do not take into account the existence of unemployment, which is generally not only persistent but also strongly fluctuating. The assumptions and basic hypotheses of neoclassical growth models give rise to a very simple dynamic behavior: either an equilibrium point or a regular cycle. The irregular behavior observed in the real world is, in general, exogenously generated.

Nevertheless, over the last three decades a number of works have presented economic growth models in which the labor market situation affects economic fluctuations and growth. Although different in their objectives, so far all of these have introduced the possibility of labor market disequilibrium. Specifically, taking the pioneering work of Goodwin [1] as a starting point, the flexibility of the labor market has been represented by wage dynamics—the Phillips curve. In particular, wages are not very sensitive to unemployment due to various labor market imperfections [5]: mobility costs, information problems, mismatch between the individuals seeking jobs and the positions available, minimum wage, and union wage-fixing.

We briefly review works that focus on how labor market disequilibrium is introduced, and the dynamics that emerge from it. The dynamics that result from these models show that unemployment rate and per capita income fluctuate between a sequence of stable points, and may even follow chaotic paths. Therefore, in these models instability is endogenously generated. In most of them, this complex behavior is due to the introduction of disequilibrium or different imperfections in labor and goods markets.

There are three main groups of growth models in which the possibility of unemployment is contemplated: Regime-Switching Models [17], [18], [19]; Disequilibrium Macroeconomic Models with Money [20], [21] and, more recently, Demo-Economic Fluctuation Models [22], [23], [24]. Besides unemployment, this last group combines demographic-economic variables and long-run fluctuations. We begin this review with the Goodwin model. This is a seminal work that studies cycles, growth and unemployment together.

1.1. Goodwin's Growth Cycle Model

The first model of growth with unemployment we will analyze is Goodwin's class struggle model [1]. In this work, Goodwin gives an endogenous explanation of economic cycles based on the interaction between wages, benefits and unemployment. The model is an application to the economy of that originally proposed in biology by Volterra [25]. It considers the interaction between two species, one of which, the predator, y, feeds on the other, the prey, x, in order to survive. In the absence of predators, the prey grow at a constant rate, a, but their presence causes a decrease in that rate directly proportional to the number of predators. As for predators, their sole source of food is their prey, so in the absence of these, they decrease at a constant rate, c, whereas if there are prey, this rate increases in proportion to their number. Bearing in mind these assumptions, we obtain the following system of differential equations:

$$\begin{cases} \dot{x} = x(a - by) \\ \dot{y} = y(-c + dx) \end{cases} \quad a, b, c, d > 0 \tag{1}$$

where b is a constant that measures predatory efficiency and d is a constant that measures the stimulus to the reproduction of the predators of the predators due to the presence of food. System (1) is known as a *Lotka-Volterra* Prey-Predator model, due to its having also been proposed by biophysicist Lotka [26] for the analysis of certain chemical reactions. Their system has two equilibrium points, $(0,0)$ and $\left(\frac{d}{c}, \frac{a}{b}\right)$. The equilibrium $(0,0)$ is globally asymptotically stable for certain values of the parameters. For other values, the system exhibits conservative oscillations around the equilibrium point $\left(\frac{d}{c}, \frac{a}{b}\right)$. Thus the dynamics of x and y are cyclical.

The Lotka-Volterra system was initially applied to the economy by Goodwin in his article *A Growth Cycle* [1], in which he considers a closed economy that produces a single good that can be used as either a consumption or investment good. There are two factors of production, labor and capital, and two classes of agents, workers and capitalists. The assumptions of the model are:

i) Population (labor force), N, grows at a constant rate, n:

$$\frac{\dot{N}}{N} = n, \quad n \geq 0$$

ii) Labor productivity, $a = \frac{Y}{L}$, grows at a constant rate, α:

$$\frac{\dot{a}}{a} = \alpha, \quad \alpha > 0$$

iii) The capital-output ratio is constant:

$$\frac{K}{Y} = \sigma, \quad \sigma > 0$$

iv) There are two types of agents, workers and capitalists. All production is divided between wages and benefits. Workers consume all of their wages and do not save. Capitalists save all benefits and invest them. Assuming that there is no depreciation, the economy saving function is:

$$\dot{K} = Y - wL = (1-u)Y$$

where w is real wage and u is the workers' share of output.

v) Wages are assumed to change according to a linearized Phillips-curve relationship given by:

$$\frac{\dot{w}}{w} = f(v) = (-\gamma + \rho v)$$

where $v = \frac{L}{N}$ is the employment rate and $\gamma, \rho > 0$ are constants. Goodwin states that the linear approximation is "*quite satisfactory for moderate movements of l near to point 1.*"

From these hypotheses he obtains the following system:

$$\begin{cases} \dot{v} = \left(\frac{1}{\sigma} - (\alpha + n) - \frac{1}{\sigma} u\right) \\ \dot{u} = \left(\rho v - (\alpha + \gamma)\right) u \end{cases}$$

which are Lotka-Volterra equations. Hence, the employment rate (prey) and the wage share (predator) oscillate periodically, whilst the periods and amplitudes depend on the initial conditions. Given the orbit defined by the chosen parameters, employment and wage share will fluctuate cyclically in a deterministic manner—without exogenous shocks. Thus, Goodwin's class struggle cycle is endogenous to the system.

The economic cycle explanation would be as follows: A high employment rate is linked to a high level of trade union force, causing a high wage share in output and a low level of savings. This means that benefits will be low, which successively decreases the employment rate, trade union strength and wage participation. Saving increases and with it benefits and the employment rate, and so the cycle begins once again.

As regards the growth of the economy from hypothesis iii):

$$\frac{\dot{Y}}{Y} = \frac{\dot{K}}{K} = \frac{1-u}{\sigma}$$

The rate of economic growth is endogenous, its being dependent upon how income is distributed between wages and benefits. It follows that the evolution of the rate of growth, as well as the evolution of v and u, is cyclical.

1.2. Disequilibrium Macroeconomic Models with Money

Macroeconomic models of growth and money with disequilibrium arise as an alternative to Tobin's neoclassical model [27]. Taking this, the Tobin model, as their starting point, these disequilibrium models incorporated a series of extensions, including the possibility of unemployment in the use of factors (both labor and capital). The Tobin model is a first attempt to integrate the effects of the growth in the amount of money in the economy and the accumulation of capital within a Solow-type growth model. However, in this model market goods and labor are in equilibrium, and disequilibrium exists only in the money market. Prices are not perfectly flexible and are adjusted depending on the money market imbalance.

Macroeconomic models of growth and money with disequilibrium are also called Keynes-Wicksell models of monetary growth, and were initially developed by Rose [28] and Stein [29]. These models differ from others as they introduce the following main two assumptions: a) savings and investment decisions are made independently, so that the market does not have to be in equilibrium[1] (savings could be not equal to investment), and (b) prices and wages are fixed temporarily—an equation of adjustment depending on market disequilibrium is introduced to represent their dynamics.

[1] For this reason, and in order to include the money market (via an LM equation), these models are called Keynes models. They are also called Wicksell models, due to the characteristics of the investment function they consider and how inflation is determined.

These are high-dimensional macroeconomic models in continuous time that cover disequilibrium in both markets, i.e. those for goods and factors. Specifically, they analyze the interaction of three markets: money, goods and labor. Furthermore, they consider three types of agents: households, firms and government. Households supply labor and acquire different financial assets: cash, bonds issued by the government, and equities issued by firms. The firms produce and invest. Their investment decisions depend on the expected profit ratio, the real interest rate and an exogenous trend that coincides with the natural growth rate. They issue equities to finance their investment projects and adjust their stock of inventories to unsold production. The government intervenes in the economy through monetary and fiscal policy by issuing bonds and collecting taxes. The labor market depends on the market for goods, which—either via household savings decisions or via firms' investment decisions—depends on what happens in the monetary and financial markets.

Although these models may differ in some equations according to the assumptions made, the general macrostructure—as it is referred to by the authors—of these models are the blocks formed by the markets and agents mentioned above. They also include three common elements: the Phillips curve (including inflation expectations, as in Rose [4]), the inventory adjustment process according to the disequilibrium in the goods market [30], and the interaction of capital accumulation and income distribution (Goodwin cyclical growth model). These types of models can be used as a basis for discussing diverse subjects: international trade, technological change, monetary and fiscal policy, and so on. Due to their enormous scale and complex notation, we do not describe them here, instead focusing only on a number of examples of how such models introduce disequilibrium into the goods and labor markets[2]. In order to introduce disequilibrium into the market for goods, prices are considered to be not perfectly flexible and to adjust according to the following equation:

$$\frac{\dot{p}}{p} = \beta_p\left(\frac{I-S}{K}\right) + k_p\left(\frac{\dot{w}}{w} - \pi^e\right) + \pi^e$$

where β_p and k_p are parameters which represent the adjustment speed; I, S and K are the investment, savings and capital of the economy; w is nominal wages, and π^e is the expected rate of inflation. Some of these models still maintain neoclassical characteristics and consider production to be determined by the supply side: all goods produced are consumed or invested. If $S > I$, firms invest their excess supply in new capital goods and, in contrast, if $S < I$, they are forced to cancel some of their investment plans. Hence, saving determines capital accumulation $(\dot{K} = S)$ and, therefore, the output of the economy. The economy always produces at its maximum capacity and prices adjust partially, based on the disequilibrium of the goods market rather than the money market (the latter is in equilibrium because firms issue equities to finance their investment projects), as in the Tobin model.

In these models, disequilibrium situations are not limited to the market for goods, and extend into the labor market. It is assumed that the labor supply is perfectly inelastic and coincides with the population, which grows at a constant exogenous rate. Demand for labor is

2 For a full review of these models see [20],[21].

given by the production and labor requirements per unit of product. Assuming a fixed coefficients production function:

$$Y = \min\left(\frac{L}{x}, yK\right)$$

labor demand is obtained by

$$L^d = \frac{Y}{x} = \frac{yK}{x}$$

where Y is output, x is labor productivity, and y is the inverse of capital productivity, which is considered constant. Labor demand is determined by the capital stock in each period, which is always used to full capacity and is the result of households' saving decisions $(\dot{K} = S)$. In models that introduce exogenous technical progress, labor productivity grows exponentially at the same rate as technical progress, n, $x = x_0 \exp(nt)$.

It is assumed that $L^d \neq L^p$ (the full employment level) and a wage adjustment equation —as a function of the disequilibrium in the labor market—is added to the model. Prices and wages are not perfectly flexible and adjust partially to the goods and labor market disequilibrium. The wage adjustment equation is introduced by a Phillips curve. This way of introducing unemployment is not new, as we already saw in the Goodwin model. However, while Goodwin considers a linear approximation of the Phillips curve in real wages, these works consider different nonlinear approaches to this curve and study the dynamics that emerge from them. The nonlinearities modify such dynamics radically, limiting them to domains with economically plausible outcomes; furthermore, for some parameter choices the dynamics may become chaotic. For example, Rose [4] considers a Phillips curve in monetary wages, and in doing so introduces the expected rate of inflation. This curve is very usual in these kinds of models:

$$\frac{\dot{w}}{w} = \beta_w (V - \bar{V}) + k_w\left(\pi - \pi^e\right) + \pi^e$$

where V is the rate of employment, $\bar{V}$ the NAIRU rate of employment, π the inflation rate, and π^e the expected rate of inflation. This modeling gives rise to a unique limit cycle or persistent cyclical motion in real wages.

Other models that include money and disequilibrium assume the so-called *kinked* Phillips curve:

$$\frac{\dot{w}}{w} = \max\left\{b\left(V - \bar{V}\right) + \pi^e, 0\right\}$$

This is an extreme case of the nonlinear Phillips curve because it introduces downward rigidity in nominal wages; wages are constant if the growth rate is negative. In this literature, it is affirmed that this curve is more realistic than assuming the possibility of wage decreases. The objective is to extend the habitual nonlinearity of the Phillips curve, a *kinked curve*, and to use numerical simulations to show how the dynamic behavior of the model changes considerably and could generate chaotic paths.

Furthermore, this literature develops models of growth incorporating the Keynesian view of production determined by the demand side. This assumption is easily inserted into K-W models by assuming $\dot{K} = I$. Firms increase their stock of inventories if production exceeds demand $(S > I)$, and decreases otherwise $(S < I)$. This assumption seems to be much more valid than the capital stock adjustment of the K-W models; it is much easier for firms to adjust their level of production than their capital stock in the presence of disequilibrium in the goods market. If firms produce what individuals demand, they may not produce at their maximum capacity. So apart from unemployment, these models introduce the underutilization rate of productive capacity in the economy.

As regards the labor market, disequilibrium is introduced in a similar way to that of the K-W models by considering nonlinear dynamic adjustment of prices and wages, which depend on the disequilibrium of the goods and labor markets. For example, Chiarella *et al.,* [21] introduce deviations of the utilization rate of productive capacity to its natural rate in the Phillips curve:

$$\frac{\dot{p}}{p} = \beta_p \left(U - \bar{U}\right) + k_p \left(\frac{\dot{w}}{w} - \pi^e\right) + \pi^e$$

$$\frac{\dot{w}}{w} = \beta_w (V - \bar{V}) + k_w \left(\pi - \pi^e\right) + \pi^e$$

where U is the rate of capacity utilization in the economy, and $\bar{U}$ is the normal rate of capacity utilization.

Some models also introduce several key concepts associated with *New Keynesian Economics*: efficiency wage models, insiders-outsiders, and wage bargaining between employers and unions [5]. They explain the relative rigidity of wages resulting from various market imperfections: mobility costs, information imperfections, mismatch between the number of workers seeking jobs and the vacancies available, minimum wage and union wage-fixing, all of which explain wage dynamics based on the optimizing behavior of individuals. In addition to these imperfections, some of these models introduce unemployment *hysteresis*: the equilibrium unemployment rate depends on the history of the actual unemployment rate.

For example, following the literature of insiders-outsiders models, Chiarella and Flaschel [20], chapter 7, distinguishes between the employment rate of the economy and the employment rate of insiders. The latter is determined by the demand, which is known by the firms:

$$L^w = \gamma L^w + \beta_v \left(L^d - L^w\right)$$

where L^w is the insiders' employment rate and γ is the expected growth rate. Then, the insiders-outsiders effect is introduced into the wage equation:

$$\frac{\dot{w}}{w} = \beta_{w1}(V - \bar{V}) + \beta_{w2}(V^{w} - 1)k_{w}\left(\pi - \pi^{e}\right) + \pi^{e}$$

where the normal rate of capacity utilization is assumed to be one. As regards the NAIRU, it is assumed that:

$$\dot{\bar{V}} = \beta_{\bar{V}}\left(V - \bar{V}\right)$$

Finally, population growth, which depends positively on the employment rate of the economy, V, and the expected growth rate, γ, are regarded as endogenous. This assumption seeks to reflect the fact that there is a segment of the population that expects to be incorporated immediately into the labor force when the forecast is optimism. The forecast is measured by the variables V and γ.

Chiarella *et al.* [21], chapter 6, introduce the results of Carlin and Soskice's wage-bargaining model [31] in order to endogenize the NAIRU. This model introduces imperfections in the labor and goods markets through two equations for each market. The first corresponds to the setting of wages, which results from a process of bargaining between unions and firms:

$$w^{B} = p^{e}B(1 - V) \quad B < 0$$

where the bargaining wage, w^{B}, depends on the expected level of prices, p^{e}, and the employment rate, *V*. In order to obtain this result, it is assumed that each firm's union maximizes the utility of its representative member.

The second equation is derived by assuming that a goods market is imperfectly competitive:

$$p = \frac{1}{1 - 1/\varepsilon}CM = \frac{1}{1 - 1/\varepsilon}\frac{w}{PM}$$

where CM and PM are cost and the marginal product respectively. Both equations can be drawn in the plane ($w/p, V$), their intersection defining a unique equilibrium of V^{*} (NAIRU).

To introduce this result, the authors rewrite the macroeconomic model in discrete time and introduce the following adjustment equations:

$$\hat{w}_{t} = \frac{w_{t} - w_{t-1}}{w_{t}} = \frac{w^{B}(V_{t}) - w_{t-1}}{w_{t-1}} + \pi_{t}^{e}$$

$$\hat{p}_{t} = \frac{p_{t} - p_{t-1}}{p_{t}} = \hat{w}_{t}$$

$$\pi_{t+1}^{e} = \pi_{t}^{e} + \beta_{\pi^{e}}\left(\hat{p}_{t} - \pi_{t}^{e}\right)$$

Furthermore, they analyze the dynamics that characterize the system for an alternative modeling of the Phillips curve. They conclude that the introduction of nonlinear behavior through a Phillips curve in these integrated dynamic systems gives rise to very complex dynamics. In some cases, government policies may sometimes stabilize the economy. Specifically, for a kinked Phillips curve the system dynamics are cyclical and the government can bring the economy to a steady state with a positive growth rate in the money supply.

1.3. Regime-Switching Growth Models with Disequilibrium

Another type of growth models that introduce unemployment are the so-called Regime-Switching Models [17], [18], [19]. In thesc, macroeconomic disequilibrium is extended to deal with capital accumulation in the long run. A growth model à la Kaldor or à la Solow is chosen as a framework. The real wage is supposed to be adjusted slowly, whilst the labor market is under a regime of excess supply (unemployment), excess demand (over-employment), or (exact) full employment. The actual transactions are assumed to take place at the minimum level of labor force demand and supply. In the unemployment regime, workers cannot satisfy their notional wage income, whereas in the over-employment regime, the owners of firms cannot fulfill their notional plan of production and profit. Therefore, the amount of saving depends not only on the wage rate but also on which regime the labor market is in. The amount of saving determines a path for capital accumulation, while the wage rate may be partially adjusted according to the regime of the labor market. Movements in capital per capita and the wage rate will trace a path characterized by disequilibrium and economic growth. Next we briefly analyze a pioneering model of this literature, that of Ito [18].

We assume a neoclassical well-behaved production function $Y_t = F(K_t, L_t)$. Capital stock is given and the wage rate is fixed. The representative firm maximizes the flow of profit with respect to labor input. The demand for labor, L_t^d, is the level of labor input which satisfies:

$$w_t = F_L(K_t, L_t)$$

where $F_L \equiv \frac{\partial F}{\partial L}$. Since F is homogeneous of degree one, F_L is homogeneous of degree zero. Therefore we have:

$$L_t^d = \Omega(w_t)K_t \qquad \Omega < 0$$

It is assumed that the labor supply per capita, l, is inelastic, therefore, the aggregate labor supply, L, is

$$L_t^s = lN_t$$

where N is the population, which is assumed to grow at a constant rate, $\frac{\dot{N}}{N} = n$. Employment in the economy is the minimum of demand and supply:

$$L_t = \min\left[L_t^d, L_t^s\right]$$

There are three possible regimes in the labor market: full-employment, unemployment and over-employment, respectively, $L^d = L^s$, $L^d < L^s$ and $L^d > L^s$.

Ito distinguishes between two levels of capital. First, he defines capital per capita as $k_t = \frac{K_t}{N_t}$—which does not depend on the current wage rate or the actual level of employment—and the desired capital/labor ratio, $k_t^d = \frac{K_t}{L_t^d} = \frac{1}{\Omega(w_t)}$. This variable is a function of the current wage rate, although capital per capita is not. Using this and the Euler equation:

$$w_t = f(k_t^d) - k_t^d f(k_t^d)$$

Capital accumulation is determined solely by the savings decision, as in a neoclassical growth model:

$$\dot{K} = s_w wL + s_K(Y - wL)$$

where $0 < s_w < 1$ and $0 < s_k < 1$. This equation is rewritten as:

$$\dot{K} = s_k Lf\left(\frac{K}{L}\right) + \left(s_w - s_K\right)wL$$

hence, the capital accumulation equation is different for each regime. The demand and supply for output is always in equilibrium since unconsumed output becomes a saving, which is equivalent to investment.

Finally, we consider a wage adjustment equation, where the adjustment speed, ξ, is different in each regime:

$$\dot{w} = \xi_1 \frac{L^d - L^s}{L^s} \quad \text{si } L^d \geq L^s, \quad \xi_1 > 0 \tag{2}$$

$$\dot{w} = \xi_2 \frac{L^d - L^s}{L^s} \quad \text{si } L^d < L^s, \quad \xi_2 > 0 \tag{3}$$

In the full-employment regime, the dynamic equation of capital accumulation per capita is:

$$\dot{k} \equiv k\left(\frac{\dot{K}}{K} - \frac{\dot{N}}{N}\right) = s_w f\left(k\right) + \left(s_w - s_K\right)kf(k) - nk_t$$

and, since the labor market is in equilibrium, $\dot{w} = 0$.

In the unemployment regime, the dynamic of capital accumulation is:

$$\dot{k}_t = k_t\left[s_w\left(\frac{f(k^d)}{k^d}\right)+(s_K - s_w)f(k_t^d - n)\right]$$

and the wage equation is (2).

Finally, in the over-employment regime, the dynamic of capital accumulation is:

$$\dot{k}_t = s_K f(k_t)+(s_w - s_K)w_t - nk_t$$

and the wage equation is (3).

In all these regimes, capital dynamics are determined by savings and wages. When $s_K \leq s_w$, unemployment and over-employment regimes have a single global and asymptotically stable stationary state. However, when $s_w < s_K$ the global stability of the stationary state cannot be guaranteed and local stability is difficult to establish. The economy remains on a path of disequilibrium that oscillates between the regimes of unemployment and over-employment, straying from or converging towards the stationary equilibrium.

From the pioneering model of Ito, various extensions have been developed that primarily focus on endogenizing the savings rate, introducing the money market, and considering the possibility of disequilibrium in the goods market [32]. In order to endogenize the savings rate, agents solve a Ramsey-type optimization problem [33]. As regards the introduction of money and disequilibrium in the goods market, this is done in the same way as in the macroeconomic disequilibrium models with money seen in the last section.

1.4. Demo-Economic Fluctuation Models

These models study the dynamic interaction between economic growth, unemployment, income distribution and population growth [34], [22], [23], [35]. In doing so, they consider two main elements: a) unemployment and b) wages dynamically related to unemployment according to a linear Phillips curve, based on labor market theories of union, job search and efficiency wage. Some of these also include c) labor supply determined by the micro-founded fertility choices of individuals, d) age structure and the participation rate in the labor market, and e) heterogeneous fertility of employed and unemployed individuals. The model that we will present in section 3 is based on this literature. The common theoretical framework is the Goodwin model [22], [23]. However, the assumption of Leontief or Cobb-Douglas technologies is easily adaptable to consider profit-maximizing firms in a Goodwin-type model [34], [35]. Manfredi and Fanti [22], [23] consider different extensions of the Goodwin model in order to analyze the mechanisms that explain the long-run oscillation of the economy and population. Now, let us briefly analyze these. A first extension is to consider that employed and unemployed individuals have different exogenous fertility rates, denoted by b_e and b_u respectively. Hence, the labor supply growth rate n can be written as:

$$n_s = n = (b_e - \mu_e)E + (b_u - \mu_u)(1-E) = n_e E + n_u (1-E) \quad (4)$$

where $E = \frac{L}{N_s}$ is the employment rate (L is labor actually employed and N_s is the labor supply), and μ_e and μ_u denote the exogenous mortality rates in the employed and the unemployed populations respectively.

Next, they introduce equation (4) into the Lotka-Volterra system (1). In the presence of heterogeneous fertility rates, Goodwin's conservative oscillations are replaced by regimes of local stability or instability, depending on whether the fertility rate of the employed is greater or less than the fertility rate of the unemployed. In particular, when $n_e > n_u$—i.e. where Malthusian conditions exist—a positive equilibrium is stabilized, and is destabilized in the opposite case, $n_e < n_u$, i.e. when there are Post-Malthusian conditions.

Secondly, they incorporate the age structure of the population.

Let the functions $P_1(t)$, $P_2(t)$, $P_3(t)$ be the number of individuals—young, adults and the retired respectively—at time t:

$$\begin{aligned} P_1(t) &= B(t) - D_1(t) - P(A_1,t) \\ P_2(t) &= P(A_1,t) - P(A_2,t) - D_2(t) \\ P_3(t) &= P(A_2,t) - D_3(t) \end{aligned} \quad (5)$$

where $B(t)$ is the birth function at time t, $D_i(t)$ denotes the number of deaths in each group at time t, and $P(A_i,t)$ denotes the flows between groups as a consequence of aging.

Using several simplifying assumptions, system (5) can be rewritten in a dynamic equation for n:

$$\dot{n} = (-1)\left[n^2 + Pn - B(w,E)\right] \quad (6)$$

where w is the real wage. Equation (6) is embedded into the Lotka-Volterra equations (1). This dynamic analysis shows that the system always admits the zero equilibrium. This equilibrium is only stable when the fertility of the unemployed is very high, otherwise, the equilibrium becomes unstable and a positive equilibrium appears.

Another extension considered is the optimal fertility choices of employed individuals [6], [7], [8]:

$$\begin{aligned} &U(c,b) = c^a (b - b^o)^{1-a}, \quad 0 < a < 1 \\ &\text{s.a } c + qb \le w \end{aligned}$$

where b is the birth rate, c consumption, and q is the real cost per child. Simple calculations give the demand for children:

$$b = ab^o \frac{(1-a)w}{q}$$

which is a linear Malthusian-fertility function. In this literature, fertility is termed Malthusian when the fertility rate is an increasing function of wages. It summarizes the known Malthusian mechanism by which phases of increasing wages usually yield increases in the workers' number of children.

The endogenous fertility rate is introduced into the model, and the dynamics that emerge from it are analyzed. When the fertility rate of the unemployed is below that of the employed the interaction between heterogeneous fertility and age structure may lead to sustained oscillations depending on the age of entry into the labor force. This is an example of the *Malthusian cycle*: sustained oscillations depend on the age of entry into the labor force [36]. In addition, the analysis shows that when the fertility rate of the employed is lower than that of the unemployed, both transient and robust chaotic phenomena may appear, depending largely on the age patterns of entry into the labor market.

Finally, another extension considered in Manfredi and Fanti [23] is to introduce a participation schedule dependent on the state of the labor market via a *discouraged worker* hypothesis [37], [38], [39], whereby groups of secondary workers have a tendency to move into and out of the labor force with the business cycle, looking for jobs when these are available, while giving up their job search during recessions. The participation rate $s(t) = \frac{N_s(t)}{N_s(t)}$,

and n_s satisfies $n_s = \frac{\dot{N}_s(t)}{N_s(t)} = \frac{\dot{s}(t)}{s(t)} + n$. The authors take a linear approximation of s:

$$\frac{\dot{s}}{s} = -\delta + q_1 U + q_2 w, \qquad q_1 > 0, q_2 > 0.$$

When we introduce the dynamics of s into the Lotka-Volterra system, dynamic analysis shows that oscillations are the result of the balance between delayed entrance into the labor force due to the age structure mechanism, and the stabilizing pressure due to participation.

Taking as the starting point the models we have just described, in the following sections we develop an economic growth model that includes both unemployment and endogenous population growth, and we also analyze its dynamics behavior.

2. A Model of Economic Growth with Unemployment

In this section we present a model of economic growth with unemployment—making the standard assumptions of economic growth literature—, though with disequilibrium in the labor market. Our intention in doing so is to consider the origin and nature of economic fluctuations in greater depth by studying the interaction between economic growth and the unemployment rate. In particular, we will show how the simple introduction of nonlinear modeling in the labor market can generate large irregularities in the fluctuation of the economic variables, and temporal evolutions with complex dynamics.

2.1. Basic Model

Final Good and Knowledge Production

A single economy exists that produces a final good, Y_t , at the end of period t. The market for this good is perfectly competitive. The aggregate production function is:

$$Y_t = F(L_t, h_t) = \mu(\gamma h_t L_t)^{\alpha}\, \hat{h}_t^{\beta}, \quad 0<\alpha<1,\ 0<\gamma<1,\ \beta>0, \mu>0$$

where μ is sector productivity and γ is the fraction of time that people devote to the production of the final good. We assume both are exogenous and constant. L_t denotes physical labor and h_t represents the individual level of knowledge. Labor input is measured in efficiency units, $h_t L_t$, or labor-augmenting technical progress.

$\hat{h}_t$ denotes the average level of human capital in the productive sector [13]. Its introduction into the production function is intended to reflect the fact that people are more productive when they are surrounded by people with a high level of knowledge; thus, the level of knowledge of an agent affects not only their own productivity but also that of the rest of the agents.

If we assume the absolute homogeneity of agents, all individuals have the same level of knowledge and $\hat{h}_t = h_t$. Therefore, the production function can be rewritten as:

$$Y_t = F(L_t, h_t) = \mu(\gamma L_t)^{\alpha}\, h_t^{\alpha+\beta} \tag{7}$$

For the sake of simplicity, physical capital is assumed constant. It could be included in the parameter μ, which reflects the effect of different inputs on production. This hypothesis is considered in traditional models of endogenous economic growth which, like ours, focus mainly on explaining knowledge or human capital as engineers of economic growth [40].

Besides final goods, the productive sector also produces knowledge. In the spirit of Lucas [13], who identifies knowledge with human capital, we consider knowledge to evolve according to

$$\frac{h_{t+1}}{h_t} = 1+\delta(1-\gamma) \qquad 0<\delta<1$$

where $(1-\gamma)$ is the fraction of time devoted to knowledge production and δ is the productivity of the sector. To simplify the subsequent analysis, the above equation is rewritten as:[3]

[3] Since $1+x \sim e^x$ for $x \sim 0$, then $1+\delta(1-\gamma) \sim e^{\delta(1-\gamma)}$ for $\delta(1-\gamma) \sim 0$.

$$\frac{h_{t+1}}{h_t} = e^{\delta(1-\gamma)} \tag{8}$$

In our model, the acquisition of knowledge does not result from decisions by individuals. Instead, this decision (represented in our model by the exogenously given parameter γ) can best be interpreted as cultural or social in nature. This idea is similar to that of Lucas ([13], p. 19), who defined human capital as a social activity involving groups of people. Similarly, Jones [8] relates the exogenous fraction of time devoted to knowledge accumulation to the role of institutional development, which promotes the production of knowledge by creating, defining, and enforcing property rights.

Consumers-Workers

It is assumed that the labor supply is perfectly elastic and equal to the labor force A_t. The labor force grows at the same (constant and exogenous) rate n as the total population N, hence:[4]

$$\frac{A_{t+1}}{A_t} = \frac{N_{t+1}}{N_t} = 1+n, \quad n>0 \tag{9}$$

All consumers are equal and are endowed with one unit of time that they supply inelastically to the productive sector at the beginning of each period. A constant fraction of their time is used in producing the final good and the rest is used in producing knowledge. Both activities are paid at the same wage, denoted by w_t, at the end of the period.[5] This is the only income they receive and is spent entirely on consumption (there is no domestic saving). So the total demand in each period is for the final good and is equal to the wage income paid at the end of the previous period:

$$D_{t+1} = C_{t+1} = w_t L_t \tag{10}$$

where D_{t+1} is the total demand in period $t+1$, C_{t+1} is the total consumption in period $t+1$, L_t is employment, and $w_t L_t$ is the total wage income paid at the end of period t.

Final Good Production and Labor Demand

The productive sector produces whatever individuals demand. The production process for the final good takes one period. In each period, final production is equal to the total demand in the next period, which we assume is known by the productive sector,

---

[4] That is, we assume that $N = \lambda A$, with $\lambda > 1$. In Spain in particular, this relation is very stable.

[5] The model can easily be rewritten in terms of a two-sector economy (final good and knowledge), in which there exists a constant proportionality between the populations devoted to the production of final good and knowledge, and workers are paid at the same wage.

$$Y_t = D_{t+1} \tag{11}$$

From this equation we obtain the total demand for labor. At the beginning of each period, the productive sector hires the number of workers for which the supply is equal to the demand of goods in the next period. Substituting the demand and supply expressions:

$$\mu(\gamma L_t)^{\alpha} h_t^{\alpha+\beta} = w_t L_t$$

and solving for L_t, we obtain the total labor[6] demand of the economy:

$$L_t = \left(\frac{\mu \gamma^{\alpha} h_t^{\alpha+\beta}}{w_t} \right)^{\frac{1}{1-\alpha}}$$

This decision rule is clearly Keynesian in nature because production adjusts to demand. The supply side makes a prediction, which we have assumed is perfect, regarding demand and this is what it produces.

Saving and Knowledge Investment

If Lt is used in the production of final goods and if the economy does not invest in knowledge, final production (potential product) would be $\tilde{Y}_t$:

$$\tilde{Y}_t = \mu L_t^{\alpha} h_t^{\alpha+\beta}$$

So, if all employment were used in final good production and none in the production of knowledge, a great amount of output would be obtained. The difference between the production levels is positive:

$$\tilde{Y}_t - Y_t = \mu L_t^{\alpha} h_t^{\alpha+\beta} - \mu(\gamma L_t)^{\alpha} h_t^{\alpha+\beta} = (1-\gamma^{\alpha})\tilde{Y}_t$$

and shows the opportunity cost of using labor inputs in the production (investment) of knowledge instead of final goods. This difference is interpreted as the total savings of the economy, which is invested a priori in knowledge accumulation. Consequently, γ^{α} would be the fraction of income or output spent on final good consumption, while $1-\gamma^{\alpha}$ would be the fraction spent on saving and investment in knowledge.

[6] Although the labor supply could be lower than demand—which would generate excess output in the next period -, we assume that $L_t \leq A_t$, hence the goods market is always in equilibrium.

Wage Dynamics

Unlike in the neoclassical framework of perfect competition, wages are not perfectly flexible. Wage dynamics are determined by the disequilibrium of the labor market, and are represented by a Phillips equation, where wages are increasing with the rate of employment:

$$\frac{w_{t+1}-w_t}{w_t}=\phi(l_t), \quad \phi'(l)>0$$

or equivalently:[7]

$$\frac{w_{t+1}}{w_t}=h(l_t), \quad h'(l)>0$$

where $l_t=\frac{L_t}{A_t}$ is the rate of employment. This modeling shows how the situation in the labor market affects the growth of wages. Near to full employment, firms raise wage rates in order to attract the most suitable workers. This idea can be interpreted in terms of workers' bargaining power, because we assume that this power increases, and so wages grow, when the economy is closer to full employment.

As we discussed in the introduction, for simplicity, it is very common to introduce a lineal approximation of $h(l_t)$ in line with Goodwin [1]:

$$h(l_t)=1-r+sl_t \qquad s,r>0$$

However, we consider the following nonlinear Phillips curve:

$$\frac{w_{t+1}}{w_t}=\exp(-a+bl_t), \; b>a>0 \tag{12}$$

which is illustrated in figure 1. Nonlinear modeling allows the behavior of the Phillips curve to be reflected in a more appropriate way; in particular for values of the employment rate l far from full employment, for which the linear approximation does not adapt appropriately.

[7] Although function $\phi(l)$ is normally called the Phillips curve, we will also call function $h(l)$ the Phillips curve, for the sake of argument. Notice that both functions have the same characteristics because $h(l)$ is a translation of $\phi(l)$: $h(l)=1+\phi(l)$.

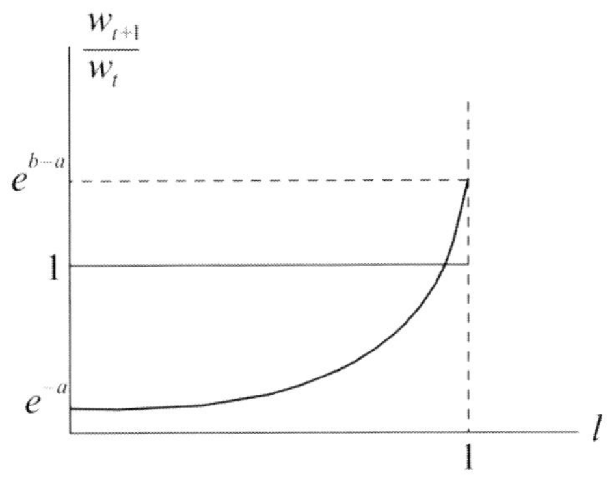

Figure 1. Wage dynamics and rate of employment.

Regarding parameters a and b, we make the following assumptions: On the one hand, in order to guarantee that wages do not rise when $l = 0$, it is necessary that $a > 0$, that is, $e^{-a} < 1$. On the other hand, under full employment, the growth of wages must be high, in order for $b - a$ to be large; in particular, we require that $e^{b-a} > 1$. Therefore, we assume $b > a$ and $a > 0$.

Dynamic Analysis of the Model

The model is formalized by equations (7)-(12). Then, from condition (7) of supply equal to demand, we get:

$$\frac{Y_{t+1}}{Y_t} = \frac{D_{t+2}}{D_{t+1}}$$

and substituting the expressions for production (7) and demand (10) we obtain:

$$\left(\frac{h_{t+1}}{h_t}\right)^{\alpha+\beta}\left(\frac{L_{t+1}}{L_t}\right)^{\alpha} = \frac{w_{t+1}}{w_t}\frac{L_{t+1}}{L_t}$$

Taking logarithms in the last expression:

$$(1-\alpha)\ln\frac{L_{t+1}}{L_t} = (\alpha+\beta)\ln\frac{h_{t+1}}{h_t} - \ln\frac{w_{t+1}}{w_t}$$

And taking into account (8) and (12), we get:

$$(1-\alpha)\ln\frac{L_{t+1}}{L_t} = (\alpha+\beta)\delta(1-\gamma) - (-a + bl_t)$$

This expression can be rewritten in terms of l_t :

$$\ln\left(\frac{L_{t+1}}{L_t}\frac{A_{t+1}}{A_t}\frac{A_t}{A_{t+1}}\right)=\frac{(\alpha+\beta)\delta(1-\gamma)+a-bl_t}{(1-\alpha)}$$

that is:

$$\frac{l_{t+1}}{l_t}=\frac{1}{1+n}\exp\left(\frac{(\alpha+\beta)\delta(1-\gamma)+a-bl_t}{(1-\alpha)}\right)=\frac{1}{1+n}\exp\left(\frac{(\alpha+\beta)\delta(1-\gamma)+a}{(1-\alpha)}\right)\cdot\exp\left(\frac{-bl_t}{(1-\alpha)}\right)$$

Letting $r=\frac{1}{1+n}\exp\left(\frac{(\alpha+\beta)\delta(1-\gamma)+a}{(1-\alpha)}\right)$ and $s=\frac{b}{(1-\alpha)}$, we obtain the nonlinear dynamic equation of the employment rate:

$$l_{t+1}=f(l_t)=re^{-sl_t}l_t \tag{13}$$

Equation (13) is known as the Ricker-Moran equation [41], [42], [43], [44], and has been employed in ecology, especially in the study of fish populations. It has been used subsequently in various sciences (epidemiology and entomology, for example). Its dynamics and the possibility of chaos behavior are well documented in ecology and mathematics literature [45], [46].

The graph of $f(l_t)$ is a function passing through $(0,0)$, and $\lim_{l\to\infty}f(l)=0$. Its maximum point is $(\frac{1}{s},\frac{r}{es})$ and solving

$$l=re^{-sl}l$$

$f(l_t)$ has two fixed points, $l_1^*=0$ and $l_2^*=\frac{\ln r}{s}$. In figure 2, $f(l_t)$ is drawn for different values of r.

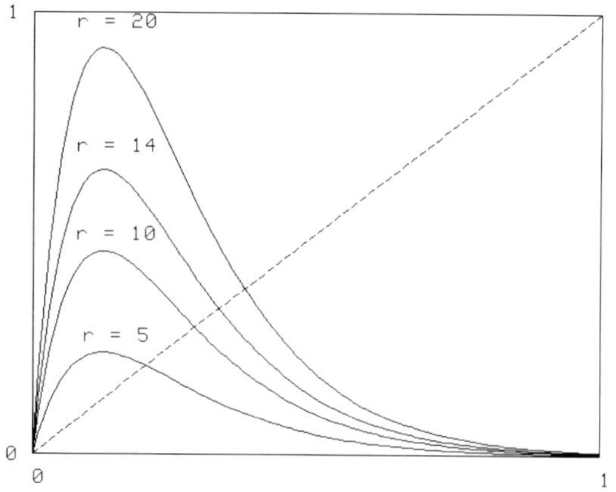

Figure 2. Function $f(l)$ for different values of r.

Although equation (13) depends on two parameters,[8] as we will show, its dynamic behavior will depend mainly on the value of parameter r, while the value of parameter s will only affect the values of the fixed and periodic points.

For $r<1$, the unique fixed point is zero because l_2^* is negative. In order to study the local stability of the fixed point, we evaluate the absolute value of the slope of f:

$$\left|f'(l)\right| = r\left|1-sl\right|e^{-sl}$$

at the fixed point. Since $\left|f'(l_1^*)\right| = r<1$, zero is a locally stable fixed point. For $r=1$, the fixed point is neutrally stable and for $r>1$, l_1^* becomes unstable and the second fixed point appears, l_2^* (now positive). The slope of f evaluated at this fixed point is $\left|f'(l_2^*)\right| = 1-\ln r$. For $r<1$, l_2^* (although negative) was unstable. Nevertheless, for $r>1$ the fixed point becomes locally stable and a *transcritical bifurcation* appears. Stability is guaranteed if $\left|f'(l_2^*)\right|<1$, that is, for $1<r<e^2$.

For $r=e^2$, the behavior starts to become complex. For this value, l_2^* becomes unstable and a cycle of period two emerges, and now a *period doubling bifurcation* appears. In order to study the dynamic behavior in this zone and the appearance of cycles of period two, we analyze the second iteration of f:

$$l_{t+2} = f(l_{t+1},r) = f\left(f\left(l_t,r\right),r\right) = f^2(l_t,r) = r^2\left(l\exp(-sl)\right)\exp(-s\left(rl\exp(-sl)\right))$$

The stability of the cycle of period two is analyzed using the absolute value of the scope of f^2 evaluated at the fixed points of f^2, given by the equation:

$$l = r^2\left(l\exp(-sl)\right)\exp(-s\left(rl\exp(-sl)\right))$$

Since it is not possible to have an expression of the fixed points for any value of r, from now on we will limit ourselves to a numerical analysis of particular values of r. For $r>12.504$, the cycle of period two becomes unstable and a new fixed point of four period emerges (a new period-doubling bifurcation). If we continue increasing the value of r, the same process of period-doubling bifurcation is repeated: the cycle of period four becomes unstable and a cycle of period eight appears, which loses its stability, followed by a cycle of period sixteen, and so on and so forth. In figure 3, the time evolutions for different values of r are drawn, and the dynamic behaviors we have just described are shown. Specifically, for $r=5$, a stable fixed point; for $r=10$, a stable cycle of period two; for $r=13$, a stable cycle of period four, and for $r=14.5$, a stable cycle of period eight.

---

[8] In our case, the values of the parameters must guarantee that $L_t < A_t$ ($l<1$), so $\frac{1}{s} = \frac{(1-\alpha)}{b} < 1$ and $f(\frac{1}{s}) = re^{-1}\frac{1}{s} < 1$ must be satisfied; that is, $b+\alpha>1$ and $r<es$.

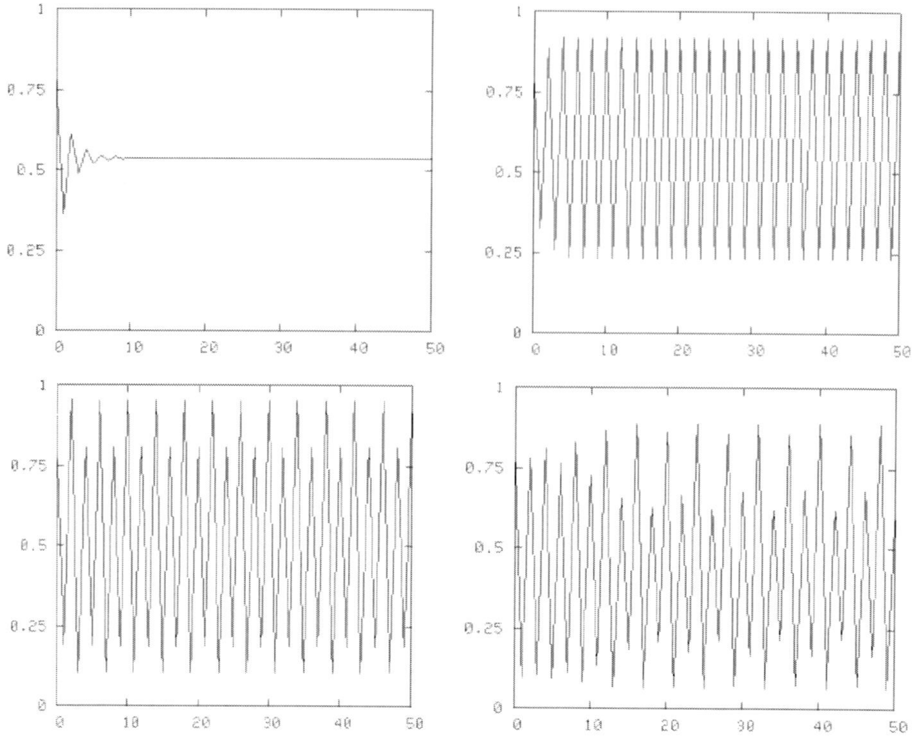

Figure 3. Time evolutions of *l* for different values of *r*.

This bifurcation process produces an infinite sequence of cycles of 2^n $(n \to \infty)$ that are bound by a certain parameter value ($r_c \approx 14.767075$). Beyond this limit, cycles of odd periods appear. These are long at first, but as *r* increases they become shorter until a cycle of period three appears. Here we enter into the "chaotic" regime, which is characterized by a finite number of attracting fixed points, an infinite number of repelling fixed points, and an uncountable number of points (initial conditions) whose trajectories are totally aperiodic. The left side of figure 4 shows (for $s = 9$) the *bifurcation diagram*, when the "route to chaos" is visible. To the right of the graph, the *Lyapunov exponents* are drawn (which measure the sensitivity to initial conditions and are positive in the chaotic area).

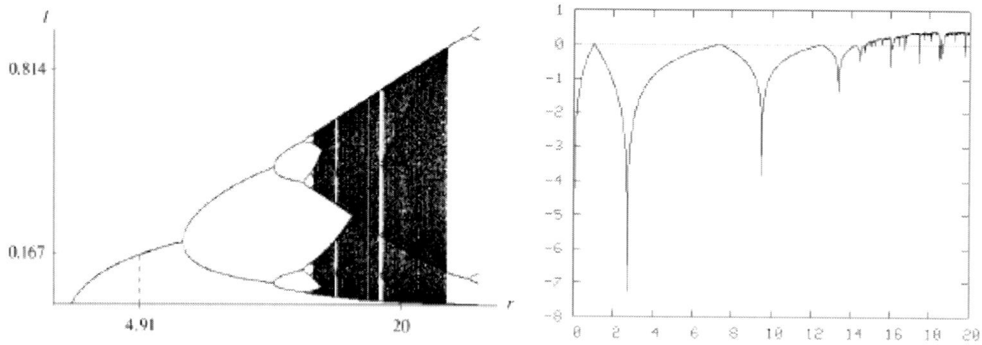

Figure 4. Bifurcation diagram and Lyapunov exponents.

The complexity of the chaotic area, for example for $r = 18$, is shown in figure 5, in which a typical temporal evolution (right) and the diagram of its orbit (left) are drawn.

Table 1 summarizes the dynamics of equation (13) for each value of parameter r.[9]

To finalize the dynamic analysis, we study how the original parameters n, a, α, b, δ, β and γ affect the qualitative behavior of the system.

Parameter b, which according to Pohjola [47] can be interpreted as reflecting workers' bargaining power, is not included in parameter r, so only affects the value of the equilibrium points: in particular, the greater the value of b, the greater the value of s and the lower the employment rate. So, as in the wage-bargaining models [48], [49], this model implies that a lower unemployment rate coincides with greater bargaining power (lower flexibility of the labor market).

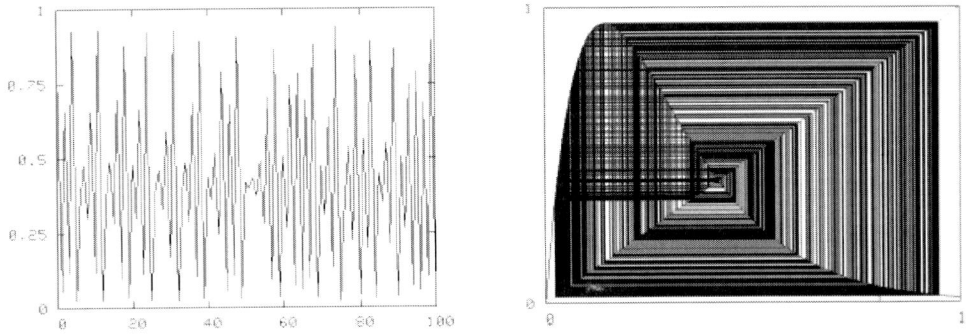

Figure 5. Chaotic time evolution and orbit diagram.

Table 1. Dynamic behavior of *l*

Dynamic Behavior	Values of r
Attracting fixed point	$1 < r < e^2$
Attracting 2-period cycle	$e^2 < r < 12.5039$
Attracting 4-period cycle	$12.5039 < r < 14.2392$
Attracting 8-period cycle	$14.2392 < r < 14.6582$
Attracting 16, 32, 64-period cycle	$14.6582 < r < 14.7611$
Chaos	$r > 14.7611$

The remaining parameters determine the value r and affect the behavior of the employment rate. Parameters a, α, δ and β increase the value of r, and then the employment rate and the possibility of complex dynamic behavior. So, the model predicts that economies in which the external effect of the average level of knowledge (β) is important, the productivity of the knowledge sector (δ) is high, and production function returns (α) are high will have less unemployment and a greater possibility of complex dynamic behavior in the employment rate.

[9] See [45], [46].

In addition, an increase in the values of parameters γ and n decreases the value of r and the employment rate, and, contrary to those discussed above, these parameters tend to stabilize the economy and decrease the possibility of chaos. Therefore, the model concludes that the greater the level of development (indicated by a lower value of γ—lesser significance of the knowledge sector—and lower value of n) the greater the employment rate[10] and the greater the possibility of complex dynamics. This last result coincides with the ideas of Keynes in *The General Theory of Employment, Interest and Money* ([50], chap. 22), and Schumpeter, in *The Theory of Economic Development* ([51], chap. 4), regarding the forms economic development can adopt in capitalist economies. As the level of development increases, rigidities and imperfections become more pronounced and oscillations become more and more irregular (this theoretical argument could be extended to parameters δ and β, since most developed economies are characterized by both greater productivity of the knowledge sector and greater relevance of the external effect).

The results obtained for employment rate extend easily to the growth rate of per capita production y_t, given by:

$$\frac{y_{t+1}}{y_t} = \left(\frac{h_{t+1}}{h_t}\right)^{\alpha+\beta} \left(\frac{l_{t+1}}{l_t}\right)^{\alpha} (1+n)^{\alpha-1} = z \cdot \left(\frac{l_{t+1}}{l_t}\right)^{\alpha}$$

where $z = e^{\delta(1-\gamma)(\alpha+\beta)} (1+n)^{\alpha-1}$.

Whenever $z < 1$, production per capita tends to zero. This is satisfied when:

$$e^{\delta(1-\gamma)(\alpha+\beta)} < (1+n)^{1-\alpha} \sim \delta(1-\gamma)(\alpha+\beta) + \alpha n < n$$

that is, when the increase in knowledge production (the result of an increase in both knowledge and labor) is insufficient to offset population growth.

Whenever $z > 1$, per capita income displays a long-term positive growth trend that is sustained by knowledge production, and its dynamic behavior depends on the dynamics of the employment rate (see figure 16, where for r = 18 the aperiodic behavior characteristic of the chaotic zone can be seen). The qualitative conclusions obtained for the dynamics of the employment rate apply directly to per capita income; the greater the value of r, the greater the possibility that the economy will fluctuate along cycles of differing periods and even along chaotic paths. In particular, the greater the investment in knowledge or the level of development (measured by the fraction of time devoted to knowledge accumulation, $1-\gamma$,

---

[10] Most economic literature has shown the negative relationship between economic growth and unemployment [52], [53], except for the positive relationship between unemployment and growth (technological unemployment) expressed in "creative destruction" models [16], based on the ideas of Schumpeter [51]. Bean and Pissarides [53] suggest that the relationship between both phenomena is ambiguous because both variables can be endogenously and jointly determined (for example, economic growth depends on the growth of knowledge, and the employment rate is the result of the labor market structure), which implies that the relationship between them depends on exactly which economic structure we are considering.

knowledge sector productivity, δ , the external effect, β ,and a low population growth rate, n), the greater the possibility of complex oscillations.

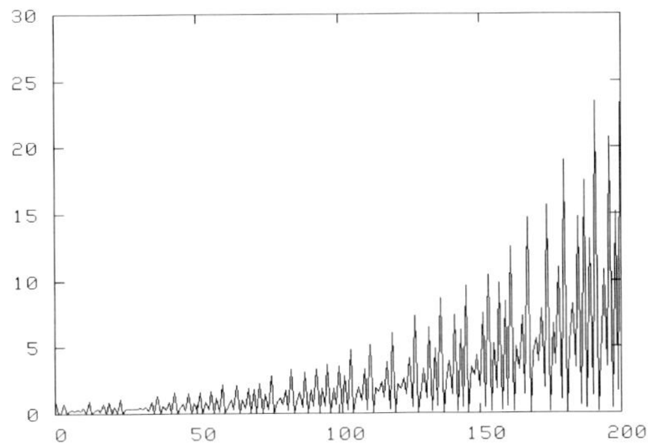

Figure 6. Time evolution of y_t .

Finally, we wish to highlight the fact that the nonlinear nature of the model can, in addition to the positive income growth trend, generate the possibility of periods in which per capita income decreases without considering exogenous shocks. However, in the same way as in traditional growth models, sustained growth is achieved through knowledge production or technological change. In conclusion, policies that promote knowledge accumulation will positively affect economic growth, though will increase instability. Additionally, policies that increase the flexibility of the labor market will also positively affect economic growth—increasing the employment rate—without changing its dynamic behavior.

2.2. Adjusted Wage Dynamics

If we look at the trajectories of employment and per capita income, we see that the size of the oscillations of the time series is large when compared to real world behavior; this result is due to the simple nonlinear modeling we have assumed for wage dynamics. In this section, we will now show how by introducing more realistic assumptions about the nonlinearity of the Phillips curve, the size of these oscillations decreases and the values of the employment rate are close to full employment.

The nonlinearity of the Phillips curve was already pointed out in the pioneering articles of Phillips [2] and Lipsey [3]. Phillips states: *"When the demand for labor is high and there are very few unemployed we should expect employers to bid wage rates up quite rapidly... On the other hand, it appears that workers are reluctant to offer their services at less than the prevailing rates when the demand for labor is low and unemployment is high so that wage rates fall only very slowly. The relation between unemployment and the rate of change of wage rates is therefore likely to be highly non-linear."* On the basis of this idea, a growing group of empirical work appeared during the nineties, which sought to prove the nonlinearity of the Phillips curve [54], [55], [56]. Using different statistical methods, they show how the empirical evidence supports the nonlinear assumption. This nonlinearity, known as "asymmetry of the Phillips curve," is based on the fact that *"excess demand conditions are much more inflationary than excess supply conditions are disinflationary"* [56]. Also, *"the linear model ignores much of the historical context underlying the original split between classical and Keynesian economics: under conditions of full employment, inflation appeared to respond strongly to demand conditions, while in deep recessions, it was relatively insensitive to changes in activity"* [57]. In the modeling (12) previously used, even though nonlinear, the logarithm is linear:

$$\ln\frac{w_{t+1}}{w_t}=-a+bl_t$$

This simple modeling is one reason why production and employment oscillations are too large and do not reflect their real behaviors. Consequently, an extension of the nonlinearity of the Phillips curve—the result of a more realistic assumption about wage behavior—could solve this problem.

Now, we consider the following alternative modeling of the Phillips curve:

$$\frac{w_{t+1}}{w_t}=h(l_t)=\exp\left(-a+bl_t^{\sigma}+c\left(1-l_t\right)^{-\varepsilon}\right) \tag{14}$$

with $a, b, c>0$, $0<\sigma<1$ and $0<\varepsilon<1$. The resulting behavior is illustrated in figure 7 and is based in the assumptions described below.

First, we assume that there is a large area, corresponding to an interval $(\varepsilon_1, 1-\varepsilon_2)$ with ε_1 and ε_2 being small, where wages are very insensitive to employment changes (in this interval the multiplicative growth rate is close to one). This assumption is in consonance with the ideas of Phillips and the empirical literature mentioned above (when unemployment is high, wages are very insensitive to changes in activity), and with the Keynesian ideas on downward rigidity in nominal wages due to market imperfections.

Secondly, we assume a vertical tangency, $l=0$, in order to capture the rapid fall in wages when the unemployment rate is very close to 100% (l close to 0). Finally, we assume a vertical asymptote at $l=1$. This assumption is very common in theoretical works that consider a Phillips curve [2], [3], [58], [4], [59], and in the empirical works mentioned above. For example, Lipsey [3] states: *"It is, however, impossible that the employment rate could be reduced below zero [...] the employment rate must approach zero (or some small value > 0) asymptotically."* In short, this asymptote is designed to reflect the fact that with near to full employment it is more and more difficult to hire workers and labor market pressure accelerates the growth of wages; with which near to full employment would be huge.

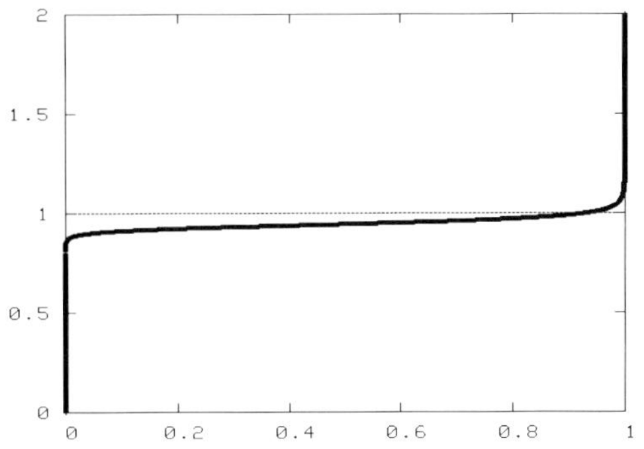

Figure 7. Adjusted wage dynamics.

Taking into consideration the Phillips curve (14), the dynamic of the employment rate is now given by:

$$l_{t+1} = f(l_t) = \frac{1}{1+n}\exp\left(\frac{(\alpha+\beta)\delta(1-\gamma)-q(l_t)}{(1-\alpha)}\right) \tag{15}$$

where $q(l_t) = -a + bl_t^{\sigma} + c(1-l_t)^{-\varepsilon}$.

Figure 8 shows the diagram of a typical orbit of $f(l_t)$ (left) and the temporal evolution of l_t (right) for the following values of the parameters: $\alpha = 0.7$, $\beta = 0.1$, $\delta = 0.1$, $\gamma = 0.7$, $n = 0.02$ and $a = 1.716$, $b = 1.455$, $\sigma = 0.01$, $\varepsilon = 0.1$. The dynamic behavior is qualitatively similar to the function $f(l_t)$ given by (13). The oscillations are complex and irregular too, though are now much closer to full employment values, which seem to adapt better to the empirical evidence.

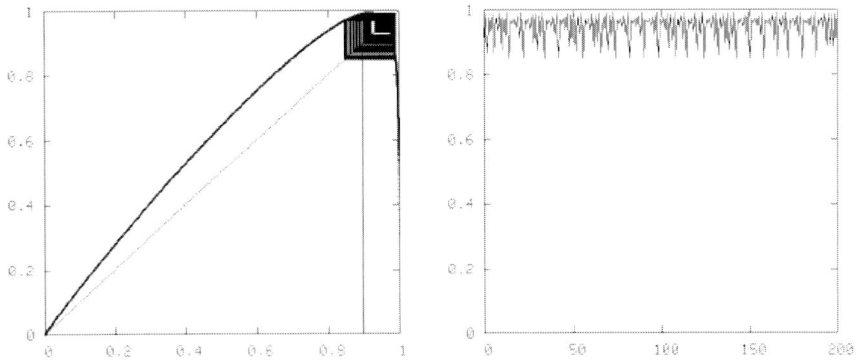

Figure 8. Orbit diagram and time evolution for adjusted model.

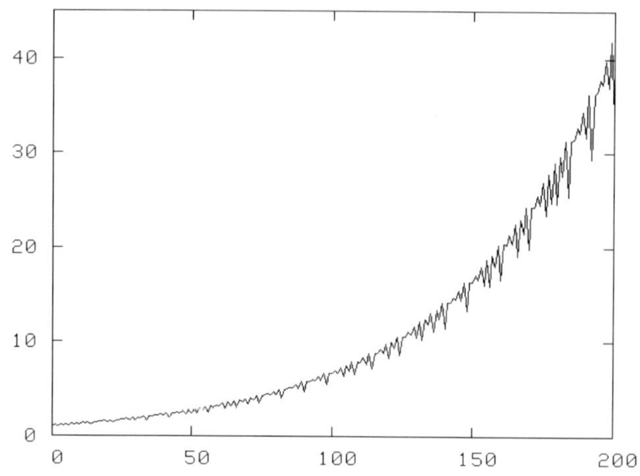

Figure 9. Time evolution of y_t for adjusted model.

As in the same approach shown in the previous section, instability is transferred to the dynamics of per capita production. As shown in figure 9, the time evolution of y_t also has a cycle behavior with a growth trend and, in particular, the possibility that, in some periods, per capita income decreases. The only difference is that now the amplitude of the oscillations is smaller.

The assumptions regarding the Phillips curve can also be justified on the basis of the work of Rose [4], who introduces a kind of nonlinearity into the Phillips curve, very similar to figure 7, in order to prevent explosive local dynamics.[11] In particular, Rose considers a vertical asymptote in the growth rate of wages for an employment rate of $b \leq 1$. Furthermore, he considers a vertical asymptote in the decrease of wages for an employment rate of $a > 0$.

The only difference between our Phillips curve modeling (equation 14) and that of Rose is that, for small values l ($l \leq a$), Rose assumes that wages decrease so much that nobody is willing to work. Nevertheless, as we now show, this difference does not significantly affect the dynamics generated by our model.

Effectively, considering a Phillips curve of the form:

$$\frac{w_{t+1}}{w_t} = h(l_t) = e^{-a(l_t - l^*)^{-\sigma} + b(1-l_t)^{-\varepsilon}} \quad \text{if} \quad l > l^* \tag{16}$$

where $0 < l^* < 1$, $a, b > 0$, $0 < \sigma < 1$ and $0 < \varepsilon < 1$. Figure 10 shows the graph of the function $h(l_t)$ for parameter values $l^* = 0.4$, $a = 1$, $b = 1$, $\sigma = 0.02$ and $\varepsilon = 0.006$.

[11] Rose tries to explain the theory of nonlinear business cycles from a Keynesian perspective (Keynes-Wicksell models). Among others, one of his objectives is to show how the Phillips curve affects not only the cycle, but also the income growth trend.

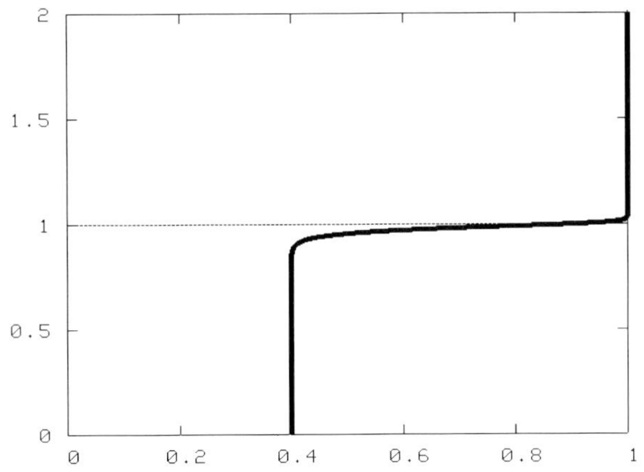

Figure 10. Rose-type adjustment for wage dynamics.

According to this modeling of the Phillips curve, the dynamic of the employment rate is given by:

$$l_{t+1} = f(l_t) = \frac{1}{1+n} l_t \exp\left(\frac{(\alpha+\beta)\delta(1-\gamma)}{(1-\alpha)}\right)[h(l_t)]^{\frac{-1}{1-\alpha}} \tag{17}$$

where $h(l_t)$ is function (16). Figure 11 shows that the dynamic behavior of $f(l_t)$ (now equation 17) is qualitatively similar to function (15) for levels of employment close to 1. The only difference is that now there is no economic activity below the critical level l^*.

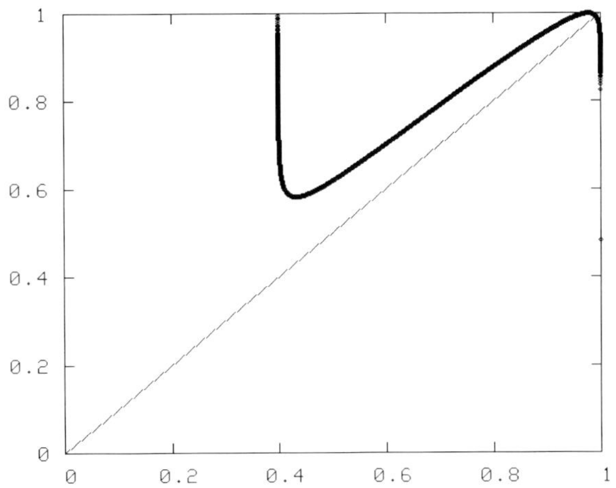

Figure 11. Function $f(l)$ given by Rose-type adjusted model.

Naturally, this similarity leads the orbits in (17) and (15) to behave in the same way, as can be seen by comparing the graphs in figure 12 and figure 8.

In order to study the effects of parameter changes on the employment rate l and per capita income y, we carried out a large number of numerical simulations, considering only standard values of the parameters for which the temporal evolutions of these variables are in the goods market equilibrium zone. We obtained the same results as in the simple nonlinear model: the greater the values of $1-\gamma$, δ and α, the lower the rate of population growth, n, the greater the employment rate, l, and per capita income, and, likewise, the greater the possibility of complex dynamics.

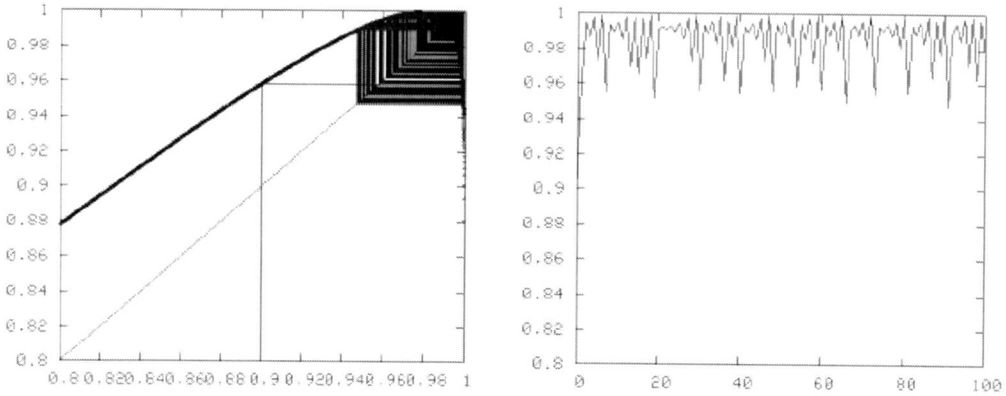

Figure 12. Orbit diagram and time evolution for a Rose-type adjusted model.

In conclusion, using appropriate nonlinear modeling based on the theoretical characteristics dictated by the economic theory of labor markets generates more realistic temporal evolutions in employment and per capita production.

3. An Extension: Endogenous Population Growth

In this section, we extend the basic model by introducing endogenous population growth. Following the standard models of endogenous population literature [7], [8], it is assumed that the labor supply is determined through the micro-founded fertility choices of individuals. Each individual is considered to be a couple or a representative family. At every point of time *t*, each family choice determines the number of children, $\hat{b}$, who will be born in the next period, $t + 1$.

Let us assume that the representative family's preferences are represented by the following standard log-linear utility function [60]:

$$U(\hat{c}_{t+1}, \hat{b}_{t+1}) = \hat{c}_{t+1}^{1-\varepsilon} \hat{b}_{t+1}^{\varepsilon}, \qquad 0 < \varepsilon < 1$$

where $\hat{c}$ is the family's per capita consumption and ε measures its preference as regards number of children.

The cost of childrearing, E_t, includes both the cost of raising a child (regardless of quality), θ_1, and the cost of educating it, $e_t = \theta_2 h_t^\rho$:

$$E_t = \theta_1 + \theta_2 h_t^\rho, \quad 0 < \rho < 1$$

θ_1 is considered a fixed cost (e.g. food and clothing), whereas the education cost, $e_t = \theta_2 h_t^\rho$, depends on a medium level of knowledge, h. The idea behind this assumption is that a higher level of knowledge within the economy would imply a higher demand for education,[12] which would be more costly. However, although this cost increases in h, following the habitual form of cost functions we assume that its growth is decreasing ($\rho < 1$).

Given these assumptions, each family's static optimization problem would be as follows:

$$\begin{cases} \text{MAX.} & U(\hat{c}_{t+1}, \hat{b}_{t+1}) = \hat{c}_{t+1}^{1-\varepsilon} \hat{b}_{t+1}^{\varepsilon} \\ \text{subject to:} & \hat{c}_{t+1} + (\theta_1 + \theta_2 h_t^\rho)\hat{b}_{t+1} = \hat{y}_t \end{cases} \tag{18}$$

with $\hat{y}_t = 2y_t$ being the representative family's income.

This problem can be rewritten as:

$$\text{MAX.} \quad \varphi\left(\hat{b}_{t+1}\right) = (\hat{y}_t - (\theta_1 + \theta_2 h_t^\rho)\hat{b}_{t+1})^{1-\varepsilon} \hat{b}_{t+1}^{\varepsilon}$$

Given that:

$$\varphi'\left(\hat{b}_{t+1}\right) = \left(\varepsilon\hat{y}_t - \left(\theta_1 + \theta_2 h_t^\rho\right)\hat{b}_{t+1}\right)\left(\hat{y}_t - \left(\theta_1 + \theta_2 h_t^\rho\right)\hat{b}_{t+1}\right)^{-\varepsilon} \hat{b}_{t+1}^{\varepsilon-1}$$

$$\varphi''\left(\hat{b}_{t+1}\right) = -\varepsilon(1-\varepsilon)\left(\hat{y}_t - \left(\theta_1 + \theta_2 h_t^\rho\right)\hat{b}_{t+1}\right)^{-\varepsilon-1} \hat{b}_{t+1}^{\varepsilon-2} < 0$$

its solution satisfies:

$$\varepsilon\hat{y}_t - \left(\theta_1 + \theta_2 h_t^\rho\right)\hat{b}_{t+1} = 0$$

Then, the optimal number of children for each adult of a representative family at each period t is:

$$b_{t+1} = \frac{1}{2}\hat{b}_{t+1} = \frac{1}{2}\frac{\hat{y}_t \varepsilon}{\theta_1 + \theta_2 h_t^\rho} = \frac{y_t \varepsilon}{\theta_1 + \theta_2 h_t^\rho} = \frac{w_t l_t \varepsilon}{\theta_1 + \theta_2 h_t^\rho} \tag{19}$$

---

[12] As Schultz [61] has claimed, citing a wide range of evidence, new technology will create a demand for individuals more qualified to work in new production processes.

According to the literature on endogenous population growth, the birth rate depends positively on per capita income and negatively on the cost of childrearing. Equation (19) also shows the inverse relation between the economic level of development, given in our model by the average level of knowledge, and the birth rate.

We assume that it is the labor force, A, which decides to have children in each period, so $b_{t+1}A_t$ is the total number of births in $t+1$. Finally, we assume a constant mortality rate, π, hence in each period, πN_t individuals die.[13]

Taking into account the above assumptions, the total population in the next period, N_t, is given by:

$$N_{t+1} = N_t + b_{t+1}A_t - \pi N_t = N_t(1-\pi) + b_{t+1}A_t$$

and remembering that $N = \lambda A$, we obtain the endogenous growth rate of A:

$$n_t = \frac{A_{t+1}}{A_t} - 1 = \frac{N_{t+1}}{N_t} - 1 = -\pi + \frac{1}{\lambda} b_{t+1}$$

Therefore, the growth rate of the labor force and the total population is:

$$n_t = -\pi + \frac{1}{\lambda}\frac{w_t l_t \varepsilon}{\theta_1 + \theta_2 h_t^{\rho}} \tag{20}$$

which replaces equation (15) in the economic growth model with unemployment presented in the previous section.

In particular, by considering the Phillips curve (14), the dynamics of employment are given by equation (15), taking into account $n = n_t$:

$$l_{t+1} = f(l_t) = \frac{1}{1+n_t} \exp\left(\frac{(\alpha+\beta)\delta(1-\gamma) - q(l_t)}{(1-\alpha)} \right) \tag{21}$$

where $q(l_t) = -a + bl_t^{\sigma} + c(1-l_t)^{-\varepsilon}$.

Due to the high analytical complexity of the model, we limit its study to numerical simulations.[14] The first property is the endogenous emergence of a logistic behavior in the population growth rate describing its historical evolution (see figure 13). These dynamic

---

[13] Blanchard [62] states that "evidence on mortality rates suggests low and approximately constant probabilities from age 20 to age 40." After this, mortality rates depend inversely and exponentially on individual age [63]. For simplicity, we set the mortality rate of children at zero. Though this might seem inappropriate for historical periods characterized by high child mortality, or for current conditions in poor countries, it can, however, easily be incorporated into the model by presuming a "diminished" fertility rate in order to include the mortality of newborns in child mortality.

[14] The large number of simulations carried out suggests that the subsequent properties are robust for acceptable changes in parameter.

results are also found in other models of endogenous fertility rate [7]. This evolution is characterized by a first stage, typically called Post-Malthusian, in which the rate of population growth increases, to be followed, after a transition phase, by a modern growth stage in which n decreases and tends to stagnate.

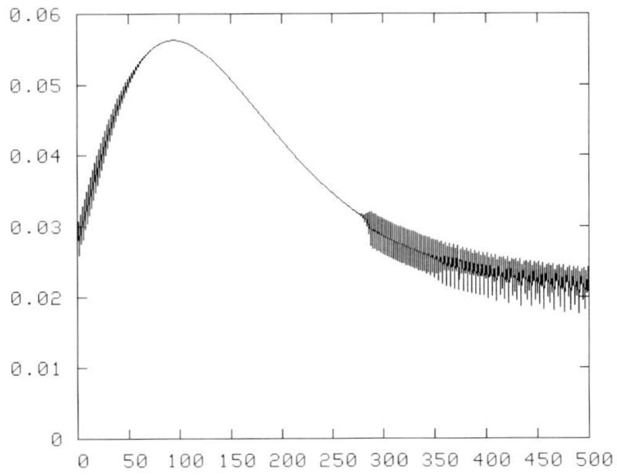

Figure 13. Time evolution of population growth rate.

Figure 14 (left) shows the temporal evolutions of y_t and h_t. We see that the stage prior to the transition corresponds to low values of income and knowledge, and increasing growth rates. In this stage, the income effect is higher than the knowledge (cost) effect, and n_t grows. This situation, described in the literature of endogenous population growth, corresponds to economies that take off from an underdevelopment stage (called the Malthusian stage) to a Post-Malthusian stage. In the latter, economic growth is positively related to population growth.

Subsequently, for populations with high levels of knowledge and income, the cost of education rises, inducing parents to have fewer but better quality children. Furthermore, as the economy develops, new technology and production processes increase the demand for human capital. This generates a demographic transition, that is, an economy transitions from a high fertility and low knowledge accumulation stage to a low fertility and rapid knowledge accumulation stage.[15]

The acceleration of the growth of h with respect to the growth of y is shown in figure 14 (right), in which the function $\ln\frac{h_t}{y_t}$ is represented. This figure shows how, in the stage prior to the transition, the function $\ln\frac{h_t}{y_t}$ is concave (the income growth rate grows more than the knowledge growth rate); whereas during the transition it is almost lineal (the growth rates of income and knowledge adapt), and in the next stage it is convex (an acceleration in the knowledge growth rate respect to the income growth rate).

[15] Because human capital is not a family choice, the model is abstracted from the so-called quantity-quality trade-off in the literature on endogenous population growth.

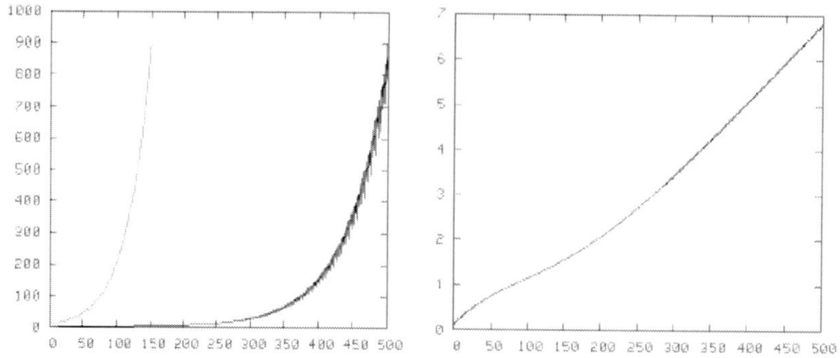

Figure 14. Time evolutions of y, h and $\ln\frac{h}{y}$.

In addition to the logistic behavior of population growth, figure 13 shows the behavior of n during different phases. In the first stage, characterized by low knowledge accumulation, remarkably regular behavior (equilibrium points or period cycles) can be noted, whilst in the last stage, characterized by high knowledge accumulation, very erratic oscillations can be seen.

The numerical simulations of the temporal evolution of n for different values of ρ show that as ρ approaches one, the regular behavior of the transition stage tends to decrease, though the irregular behavior and amplitude of the oscillations in both final and first stages tend to increase. This result is clearly observed in figure 15, which shows the dynamics of n for $\rho = 0.6$ (up) and $\rho = 0.7$ (down). As ρ approaches one, in addition to the increase in irregular behavior in the final stage, we show that the length of the initial and transition stages decreases gradually. This result is due to the fact that ρ reflects the positive effect of knowledge on the cost of education, which we assume becomes lower and lower ($\rho < 1$). As ρ moves closer to one, the effect of h on this cost increases. Parents decide to have fewer children, though children with a higher level of skills, and the population rate begins to decrease sooner.[16]

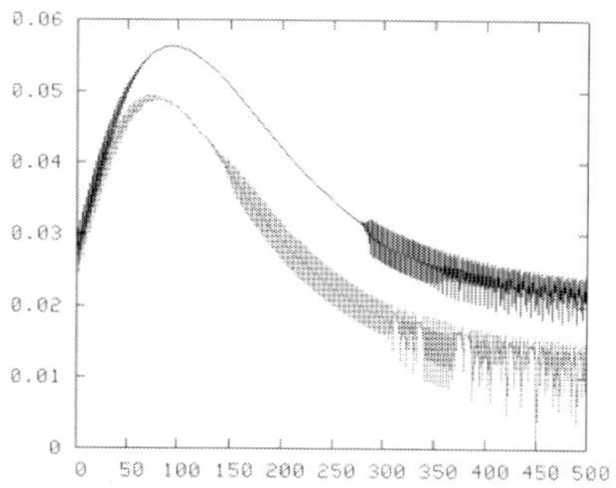

Figure 15. Time evolutions of n (up $\rho = 0.6$, and down $\rho = 0.7$).

[16] In general, the literature on endogenous population growth assumes $\rho = 1$. In this case, only the last stage is observed, and population growth—as this literature predicts [8]—stabilizes quickly.

The type of dynamic evolution that we have just described[17] does not pertain exclusively to the population growth rate. In figure 16, we have drawn the evolution, over time, of l_t (left for $\rho = 0.6$ and right for $\rho = 0.7$), which shows the same dynamic behavior.

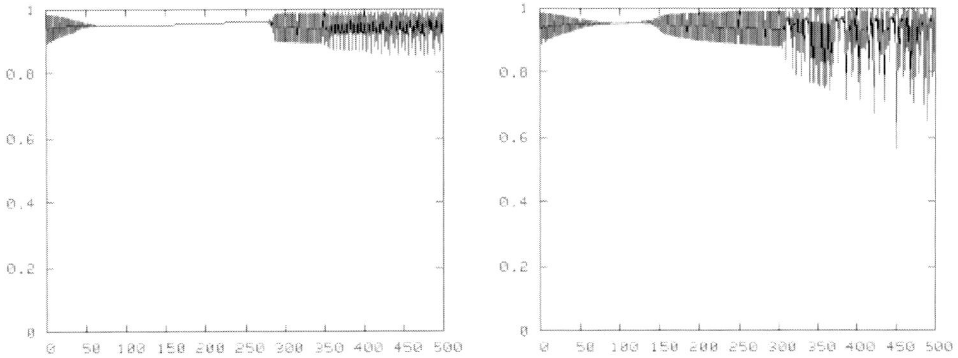

Figure 16. Time evolution of employment rate (left $\rho = 0.6$, and right $\rho = 0.7$).

Then, during the transition stage, economic variables evolve regularly. However, behind this apparent regularity lies a profound structural change that corresponds to the change of trend in population growth. The stage of initial cyclic (but regular) behavior seems to correspond to an underdeveloped economy that embarks upon a stage of sustained growth (Post-Malthusian stage). A growing economy creates more opportunities; the rigidities that cause instability have a *"safety valve"* and are less grave. The stability of l in the transition stage could be due to the fact that, during this stage, the labor force adapts to the needs of the labor market, absorbing the oscillations that result from the rigidities or imperfections of the labor market. This can cause the behavior of the variables to be stable during the transition. Later, when the economy reaches a high degree of development, the rigidities and imperfections are accentuated and fluctuations are very unstable.[18]

Introducing endogenous population growth does not affect the result of the previous section regarding how changes in the model's parameter values affect the dynamics of employment and per capita income. As for the parameters of the endogenous population growth rate, due to the inverse relationship between population and economic growth: a) the greater the value of child preference ε, the lower per capita income, and b) the lower both the cost of childrearing and the mortality rate, the greater per capita income.

[17] However, such large movements in population growth do not seem to be present in the rich world today [64]. This is a consequence of the basic assumptions of the model. Stage-dependent assumptions (e.g. regarding the birth rate, endogenous mortality, and the labor market) would help generate more realistic population growth rates over time.

[18] One possible explanation for this dynamic result could be related to the age structure of the population [65], [66], [22], [23], [24]. Although age structure has not been modeled, we could relate it to population growth if population begins to grow because young populations change. Then, at the beginning of the transition, a young population (resulting from the typical "baby boom" of the Post-Malthusian stage) joins the labor force. A young labor force satisfies the needs of the labor market more easily (e.g. thanks to training, geographic and labor mobility) than an adult population, characteristic of the modern economic growth stage. Therefore, a young labor force could smooth the fluctuations caused by labor market rigidities.

Finally, it is important to note that the logistic behavior and instability emerge solely as a result of the internal structure of the economy; they are not exogenously generated. Thus, the model might be regarded as a self-organizing system displaying emergent properties.

Conclusion

Our work complements and discusses the theoretical results of economic growth models with unemployment. Similarly, we show that the introduction of unemployment into economic growth models through nonlinear modeling of the Phillips curve enriches and completes the literature that seeks to explain the origin and nature of fluctuations.

We show how the internal dynamics of an economy in which the labor market is in disequilibrium generates both a positive growth trend and irregular behavior, which describe the intertemporal evolution of per capita income. In particular, dynamic analysis shows how per capita production and the employment rate oscillate between stable cycles of different periods to an aperiodic path. This dynamic depends on the flexibility of the labor market: the higher the rigidity of the labor market, the greater the possibility of instability. Besides cyclical behavior, per capita production shows a positive long-run growth trend. There are periods with net decreases in per capita income generated without considering exogenous shocks. Moreover, in line with wage- bargaining models, we find that the higher workers' bargaining power, the lower both the employment rate and per capita production. As far as growth determinants go, our model coincides with the results of traditional neoclassical growth models, i.e. technical progress ensures economic growth in the long term.

When we assume the presence of endogenous population growth due to optimal fertility choices, the basic model generates a demographic transition in line with the historical evolution of the population growth rate. The irregular long-run oscillations are caused by the mismatch between family fertility decisions and subsequent labor market needs. The joint study of these demographic factors and the characteristics of the labor market explains the relationship between a greater degree of economic development (human capital) and the existence of temporal evolutions with a greater number of oscillations (i.e. instability).

We find these preliminary results encouraging enough to call for further work, both at the theoretical and empirical level. Future work should consider: (1) the endogenous accumulation of human capital, (2) labor force needs for different levels of human capital, and (3) the age structure of the population.

References

[1] R. M. Goodwin, A growth cycle. In C.H. Feinstein (Ed.), *Socialism, Capitalism and Economic Growth* (pp. 54–58). Cambridge: Cambridge University Press (1967).

[2] A.W. Phillips, The relation between unemployment and the rate of change of money wage rates in the United Kingdom, 1861–1857. *Economica*, 25 (100), 283–299 (1958).

[3] R. G. Lipsey, The relation between unemployment and the rate of change of money wage rates in the United Kingdom, 1861–1957: a further analysis. *Economica,* 27, 1–31 (1960).

[4] H. Rose, On the non-linear theory of the employment cycle. *Review of Economic Studies*, 34, 153–173 (1967).

[5] N. G. Mankiw and D. Romer, (Eds.) New Keynesian Economics, Vols. I and II. Cambridge, *MA: MIT Press* (1991).

[6] R. E. Lucas, *The industrial revolution: past and future*. Chicago: University of Chicago (1998).

[7] O. Galor and D. N. Weil, Population, technology, and growth: From the Malthusian regime to the demographic transition and beyond. *American Economic Review*, 90, 806-828 (2000).

[8] I. C. Jones, Was an industrial revolution inevitable? Economic Growth over the Very Long Run. *Advances in Macroeconomics*, 1 (2), art. 1 (2001).

[9] R. Tamura, Human capital and the switch from agriculture to industry. *Journal of Economic Dynamics and Control*, 27, 207–242 (2002).

[10] R. M. Solow, A contribution to the theory of economic growth. *Quarterly Journal of Economics*, 70 (1), 65–94 (1956).

[11] D. Cass, Optimum Growth in an Aggregative Model of Capital Accumulation. *Review of Economics Studies,* 32 (July), 233-240 (1965).

[12] T. C. Koopmans, On the Concept of Optimal Economic Growth. (Study week on the) Econometric Approach to Development Planning. Amsterdam: *North Holland* (1965).

[13] R. E. Lucas, On the mechanics of development planning. *Journal of Monetary Economics,* 22, 3–42 (1988).

[14] P. Romer, Endogenous technological change. *Journal of Political Economy*, 98 (2), 71–102 (1990).

[15] G. M. Grossman and E. Helpman, Innovation and Growth in the Global Economy. Cambridge, *MA: MIT Press* (1991).

[16] P. Aghion, and P. Howitt, A Model of Growth through Creative Destruction. *Econometrica*, 60 (2), 323-351 (1992).

[17] T. Ito, A note on disequilibrium growth theory. *Economics Letters*, 1, 45–49 (1978).

[18] T. Ito, Disequilibrium Growth Theory. *Journal of Economic Theory*, 23, 380-409(1980).

[19] P. Y. Henin and P. Michel, Harrodian and Neoclassical Paths in a Constrained Growth Model. *Economics Letters*, 10, 237-242 (1982).

[20] C. P. Chiarella, and P. Flaschel, T*he Dynamics of Keynesian Monetary Growth: Macro Foundations*. Cambridge: Cambridge University Press (1999).

[21] C. P. Chiarella, P. Flaschel, G. Groh, and W. *Semmler, Disequilibrium, Growth and Labor Market Dynamics: Macroperspectives*. Heidelberg: Springer-Verlag (2000).

[22] P. Manfredi, and L. Fanti, The complex effects of demographic heterogeneity on the interaction between the economy and population. *Structural Change and Economic Dynamics*, 17, 148–173 (2006).

[23] P. Manfredi and L. Fanti, Demography in macroeconomic models: when labour supply matters for economic cycles. *Metroeconomica*, 57 (4), 536–563 (2006).

[24] M. J. Roa, D. Saura and F. J. Vázquez, Economic growth, labor market and demographic patterns. *Structural Change and Economic Dynamics*, 22 (1), 81–91 (2011).

[25] V. Volterra, Leçons sur la Théorie Mathématique de Lutte pour la Vie. Paris: *Gauthier-Villars* (1931).

[26] A. J. Lotka, Elements of Physical Biology. Baltimore: Willians and Wilkens (1925).

[27] J. Tobin, A General Equilibrium Approach to Monetary Theory. *Journal of Money, Credit and Banking*, 1, 15-29 (1969).

[28] H. Rose, Unemployment in a theory of growth. International Economic Review, 7, 260-282 (1966).

[29] J. Stein, Money and Capacity growth. *Journal of Political Economy*, 74, 451-465 (1966).

[30] L. A. Metzler, The nature and stability of inventory cycles. *Review of Economics Statistics,* 23, 113-129 (1941).

[31] W. Carlin and D. Soskice, *Macroeconomics and the Wage Bargain*. Oxford: Oxford University Press (1990).

[32] P. Picard, Inflation and Growth in a Disequilibrium Macroeconomic Model. *Journal of Economic Theory,* 30, 266-295 (1983).

[33] V. Ginsburgh, P. Y. Henin and P. Michel, A Dual Decision Approach to Disequilibrium Growth. *Oxford Economic Papers*, 37 (3), 353-61 (1985).

[34] P. Manfredi and L. Fanti, Cycles in continuous-time economic models (with application to Goodwin's and Solow's models). *Discussion Papers* 2003/9, Dipartamento di Scienze Economiche, University of Pisa, Italy (2003).

[35] P. Manfredi and L. Fanti, Is Labour Market Flexibility Desirable or Harmful? A Further Dynamic Perspective. *Metroeconomica,* 61 (2), 257–266 (2010).

[36] R. D. Lee, Population dynamics: equilibrium, disequilibrium, and consequences of fluctuations. In M. R. Rosenzweig and O. Strak (Eds.), *Handbook of Population and Family Economics.* Amsterdam: North Holland (1997).

[37] C. Long, Impact of effective demand on the labor supply. *American Economic Review, Papers and Proceedings* 43, 458–467 (1953).

[38] A. J. Tella, The Relation of Labor Force to Employment. *Industrial and Labor Relations Review*, 17 (1964).

[39] A. J. Tella, Labor Force Sensitivity to Employment by Age, Sex. *Industrial Relations,* 4 (1965).

[40] P. Aghion and P. Howitt, Endogenous Growth Theory. Cambridge, *MA: The MIT Press* (1998).

[41] P. A. P. Moran, Some remarks on animal population dynamics. *Biometrics,* 6, 250–258 (1950).

[42] W. E. Ricker, Stock and recruitment. *Journal of The Fisheries Research Board of Canada*, 11, 559–623 (1954).

[43] A. Macfadyen, *Animal Ecology: Aims and Methods*. London: Pitman (1963).

[44] L. M. Cook, Oscillation in the simple logistic growth model. *Nature*, 207, 316 (1965).

[45] R. M. May, Biological populations obeying difference equations: stable points, stable cycles, and chaos. *Journal of Theoretical Biology*, 49, 511–524 (1975).

[46] R. M. May and G. F. Oster, Bifurcation and dynamic complexity in simple ecological models. *The American Naturalist*, 110, 573–599 (1976).

[47] M. J. Pohjola, Stable and Chaotic Growth: the Dynamics of a Discrete Version of Goodwin's Growth Cycle Model, *Zeitschrift für Nationalökonomie* 41, 27-38 (1981).

[48] R. Layard and S. Nickell, *Unemployment, real wages, and aggregate demand in Europe, Japan and the United States*. Carnegie–Rochester Conference Series on Public Policy, 23 (1), 143–202 (1985).

[49] R. Layard and S. Nickell, Unemployment in Britain. *Economica,* 53, 121–169 (1986).
[50] J. M. Keynes, *The General Theory of Employment, Interest and Money.* Cambridge: MacMillan Cambridge University Press (1936).
[51] J. A. Schumpeter, *The Theory of Economic Development.* Cambridge MA: Harvard University Press (1934).
[52] C. A. Pissarides, Equilibrium unemployment theory. Basil Blackwell, Oxford (1990).
[53] C. Bean and C. A. Pissarides, Unemployment, consumption and growth. *European Economic Review*, 37 (4), 837-854 (1993).
[54] B. Chadha, P. Masson, and G. Meredith, Models of inflation and the costs of disinflation. *IMF Staff Papers* 39, 395–431 (1992).
[55] D. Laxton, G. Meredith and D. Rose, Asymmetric effects of economic activity on inflation: evidence and policy implications. *IMF Staff Papers* 42 (2) (1995).
[56] P. Clark, D. Laxton and D. Rose, Asymmetry in the U.S. output-inflation nexus. *IMF Staff Papers* 43, 216–251 (1996).
[57] E. Schaling, The Nonlinear Phillips Curve and Inflation Forecast Targeting – Symmetric Versus asymmetric Monetary Policy Rules. *Discussion Paper* 1998–136, Tilburg University, Center for Economic Research (1998).
[58] P. A. Samuelson, and R. M. Solow, Analytical aspects of anti-inflation policy. *The American Economic Review*, 50, 177–194 (1960).
[59] C. P. Chiarella and P. Flaschel, Real and monetary cycles in models of Keynes–Wicksell type. *Journal of Economic Behavior and Organization*, 30, 327–351 (1996).
[60] R. H. Day, K. H. Kim and D. Macunovich, Complex demoeconomic dynamics. *Journal of Population Economics*, 2 (2), 139–159 (1989).
[61] T. W. Schultz, The value of the ability to deal with disequilibria. *Journal of Economic Literature*, 13 (3), 827–846 (1975).
[62] O. J. Blanchard, Debt, deficits, and finite horizons. *Journal of Political Economy*, 93 (2), 223–247 (1985).
[63] W. H. Wetterstrand, Parametric models for the life insurance mortality data: Gompertz's law over time. *Transactions of Society of Actuaries*, 33, 159–179 (1981).
[64] N. Lagerlof, The Galor–Weil model revisited: a quantitative exploration. *Review of Economic Dynamics*, 9, 116–142 (2006).
[65] D. E. Bloom and D. Canning, Economic Development and Demographic Transition: The Role of Cumulative Causality. *CAER II Discussion Paper* 51 (1999).
[66] D. E. Bloom and D. Canning, Global Demographic Change: Dimensions and Economic Significance. *PGDA Working Papers* 0105 (2005).

In: Labor Markets: Dynamics, Trends and Economic Impact
Editor: Samir Amine
ISBN: 978-1-61470-825-4

Chapter 3

PRODUCTIVITY AND DURATION OF EMPLOYMENT IN A MATCHING MODEL

Samir Amine *
Université of Quebec and CIRANO, Canada

ABSTRACT

We consider a matching model where firms face a trade-off between the productivity and the expected duration of employment. As firms ignore the effect of their decision on the unemployment costs, hence the payroll taxes they must pay, the productivity as well as the destruction rate are too high. Financing the unemployment costs by lay-off taxes lead the firms to internalize the budgetary consequences of their technological choice, lowering then unemployment.

INTRODUCTION

It should be clearly distinguished both forms of employment protection. Under protection regulation (employment protection laws), the index constructed by the OECD (OECD, 2004) clearly shows that the law is less binding in the United States than in Europe. However, in terms of tax shield, the measure of experience rating reverses this classification. Thus, in the State of New York, modulation of social contributions made to support firms with a surtax which funds 80 % of benefits paid to employees they lay off (Fougère and Margolis, 2000).

In general, economists put forward the argument whereby the employment protection leads firms to internalize the external effects of their dismissal decisions (costs for compensation and reclassification of the unemployed). On this point, the article of Blanchard and Tirole (2004) provides a rigorous and convincing analysis. However, the literature ignores a significant effect of protection employment, that it is administrative or tax. This effect concerns the technological choices of firms. The argument that we develop in this

* E-mail address: samir.amine@uqo.ca.

article is intuitive. The employment protection which increases the consequences of a possible failure encourages firms to focus on the safest investment projects.

Our analytical framework is a matching model with wage bargaining and free-entry (Pissarides, 2000), in which we introduce two additional assumptions. First, the destruction rate of jobs is endogenous here. Indeed we consider that technology can be described by an increasing relationship (and convex) between destruction rate and jobs productivity. Higher productivity can be achieved only at the price of a greater risk of failure. These two variables are chosen by firms when they enter the labor market by maximizing the value of jobs.

Secondly, as Blanchard and Tirole (2004), we assume that employment protection takes the form of a tax on dismissals which will be added to social security contributions in order to finance unemployment costs. These costs are the expenses of a public agency responsible for reclassification and placement of unemployed. In summary, firstly, we propose an original analysis of the behavior of dismissal. On the other hand, the identification of two conditions of stability allows us to obtain analytical results in the presence of a budget constraint.

Section 1 describes the analytical framework. Then, section 2 presents the two conditions stability that allows us to study the effects of tax dismissals on the decentralized equilibrium.

1. The Model

The analysis is based on a matching model (Pissarides, 2000) in which firms choose between productivity and risk of job destruction. The labor market frictions preclude the instantaneous association between firms and workers. We consider that workers, non-countable, are identical and insensitive to risk. They have an infinite horizon and receive a wage, w, when they are employed and have a domestic production, d, when they are unemployed.

Concerning firms, they are also non-countable, identical and insensitive to risk. In addition, they freely enter the market and have a single job. While it is vacant, the job costs c per period to stay open. Once filled, the job creates a production y there until the arrival of an idiosyncratic shock probability s. This permanent shock has the effect of cancel the productivity of the job. In that event the firm is therefore bound to dismiss its employee. She must pay a tax f ($f \geq 0$).

As mentioned in the introduction, our analysis assumes that jobs more productive are also more risky. This hypothesis can be regarded as an illustration of the very general principle according to which a higher average yield cannot be obtained only at the cost of greater variance. Formally, the relationship between productivity and the destruction rate is assumed increasing and convex. We have:

$$s = s(y) \tag{1}$$

With $s'(y) > 0$ and $s''(y) > 0$.

When the job is filled, firm must pay a fee τ ($\tau \geq 0$). As time is continuous, the value of a filled job, with a productivity y, denoted $J(y)$, thus satisfies:

$$rJ(y) = y - w(y) - \tau - s(y)(J(y) - V + f) \tag{2}$$

where r is the interest rate and V is the value of a vacant job.

Market frictions are synthesized by a constant returns matching function. Let θ the labor market tightness (number of vacancies compared to a number of unemployed). Using the matching function, we deduce the probability, $q(\theta)$, (instantaneous) to fill a vacancy and the probability, $p(\theta)$, of finding a job ($p=\theta q$). The tightness θ reduces the probability q and the increases the probability p. With these notations, the value of a vacant job is defined as follows:

$$rV = -c + q(J(y) - V) \tag{3}$$

Concerning Workers, $W(y)$ denote the intertemporal utility of an employee, in a firm with productivity y, and U of an unemployed. In a steady state, the utilities jointly verify the following two relationships:

$$rW(y) = w(y) - s(y)(W(y) - U) \tag{4}$$

$$rU = d + p(W(y) - U) \tag{5}$$

According to the generalized Nash rule, the total surplus, denoted S, created by a couple employer/employee is distributed between both agents according to their respective bargaining strength. We shall note β ($0<\beta<1$) the workers bargaining strength. Using equations (2) and (4), we deduce:

$$S = \frac{y - \tau - s(y)f - r(V + U)}{r + s(y)} \tag{6}$$

This expression of total surplus allows us to easily analyze the technological choice of firms. Rationally, firms are assumed to arbitrate between productivity and risk of destruction by studying the value of their vacant job. In view of the above relations, this means that each firm maximizes S. In the symmetric state, the first order condition satisfies:

$$1 - s'(y)(S + f) \tag{7}$$

As mentioned above, taking into account the budget constraint of the State is an essential element of our model. Credit side, the State has every moment a stream of revenue, relative to employment, is given by: $\tau + s(y)f$. Finally, as regards job creation, we retain the assumption usual of free-entry. Under this assumption, the equilibrium value of vacant job is zero ($V = 0$).

2. Equilibrium and Results

Using the bargaining rule and equations (3) and (5), we can express the value of the vacant job, V, and the utility of the unemployed, U, according to the surplus S. We get:

$$rV = -c + q(1-\beta)S \tag{8}$$

$$rU = d + p\beta S \tag{9}$$

The equilibrium values of variables can then be obtained by combining equations (1), (6), (7), (8) and (9). To these equilibrium equations, we add two conditions. The first is a stability condition of technological choices, while the second concerns the jobs creation. Because it results from an individual choice, determining productivity (and the rate of destruction) may pose a stability problem. Indeed, when they decide, firms ignore the fact that an increased rate of destruction is reflected by an increase in the payroll tax which tends to reduce private surplus S. It is possible that an increased rate of destruction will lead firms to raise it further. We must therefore impose that in the equilibrium, technological choices are stable. Formally, this means that an increase in y will increase the product $(s'(y)(S+f))$ (see the optimality condition (7)). By differentiation of the equilibrium equations (8) and (9) given above, we establish then Lemma 1:

Lemma 1. For a given level of the variable θ, an increase of y increases the expression $(s'(y)(S+f))$ if and only if the following stability condition is satisfied:

$$\sigma \equiv r + s(y) + \beta p + q(1-\beta) - \frac{\tau(s'(y))^2}{s(y)s''(y)(S+f)} > 0 \tag{10}$$

As suggested by the above reasoning, the stability condition (10) requires that the impact of the destruction rate on contributions (which is given by) is not too high.

Returning now to the free-entry assumption. In the usual matching models (Pissarides, 2000), free-entry serves only to cancel the equilibrium value of vacant jobs. In these models, increasing the number of vacancies reduces their value by making recruitment more slowly (average). Here, an increase in the labor market tightness θ causes a decrease in social security contributions, which could offset the congestion effect and thus increase the value of vacant jobs. Clearly, this possibility must be rejected. By differentiation of the equilibrium equations (8) and (9), we establish then Lemma 2:

Lemma 2. Under the condition (10), an increase in the labor market tightness θ decreases the value of vacant jobs, V, if and only if the following stability condition is satisfied:

$$E \equiv (\sigma - q(1-\beta))Sq'(\theta) + q\left(\frac{s(y)h}{p^2} - \beta S\right)p'(\theta) < 0 \tag{11}$$

According to intuition, this stability condition of job creation implies that the impact of θ on the unemployment costs (measured by the term $s(y)hp'(\theta)/p^2$) is not too large. In summary, the labor market equilibrium (stable) may be defined as follows:

Definition 1. A labor market equilibrium is a set of variables () that simultaneously satisfy equations (1), (6), (7), (8), (9), (10) and (11).

Concerning the effect of the tax on layoffs, we consider that social contributions are (strictly) positive to demonstrate the following proposition:

Proposition 1. Under the conditions (10) and (11), an increase in the tax on layoffs (f) leads to increase in the labor market tightness (θ) and to decrease in the rate destruction (s) causing the fall in unemployment.

To make this result more intuitive, we focus on the direct effects of the tax on layoffs (*i.e.* the effects for a given value of θ). On the one hand, for given productivity, increasing the tax on layoffs leads to lower social contributions which cancels the effect on the surplus S, so on the value of newly created jobs. On the other hand, a fall of the destruction rate decreases the unemployment costs. In total, the tax increase induces a net decrease of withdrawals that stimulates job creation. In fact, taxing the dismissals leads firms to decide on a lower destruction rate that takes better account of its budgetary implications. In other words, firms internalize the fiscal effects of their technological choices (Amine and *al.*, 2007).

CONCLUSION

When firms establish their technological choices, they tend to opt for high productivity at the expense of job stability. They thus ignore the impact of their decisions on the level of social contributions that they have to pay. This externality poses a problem of optimal taxation that we have shown that it could be solved by introducing a tax on layoffs. Indeed, when the unemployment costs are also funded by a tax on layoffs, firms tend to decrease productivity to reduce the destruction rate of job. It follows that the unemployment rate decreases with increase in the tax on layoffs. Indeed, firms fully internalize the consequences of their technological choices on the unemployment cost.

REFERENCES

Amine, S., Chatraoui, A., Gavrel, F., Lebon, I. (2007). Productivité et risque de destruction des emplois: Un argument favorable à l'instauration d'une taxe sur les licenciements. *Revue d'économie politique*, *117*, 921-936.

Blanchard, O., Tirole, J. (2003). *Protection de l'emploi et procédures de licenciement. Conseil d'analyse économique*. Paris: La Documentation française.

Blanchard, O., Tirole, J. (2004). The Optimal Design of Labor Market Institutions. A First Pass. *NBER working paper, 10443.*

Fougère, D., Margolis, D. (2000). Moduler les cotisations employeurs à l'assurance-chômage: Les expériences de bonus-malus aux États-Unis. *Revue française d'économie*, *15*, 3-76.

Pissarides, C. (2000). *Equilibrium Unemployment Theory* (2nd edition). Cambridge: MIT Press.

In: Labor Markets: Dynamics, Trends and Economic Impact ISBN: 978-1-61470-825-4
Editor: Samir Amine

Chapter 4

A SINGLE EUROPEAN LABOR MARKET? HOW DIFFERENCES IN SKILLS, COMPETITIVENESS, AND PRODUCTIVITY ARE SHAPING THE 'NEW' MAP OF EUROPE

Manuel Salas Velasco*
University of Granada, Spain

ABSTRACT

Free movement of workers is a fundamental right in the EU. And labor flows across regions have the potential to undo some of the direct effects of labor market shocks. However, the unemployment rates still vary significantly among European countries, ranging in 2010 from 4.4% in Austria to 20.1% in Spain. Why the European labor market is unable to allocate resources on an intra-EU basis (e.g., shifting labor from one region to another)? Differences in skills across countries, language barriers, and cultural aspects, among others, are behind the geographical labor immobility. On the other hand, as expected, lower rates of unemployment correspond with those countries which are recovering after the crisis. In this book chapter we prove that the main engine for growth is competitiveness which requires a highly skilled and adaptable workforce, along with efficient labor markets and an innovation-conducive environment and a sophisticated business culture. However, there is an important spatial heterogeneity which allow us to present the first systematic mapping and analysis of regional clusters across the EU, Norway, and Switzerland. Understanding the causes and the consequences of agglomeration of economic activity is crucial to understanding the economic rationale for location-based policies and their welfare consequences. By equipping people with the right skills governments can help boost the competitiveness of their economies as a whole, but the question remaining is whether all the European economies are equally prepared and qualified to face the globalization, technological and organizational changes, and new patterns of international trade.

* E-mail address: msalas@ugr.es.

Introduction

Understanding local labor markets is important for labor economists. The last three decades have witnessed a growing amount of empirical research on the causes and consequences of localization of workers and firms within a country. This area, at the intersection of labor and urban economics, contains important and challenging questions and is likely to generate an increasing share of high quality empirical research in the next decade (Moretti, 2011). At European Union level, concern is primarily with the free geographical movement of workers but additionally with other forms of regulation that shape Europe's labor market.

Although the EU has set ambitious objectives on employment–along with innovation, education, social inclusion, and climate/energy–to be reached by 2020, the reality is that the European labor market is complex and, in contrast with the American one, there are numerous impediments to labor mobility, suggesting that in reality there are numerous markets for labor rather than a single general market. Frequently cited reasons for barriers to geographical labor mobility within the EU include (Heinz and Ward-Warmedinger, 2006): the existence of legal and administrative barriers; the lack of familiarity with other European languages and cultures; the monetary costs of moving; inefficient housing markets; the limited portability of pension rights; the lack of clarity in the international recognition of professional qualifications; and non-formal learning and the lack of transparency of job openings. In addition, and in opposition to American mentality, one of the biggest obstacles to mobility in Europe is people's attitudes.

The efficiency and flexibility of the labor market are critical for ensuring that workers are allocated to their most efficient use in the economy and provided with incentives to give their best effort in their jobs. Labor markets must therefore have the flexibility to shift workers from one economic activity to another rapidly and at low cost, and to allow for wage fluctuations without much social disruption. Yet a perfectly competitive labor market amounts to an absence of both noneconomic and economic barriers to the transfer of labor between sectors. However, although differences in culture and language add diversity and richness to European societies, they make up significant barriers to labor mobility as well. In addition, we must bear in mind the nonhomogeneity of the labor force in terms of skills across European countries, with areas experiencing high unemployment rates of unskilled workers (e.g., bricklayers in Spain) co-existing with regions suffering from skills shortages (e.g., engineers in the UK). So even though textbooks in labor economics teach us that enhancing geographic mobility can be considered as an allocative mechanism to shift resources efficiently from sector to sector, the reality is different, with unemployment rates that vary significantly among European countries, ranging in 2010 from 4.4% in Austria to 20.1% in Spain.

The possibility that the labor market in the EU is failing to perform its role as an allocator of scarce resources has significant policy implications. In Europe, like in the USA, jobs are becoming more knowledge- and skill-intensive–technology and knowledge are nowadays the key factors of production. A better labor force in terms of qualifications and competences should help the EU and the Member States deliver high levels of employment, productivity, and social cohesion. But, are all the European countries equally well prepared and qualified? We try to answer this question and other related issues in this book chapter. We start wondering what skills the EU will need in the coming years. The second section summarizes the most comprehensive and consistent set of skill demand projections ever produced for Europe. Quantitative projections should not be seen as deterministic or prescriptive. Structural change, and its implications for changing skill needs, should not be mechanistically predicted. The third section discusses whether or not people in Europe have the right skills to match these jobs. Next section focuses on competitiveness, which requires a highly skilled and adaptable workforce along with efficient labor markets and an innovation-conducive environment and a sophisticated business culture. However, the important spatial heterogeneity observed in these factors allows us to present the first systematic mapping and analysis of regional clusters across the EU, Norway, and Switzerland. The fifth section takes the perspective of the cluster categories to document how economic activity in these categories is geographically located. The penultimate section presents a simultaneous equations model of wage determination from a macroeconomic perspective. Here we prove that although the free movement of labor is one of the key foundations of the single market there are still important differences across Europe in the levels of labor productivity and levels of skills of the labor force which explain wage dispersion. Last section concludes.

Changing Demand for Skills in Europe

The European Centre for the Development of Vocational Training (Cedefop) is an agency of the European Union based in Thessaloniki, Greece, and it supports European policy-making in the field of vocational education and training. Cedefop current project 'Forecasting Skill Supply and Demand in Europe' aims to provide short and medium term forecasts of employment and other labor market indicators of interest for Europe up to 2020 (Cedefop, 2009, 2010). The project involves developing consistent databases and related tools to produce a comprehensive and consistent set of skill projections for the 27 EU countries plus Norway and Switzerland (EU-27+).[1] In this book chapter I use data from this center.[2]

Cedefop's medium-term forecast of occupational skill needs in Europe shows a considerable shift in labor demand towards skilled workers implying that future jobs will become more knowledge- and skills-intensive (Figure 1). The basic trends observed in recent years are expected to continue. Most of the projected increases are expected for high-skilled non-manual occupations, such as management, professional and associate professional jobs–more than 8.5 million in total between 2010 and 2020. Conversely, demand for skilled manual occupations (such as skilled agricultural, craft and trade workers, machine operators) is expected to decline substantially. In short, the demand for skills is likely to continue to rise, although at the same time there are concerns about polarization, with significant increases in the number of some low level jobs.

---

[1] The Schengen area represents a territory where the free movement of persons is guaranteed. The big majority of the EU countries and non-EU members such as Norway and Switzerland have signed the Schengen agreement.

[2] Basically, the so called E3ME model developed by the consultancy Cambridge Econometrics is used to provide the employment projections for Cedefop's forecasts of skills supply and demand. The author is grateful to Cedefop for providing him with detailed forecast results (including country workbooks).

What exactly is behind these developments still needs to be analyzed. Sectoral change is one of the key drivers of occupational structures, but globalization, technological and organizational changes, and new patterns of international trade, contribute substantially as well. Employment prospects by countries and occupations (Cedefop, 2010) suggest that the European countries will continue shifting away from the primary sector (especially agriculture) and traditional manufacturing industries towards services and the knowledge intensive sectors. In particular, technicians and associate professionals will be required in Italy, Spain, and the UK. On the other hand, professionals will be needed in Germany and Switzerland (Cedefop, 2010).

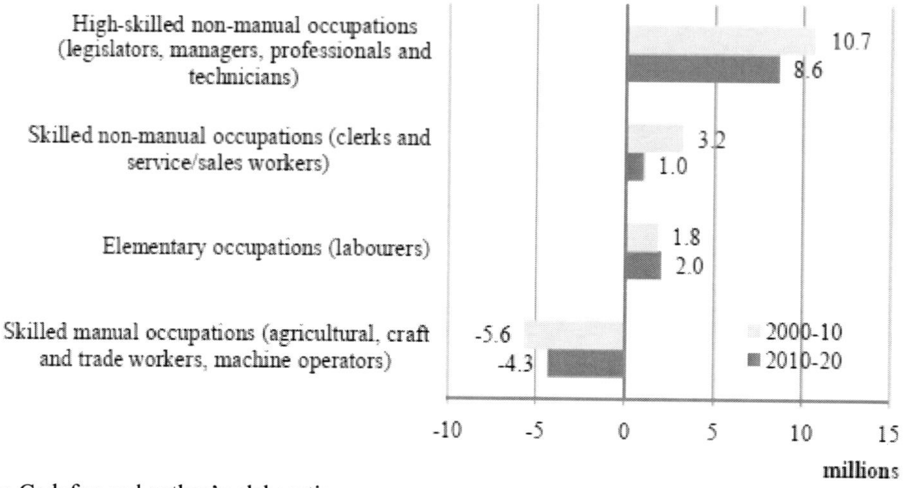

Source: Cedefop and author's elaboration.

Figure 1. Net Employment Change by Broad Occupational Groups, 2010-20, EU-27+.

With regard to employment trends by country and qualification, Cedefop (2010) focuses on three qualification levels as highest educational attainment: high, ISCED 5-6 (tertiary education); medium, ISCED 3-4 (upper secondary education); and low, ISCED 0-2 (lower secondary education or less). Substantial change is expected for high skilled labor force with around 15.6 million additional jobs being created between 2010 and 2020 in EU-27+. Changes in industrial structure combined with skill biased technological change will increase the demand for the highly qualified and intermediate level qualified categories, at the detriment of the low qualified group. This is more likely to happen in France, Italy, Spain, and the UK (Cedefop, 2010).

THE SUPPLY OF SKILLS: IS EUROPE ON THE RIGHT TRACK?

Anticipating skills needs can help to fill information deficits and avoid future imbalances and mismatches, as well as guiding and informing individual decision making and choices. In this respect, if Cedefop's skills forecasting is accurate, and we focus on high-skilled labor, it seems that the majority of European countries will not be prepared in ten years time to face a knowledge based society. According to EU statistics agency Eurostat, the population between

25 and 65 years old holding an university degree was on average by 25% in 2008 (last column in Table 1). And even though significant progress is being made across Europe with more well-qualified young people entering the workforce, and older less well formally qualified workers will retire in ten years time (penultimate column), still an important number of countries will have a relatively low proportion of highly qualified people (e.g., Czech Republic, Italy, Malta, Portugal, Romania, or Slovakia). Will these countries be able to change the picture in ten years time, without forgetting the low mobility of labor in the EU?

Table 1. Regional Imbalances in the Supply of High-Skilled Labor. Percentage of Population with Tertiary Education by Age Groups, 2008

Country	From 25 to 34 years	From 35 to 44 years	From 45 to 54 years	From 55 to 64 years	From 25 to 64 years
Finland	38.3	43.8	36.6	28.5	36.6
Norway	43.7	38.4	31.5	27.7	35.5
Cyprus	48.0	35.2	30.2	19.3	34.5
Ireland	45.6	37.7	27.5	18.9	34.4
Estonia	35.8	34.6	34.6	31.6	34.3
Switzerland	38.5	36.4	31.5	27.3	33.7
Belgium	42.3	35.3	28.7	22.3	32.3
Netherlands	39.8	32.5	30.5	26.5	32.2
Denmark	42.7	35.4	28.5	22.3	32.1
Sweden	40.8	32.7	28.4	26.4	32.0
United Kingdom	38.6	33.1	30.2	25.5	32.0
Lithuania	41.6	29.3	26.6	22.8	30.4
Spain	38.8	32.6	23.8	16.0	29.2
Luxembourg	38.7	28.4	22.0	19.4	27.7
France	40.8	30.7	20.2	17.3	27.3
Germany	23.9	26.7	25.9	24.4	25.4
Latvia	28.7	25.7	24.2	21.4	25.2
EU (27 countries)	30.9	25.8	21.4	18.1	24.3
Bulgaria	26.0	23.6	22.4	19.2	22.8
Greece	27.5	25.8	20.8	14.6	22.6
Slovenia	30.0	23.7	19.8	16.1	22.6
Poland	32.1	18.8	13.0	12.0	19.6
Hungary	24.0	19.1	16.9	16.1	19.2
Austria	19.4	19.3	17.7	15.2	18.1
Slovakia	18.4	13.9	14.2	10.9	14.8
Czech Republic	17.7	14.4	14.8	10.6	14.5
Italy	19.9	15.2	11.9	9.8	14.4
Portugal	23.2	14.5	9.9	7.7	14.3
Malta	22.7	14.1	8.1	7.6	13.2
Romania	18.8	11.3	10.8	8.9	12.8

Source: Eurostat and author's elaboration.

The average qualification levels could increase significantly in Europe iff more high school graduates go to College. But the participation rates in higher education in Europe are below the OECD average. According to the OECD (2010), EU-19 exhibits lower entry rates into tertiary education for both Type A and B tertiary programmes: 55% and 12% on average, respectively, in 2008; compared to an OECD average of 56% and 16%, respectively.[3] So I am more pessimistic than Cedefop's medium-term forecast of skill supply in Europe until 2020. Cedefop (2009) projected the change in the composition of population by level of qualification. Its results showed that the number of those with high-level qualifications will rise by almost 34% in 2020, and those with medium-level qualifications by 48.3%. This increase will be compensated by a decrease of people holding low qualifications (Figure 2).[4]

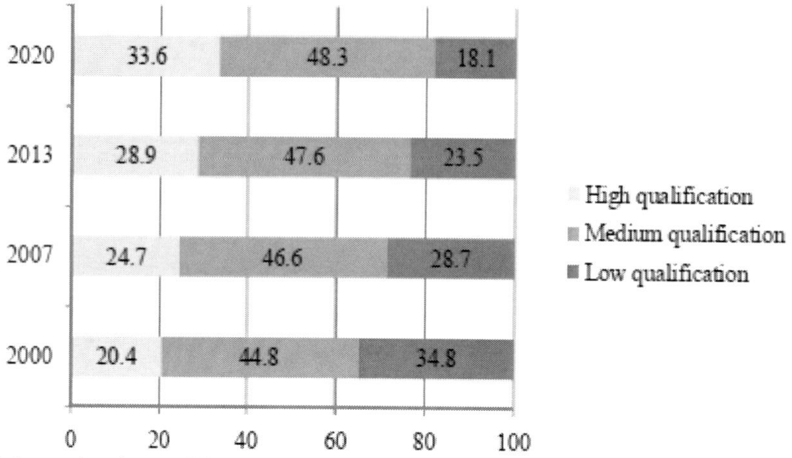

Source: Cedefop and author's elaboration.

Figure 2. Changing Qualifications Structure of the Working Age Population (25-64), in %, EU-25*.

In any case, to be more useful to both policy-makers and individual labor-market participants, more research is needed and more detail is desirable. Being restricted to formal qualifications, however, they cannot provide qualitative information on knowledge, skills, and competences people have or jobs require. And the quality of European universities is very diverse across the European countries considered here.

Spatial Segmentation of the European Labor Market

'Europe 2020' is the EU's growth strategy for the coming decade. The EU wants to become a smart, sustainable, and inclusive economy. These three mutually reinforcing priorities should help Member States deliver high levels of employment, productivity, and social cohesion. The Union has set five ambitious objectives on employment, innovation, education, social inclusion, and climate/energy to be reached by 2020. However, these are too ambitious plans, bearing in mind the imbalances in the high-skilled labor market–as we have seen, and there are important differences in levels of productivity across the European countries as well. So we could assert that there are at least more than a single labor market.

---

[3] EU-19 refers to European Union countries which belong to the OECD.

[4] Figure 2 presents the forecasts for all EU Member States excluding Bulgaria, Malta, and Romania, but including Norway. This group is referred as EU-25*. Data of future demographic development are taken from official Eurostat projections. These include too explicit assumptions about migration patterns (Cedefop, 2009).

This section aims to prove it focusing on the economic, business, and regulatory environment across Europe. Our research highlights the importance of competitiveness–fed by an excellent functioning of the labor market, well prepared workers in terms of skills and qualifications, and an innovation and business sophistication culture–for economic success (see next section). Data for the analyses come from the World Economic Forum (WEF). In 'The Global Competitiveness Report 2010-2011,' WEF included 13,600 business leaders across 139 economies. The report is comprised of 12 indicators grouped into 3 sub-indices. Data gathered through the survey provide a qualitative, timely snapshot of each nation's economic, business, and regulatory environment. Hard data are collected from various international and national sources and form part of the report too. For the 29 European countries, we take the scores given in 4 out of 12 indicators of the latest report (the four indicators with the highest and strongest positive correlation among them). Specifically, scores in: business sophistication; innovation; higher education and training; and labor market efficiency. Each indicator–for each country–has an average score which ranges from 1 to 7 (the higher the better). Figure 3 illustrates the information (dimensions) used by WEF to build those indicators. The report gives detailed information in each of these dimensions. For the EU-27+, Table 2 summaries the scores on business sophistication, innovation, highly-skilled labor force, and well-developed and efficient labor markets. It demonstrates the broad range of competitiveness in the European Union, being Denmark one of the EU's most competitive economies contrasting with the very uncompetitive Greece's economy.

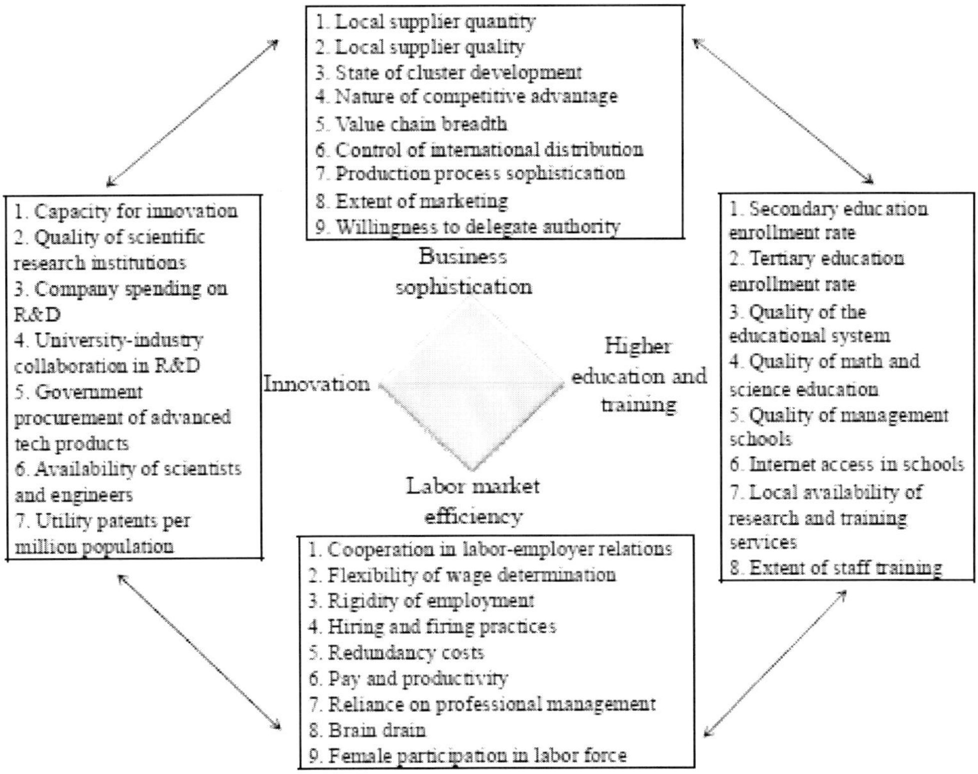

Source: Global Competitiveness Report 2010-2011 and author's elaboration.

Figure 3. The 'Diamond' of Competitiveness.

Table 2. The Competitiveness across European Countries

Country	Business sophistication scores	Innovation scores	Higher education and training scores	Labor market efficiency scores
Austria	5.46	4.48	5.38	4.75
Belgium	5.24	4.59	5.71	4.64
Bulgaria	3.52	2.91	4.14	4.51
Cyprus	4.47	3.66	4.91	4.64
Czech Republic	4.47	3.92	5.11	4.75
Denmark	5.41	4.89	5.84	5.47
Estonia	4.13	3.68	5.17	4.91
Finland	5.29	5.56	6.06	4.85
France	5.18	4.48	5.36	4.47
Germany	5.82	5.19	5.33	4.40
Greece	3.83	3.00	4.67	3.71
Hungary	3.87	3.55	4.81	4.46
Ireland	4.85	4.25	5.17	4.87
Italy	4.81	3.40	4.60	3.81
Latvia	3.73	3.02	4.81	4.58
Lithuania	4.21	3.38	5.07	4.61
Luxembourg	4.98	4.53	4.68	4.71
Malta	4.34	3.43	4.79	4.10
Netherlands	5.55	4.77	5.63	4.83
Norway	5.17	4.49	5.59	4.97
Poland	4.20	3.31	5.00	4.58
Portugal	4.19	3.77	4.76	3.85
Romania	3.55	2.94	4.47	4.32
Slovakia	4.12	2.95	4.49	4.66
Slovenia	4.42	3.73	5.27	4.26
Spain	4.46	3.47	4.85	3.88
Sweden	5.88	5.45	5.90	4.89
Switzerland	5.81	5.60	5.79	5.92
United Kingdom	5.32	4.65	5.34	5.29

Source: Global Competitiveness Report 2010-2011 and author's elaboration.

Applying Non-Hierarchical Cluster Analysis Algorithms to Region Classification

Regional clusters, the geographic concentration of economic activities in a specific field connected through different types of linkages, from knowledge spillovers to the use of a common labor market, are increasingly viewed as an interesting conceptual tool to understand the economic strength or competitiveness of a region. Regional clusters enable companies to reach higher levels of productivity and be more innovative. The cluster of IT firms in Silicon Valley in Northern California, where Google Inc. and other high-tech companies have located their corporate headquarters, or financial firms in London are notable examples. In recent years, this view has motivated more and more policy makers and economic development practitioners to turn to cluster-based concept as a new tool to strengthen regional economies. While the overall levels of skills, infrastructure, and institutional capacity in Europe seem to be on par or even better than elsewhere in the world, many researchers have identified rules and regulations that hamper flexibility, for example on the labor market, or reduce incentives, for example through high tax rates, as potential reasons for the European performance gap.

As we have seen in Table 2, there are important differences across Europe in key indicators which shape competitiveness. Accordingly, our aim now is to 'partition' the map of Europe into similar regions using those indicators. Precisely, cluster analysis is a statistical method that identifies groups of samples that behave similarly or show similar characteristics (look-alike groups). In particular, cluster analysis is useful for combining observations into groups such that:

- Each group is homogeneous or compact with respect to certain characteristics (e.g., observations in each group are similar to each other).
- Each group should be different from other groups with respect to the characteristics (e.g., observations of one group should be different from the observations of the other groups).

Two main techniques are possible: 1. Hierarchical clustering technique that considers a natural process of grouping (e.g., students/schools/school districts); 2. Non-hierarchical clustering technique: data are divided into k partitions or groups with each partition representing a cluster. In the latter case, the process, which is called 'k-means,' appears to give partitions which are reasonably efficient in the sense of within-class variance. This method was developed by MacQueen (1967). This author suggested the name k-means for describing an algorithm that assigns each item to the cluster having the nearest centroid (mean). This method is more appropriate for our data.

In general, the k-means method will produce exactly k different clusters of greatest possible distinction–maximizing intra-class similarity and minimizing interclass similarity. It should be mentioned that the best number of clusters k leading to the greatest separation (distance) is not known a priori and must be computed from the data. How do we choose the number of clusters k? In the literature, various selection criteria have been proposed for selecting k. One simple rule of thumb sets the number to (Mardia et al., 1979):

$$k \cong \sqrt{n/2}$$

where n is the number of observations. We would have between 3 and 4 clusters. However, the so called Calinski-Harabasz (1974) pseudo-F-statistic can help us determine the number of clusters. The optimal clustering is the one with the highest value for the pseudo-F-statistic; in our case: 41.87 vs. 36.34. So, three clusters have been finally identified with five countries belonging to cluster 3, eight in cluster 2, and sixteen in cluster 1 (Figure 4).

Countries that belong to the same cluster are more homogenous in terms of the variables considered–skills, labor market efficiency, business sophistication, and innovation–than are countries belonging to other clusters.

Source: Author's elaboration.

Figure 4. Mapping out the Triple Segmentation of the European Labor Market. Clusters by Country. K-Means Method.

First, in cluster 3 we have the Nordic countries (Denmark, Finland, and Sweden) and Central European regions (Germany and Switzerland); a strong 'diamond' which involves an innovation-conducive environment and a sophisticated business culture supported by highly efficient labor markets and an excellent education and training system. Companies in these countries, according to business sophistication and innovation indicators, are characterized by a high sophistication of the production processes, the use of sophisticated marketing tools and techniques, a high capacity for innovation, and a heavy spending on research and development. This demands a highly skilled labor force as well as well-functioning labor markets. In fact, these five countries scored very high on the majority of the different dimensions of both the labor market efficiency indicator–e.g., good cooperation in labor-employer relations, low redundancy costs in weeks of salary, pay related to worker productivity, and reliance on professional management–and higher education and training indicator–e.g., the educational system meets the needs of a competitive economy, and companies invest in training and employee development. Second, in cluster 2 we have Central and Western European countries (Austria, Belgium, France, Ireland, Luxembourg, Netherlands, Norway, and the United Kingdom); a good 'diamond' which involves, on the one hand, a sophisticated and innovative business culture–e.g., high production process sophistication, the nature of competitive advantage of country's companies in international markets is based mainly upon unique products and processes, and authority is mostly delegated to business unit heads and other lower-level managers; on the other hand, a skilled labor force and well-functioning labor markets–generally cooperative labor-employer relations, moderate redundancy costs, and mostly professional managers chosen for merit and qualifications. Finally, in cluster 1 we would have the regions of Southern and Eastern Europe together with Cyprus and Malta;[5] a weak 'diamond' which involves sophisticated business practices and innovation significantly behind Nordic, Central, and Western European countries.

Additionally, according to the scores given on the different dimensions of the labor market efficiency indicator, countries in cluster 1 have inefficient labor markets: confrontational labor-employer relations, pay not related to worker productivity, and management usually assigned to relatives or friends without regard to merit. The scores were very low as well in two dimensions of the higher education and training indicator: how well the educational system meets the needs of a competitive economy, and to what extent companies invest in training and employee development.

Testing Hypotheses Concerning Means by Clusters

Table 3. Analysis of Variance or ANOVA

Business sophistication	Countries	Mean	Std. Dev.
Cluster 1	16	4.15	0.36
Cluster 2	8	5.22	0.23
Cluster 3	5	5.64	0.27
Analysis of variance			
F = 56.76 Prob > F = 0.0000			
Innovation	Countries	Mean	Std. Dev.
Cluster 1	16	3.38	0.33
Cluster 2	8	4.53	0.15
Cluster 3	5	5.34	0.30
Analysis of variance			
F = 103.58 Prob > F = 0.0000			
Higher education and training	Countries	Mean	Std. Dev.
Cluster 1	16	4.81	0.29
Cluster 2	8	5.36	0.33
Cluster 3	5	5.78	0.27
Analysis of variance			
F = 23.56 Prob > F = 0.0000			
Labour market efficiency	Countries	Mean	Std. Dev.
Cluster 1	16	4.35	0.37
Cluster 2	8	4.82	0.24
Cluster 3	5	5.11	0.59
Analysis of variance			
F = 8.72 Prob > F = 0.0013			

Source: Author's calculations.

[5] Bulgaria, Cyprus, Czech Republic, Estonia, Greece, Hungary, Italy, Latvia, Lithuania, Malta, Poland, Portugal, Romania, Slovakia, Slovenia, and Spain.

Cluster analysis is an exploratory data analysis tool. Once we have classified European countries into three groups using a cluster analysis, then do an ANOVA on the clusters to see if there are in fact statistically significant differences among clusters in business sophistication, innovation, quality of the higher education and training systems, and efficiency of the labor market.

In its simplest form, ANOVA provides a statistical test of whether or not the means of several groups are all equal.[6] In Table 3 we summarize the mean values by cluster on the four indicators mentioned before. Additionally, the table gives the value of F-statistic and p-values for the null hypothesis (H_0: all k population variances are equal, against the alternative that at least two are different).[7] We reject the null hypothesis and conclude that the average values on business sophistication, innovation, quality of the higher education and training systems, and efficiency of the labor market are different in the three clusters. Therefore, it seems that our partition of Europe into tree regions is correct.

WHAT'S DRIVING THE ECONOMIC RECOVERY IN EUROPE? HIGHLY PRODUCTIVE LABOR MARKETS AS A BENCHMARK

In this section, we take the perspective of the three cluster categories and document how economic activity in these categories is geographically located. According to Eurostat, the European countries are recovering after the economic crisis. Over the whole year 2010, GDP increased by 1.7% in the EU-27. Yet the figures illustrate important differences across Europe. Whilst countries such as Sweden, Germany, Luxembourg, and Finland grew at rates over 3 per cent, other countries such as Greece, Ireland, Latvia, and Spain showed still negative growth rates. Graphic and econometric evidence on the links between competitiveness and economic growth in the short run shows a positive association between the Global Competitiveness Index (World Economic Forum, 2010) and the output growth for the 29 European countries of our analysis (Figure 5).

However, a credible and effective growth strategy for Europe can only be derived from a wider diagnosis. To do that, we regress the real GDP growth rate on some of the indicators of the Global Competition Index (World Economic Forum, 2010); specifically, the 1-to-7 scale scores on institutions, infrastructure, goods market efficiency, and financial market development. Additionally, the econometric analysis includes an indicator of human capital and three regional dummies which identify the clusters showed previously in Figure 4.[8] The results of the econometric analysis are shown in Table 4. They reveal that, controlling by other significant factors which explain the growth of the real GDP–such as the development of the financial markets and the efficiency of goods market, European countries located in region or cluster 3 (Denmark, Finland, Germany, Sweden, and Switzerland) grew at a much higher rate in 2010 (3.4% on average), shaping that we could name 'highly productive labor markets.' In other words, although a sound and well-functioning financial sector–along with

[6] It may seem odd that a procedure that compares means is called analysis of variance. However, this name is derived from the fact that in order to test for statistical significance between means, we are actually comparing (e.g., analyzing) variances.

[7] Bonferroni post test confirms too that the average scores are statistically different in the three clusters.

[8] The World Economic Forum uses enrollment rates in higher education but not education attainment.

efficient markets for goods (e.g., healthy market competition)–have a strong bearing on competitiveness and growth in Europe, there are agglomeration effects or clustering on aggregate economic activity as well. The mere geographic concentration of firms is not conclusive to economic performance. Geographically concentrated industries stimulate growth if they are characterized by a sophisticated business culture encouraged by a highly qualified labor force, supported by both an environment that is conducive to innovative activity and a labor market that is efficient.

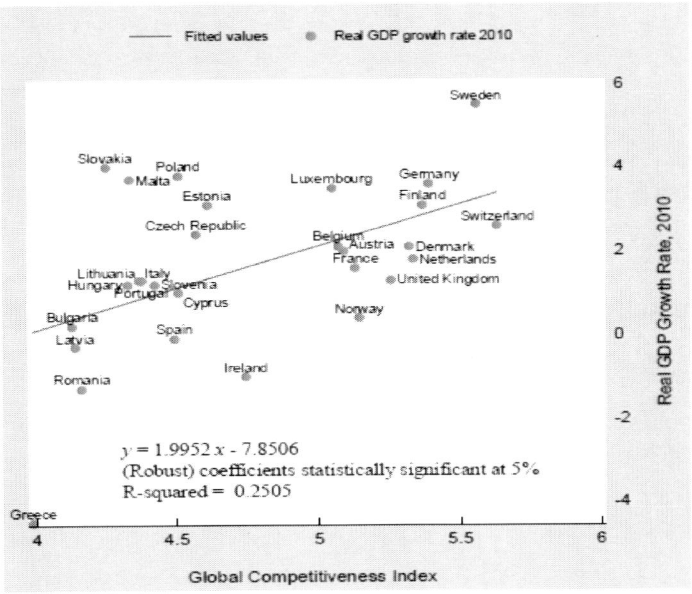

Source: Author's elaboration.

Figure 5. On the Links between Competitiveness and Aggregate Economic Growth: A Cross-Country Analysis.

Table 4. The Recovery in Europe: The Growth Engines in the Short-Run

	Coefficient		Robust Std. Err.	t
The quality of institutions	-0.787		1.03	-0.77
Extensive and efficient infrastructure	0.169		0.48	0.35
Goods market efficiency	3.579	*	1.83	1.96
Financial market development	1.718	**	0.70	2.45
(%) Population 25-64 with tertiary education attainment in 2008	-0.076		0.04	-1.69
Region 3 (cluster 3)	1.624	**	0.78	2.09
Region 2 (cluster 2)	Reference			
Region 1 (cluster 1)	1.655		1.28	1.29
Constant	-19.295		8.67	-2.23
Dependent variable = Real GDP growth rate 2010				
Number of obs. = 29				
F (7, 21) = 5.12				
Prob > F = 0.0016				
R-squared = 0.5742				

** Significance at 5%-level; * Significance at 10%-level.

Source: Author's calculations.

Evidence on agglomeration economies is particularly important for business. Firms base their location decisions on where their profits are expected to be highest, and this could be due to natural advantage or knowledge spillovers–when companies and suppliers from a particular sector are interconnected in geographically proximate groups efficiency is heightened. This concept relates to the idea of economies of scale and network effects. Firms in these countries must design and develop cutting-edge products and processes to maintain a competitive edge. This requires an environment that is conducive to innovative activity, supported by both the public and the private sectors. In particular, it means sufficient investment in research and development (RandD), especially by the private sector; the presence of high quality scientific research institutions; extensive collaboration in research between universities and industry; and the protection of intellectual property. Innovation is particularly important for economies as they approach the frontiers of knowledge and the possibility of integrating and adapting exogenous technologies tends to disappear. In the long run, standards of living can be enhanced only by technological innovation.

THE MACROECONOMICS OF THE EUROPEAN LABOR MARKET: WAGE DETERMINATION

Labor economics seeks to understand the functioning and dynamics of the market for labor. Efficient labor markets must ensure a clear relationship between worker incentives and their efforts.

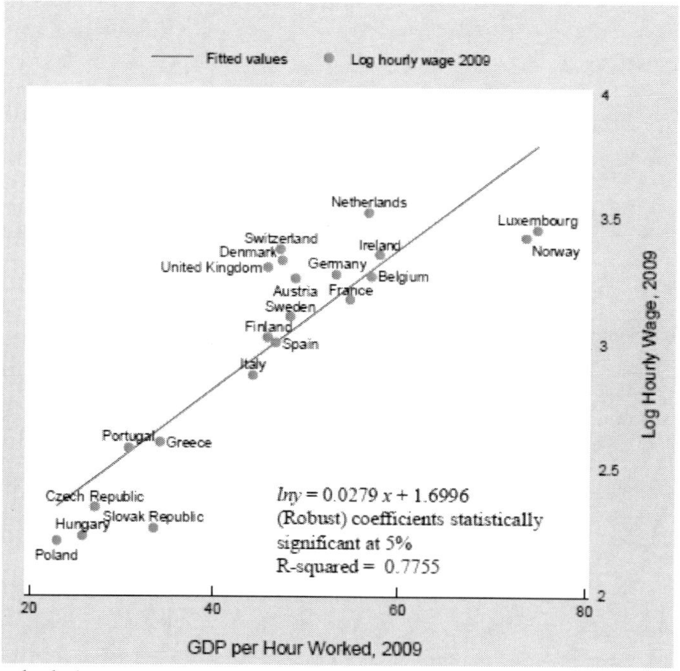

Source: Author's calculations.

Figure 6. The Relationship between Wages and Labor Productivity Levels in Europe (only 21 Countries that Are OECD Member Countries).

In a perfectly competitive market, workers' wages are equal to their productivity. In fact, the marginal productivity theory of wages has proved, over the years, to be a useful basis for analyzing wage and labor productivity relationships. Econometric evidence in Figure 6 corroborates this idea. In the horizontal axis, we measure the estimates of aggregate labor productivity levels across countries (GDP per hour worked, current prices, USD). In the vertical axis, we represent the natural log of the wage rate (2008 USD PPPs and 2008 constant prices). Data come from *OECD.Stat*, and only provided for the total economy and for one year (currently the latest available year is 2009).

However, the above analysis might represent only a partial view of the whole picture, as labor market outcomes are influenced too by the institutions and processes of collective bargaining, including the roles played by employers' organizations and trade unions. Additionally, we must bear in mind that the explanatory variable X, productivity, is not an exogenous one. Consequently, a better relationship between wages and their determinants could come from a two-equation model of wage determination:

$$Y = f(X, D) + \varepsilon_1$$
$$X = f(Z_1, Z_2, \ldots, Z_n) + \varepsilon_2$$

where: Y = wages; X = labor productivity; D = institutional aspects of the labor market affecting wages; and Z_1, Z_2,...,Z_n are the determinants of labor productivity.

Table 5 summarizes the results of the econometric estimation of the above simultaneous equations model.[9] The traditional ordinary least squares (OLS) technique is not appropriate for estimating the two-equation model, because the relationship specified by the equations violates the OLS assumption of zero covariance between the disturbance term and the independent variables. Estimation of such model via OLS would lead to biased and inconsistent estimates of the coefficients. Therefore, the estimation given in Table 5 is via three-stage least squares (3SLS) which estimates a system of structural equations (Zellner and Theil, 1962), where our wage equation contains an endogenous variable (productivity) among the explanatory variables.[10]

The first important result is that labor productivity is the key variable explaining the wages in Europe. The estimated coefficient associated to the productivity variable is positive and statistically significant, and we get a higher value than the figure shown in Figure 6, proving that not considering X as an endogenous variable would give us a downward bias in the estimation of the regression coefficient. However, the coefficient associated to D (flexibility of wage determination) does not show significance. With regard to the second equation, the results in Table 5 (second column) show that higher productivity levels are linked to higher human capital and better infrastructure–and both explanatory variables are positively correlated. Therefore, the complementarity of human and physical capital,

---

[9] In Table 5, data for the independent variables in both equations come from the Global Competitiveness Report 2008-2009, but for GDP per hour worked and percentage of people with tertiary education where figures have been taken from OECD databases.

[10] Another common avenue taken by researchers is IV estimation (or 2SLS). The purpose is to create instruments Z that are correlated with the endogenous variable X but are not correlated with Y. However, in practice, is difficult to find good instruments. Furthermore, assuming that our system is correctly specified, 3SLS is more efficient (or at least as efficient) than 2SLS.

controlling by other aspects such as macroeconomic conditions or competition, generates a positive relationship between average wages and average productivity levels. Although differences across countries in their quantity of physical capital play a central role in this model, differences in the quality of physical capital (technology) could arguably generate similar conclusions.

This is in fact the evidence from a more parsimonious model (last columns in Table 5) which shows a positive impact of both human capital and technology readiness on labor productivity–and human capital and technology readiness are positively correlated.[11] Accordingly, if skills and technology are complementary, it is plausible to assume that the optimal amount of human capital depends on both, the amount of physical capital a worker expects to use and the technological level that characterizes such capital.

As a country becomes more competitive, productivity will increase and wages will rise with advancing development.

Table 5. The Econometric Approach to Wage Determination in Europe: A Simultaneous Equations Model

Wage equation	Coef.		z	Coef.		z
GDP per hour worked, current prices, USD 2009	0.0329	**	6.21	0.0326	**	6.03
Flexibility of wage determination	-0.0446		-0.98	-0.0457		-0.97
Constant	1.6583	**	4.20	1.6772	**	4.13
R^2	0.7429			0.7462		
Chi2	70.28			68.00		
p-value	0.0000			0.0000		
Observations	21					
Dependent var. = Log hourly wage in 2009						
Productivity determination equation	Coef.		z	Coef.		z
Macroeconomy	3.0421		0.66	0.8069		0.17
(%) People 25-64 yo with tertiary education attainment in 2008	0.6953	**	2.24	0.6884	**	2.08
Infrastructure	5.5122	*	1.66			
Availability of latest technologies	1.4624		0.24	9.3245	**	2.18
Intensity of local competition	-4.8495		-1.05	-3.6605		-0.75
Constant	2.9917		0.12	-8.5731		-0.33
R^2	0.5207			0.4913		
Chi2	30.76			26.97		
p-value	0.0000			0.0000		
Observations	21					
Dependent var. = GDP per hour worked, current prices, USD 2009						

** Significance at 5%-level; * Significance at 10%-level.
Source: Author's calculations.

[11] Similarly, in long-run growth models with endogenous skill-biased technical change, an increase in the supply of educated workers increases the size of the market for skill-complementary technologies and stimulates the RandD sector to spend more effort upgrading the productivity of skilled workers (Acemoglu, 1997).

Conclusion

The structure of employment is constantly changing. Europe has seen dramatic changes in its employment structure over the past 60 years. While primary industries (including agriculture) and manufacturing are still important in economic terms, they account for an increasingly small part of total employment. The basic trends observed in recent years are expected to continue. The overall aims of the Cedefop work in this area are to provide better understanding of past trends in skill demand and supply at a pan-European level, and then to develop consistent skills projections, using existing comparable data. On the demand side, the focus is on skill needs (jobs) as measured by the numbers employed and number of job openings by sector, occupation, and qualification (including replacement demands arising from retirement, etc). Most of the projected increases are expected for high-skilled non-manual occupations, such as management, and professional and associate professional jobs. On the supply side, the focus is on the available skills, as measured by the highest qualification held by members of the population that are economically active. Cedefop's medium-term skill supply forecast for Europe up to 2020 suggests a substantial further increase in the proportion of the adult labor force with high- and medium-level qualifications. In contrast, the number of people with low-level qualifications is projected to decline in most European countries.

However, the optimistic forecasts made by Cedefop should be taken with caution. The percentage of population with higher education is still very low in an important number of European countries; and some countries have worrying rates of dropouts in secondary education which means, of course, lower higher education participation rates–without forgetting the lousy performance on international testing such as PISA of some European countries. Indeed, we observe an important spatial heterogeneity in terms of skills, quality of the education and training systems, and competitiveness. The diversity observed has allowed us to draw the first systematic analysis of regional clusters across the EU, Norway, and Switzerland. And the main engine for growth is competitiveness. But geographically concentrated economies can stimulate growth only if they are characterized by a sophisticated business culture encouraged by a highly qualified labor force, supported by both an environment that is conducive to innovative activity and a labor market that is efficient.

Knowing the causes and the consequences of agglomeration of economic activity is crucial to understanding the economic rationale for location-based policies and their welfare consequences. As a country becomes more competitive, productivity will increase and wages will rise with advancing development. Differences on workers' welfare are related with their productivity. We have proved that higher wages are strongly and positively related to higher labor productivity levels. So geographic concentration of economic activity is of fundamental importance for our understanding of how labor markets operate and have deep policy implications.

References

Acemoglu, D. (1997). Training and Innovation in an Imperfect Labour Market. *Review of Economic Studies, 64 (3)*, 445-464.

Calinski, T., Harabasz, J. (1974). A Dendrite Method for Cluster Analysis. *Communications in Statistics*, *3 (1)*, 1-27.

Cedefop (2009). Future Skill Supply in Europe. Medium-term Forecast up to 2020: Synthesis report. Luxembourg: Publications Office of the European Union.

Cedefop (2010): Skills Supply and Demand in Europe. Medium-term Forecast up to 2020. Luxembourg: Publications Office of the European Union.

Heinz, F.F., Ward-Warmedinger, M.E. (2006). Cross-Border Labour Mobility within an Enlarged EU. European Central Bank Occasional Paper No. 52.

MacQueen, J. (1967). Some Methods for Classification and Analysis of Multivariate Observations. In L. M. Le Cam, and J. Neyman (Eds.), Proceedings of the Fifth Berkeley Symposium on Mathematical Statistics and Probability: Vol. 1. Statistics (pp. 281-297). Berkeley, CA: University of California Press.

Mardia, K. V., Kent, J. T., Bibby, J. M. (1979). Multivariate Analysis. London: Academic Press.

Moretti, E. (2011). Local Labor Markets. In O. Ashenfelter, and D. Card (Eds.), Handbook of Labor Economics: Vol. 4b (pp. 1237-1313). Amsterdam: Elsevier Science.

OECD (2010). Education at a Glance 2010: OECD Indicators. Paris: OECD.

World Economic Forum (2010). The Global Competitiveness Report 2010-2011. Geneva: The World Economic Forum.

Zellner, A., Theil, H. (1962). Three Stage Least Squares: Simultaneous Estimation of Simultaneous Equations. *Econometrica*, *30 (1)*, 54-78.

In: Labor Markets: Dynamics, Trends and Economic Impact ISBN: 978-1-61470-825-4
Editor: Samir Amine

Chapter 5

SPANISH UNEMPLOYMENT AND BEVERIDGE CURVE SHIFTS

***Raquel Fonseca*[1,*] *and Henri Sneessens*[2]**
[1]Université du Québec à Montréal, CIRPÉE and RAND Corporation, Canada
[2]Université du Luxembourg, CREA, IRES and IZA, Luxembourg

ABSTRACT

This chapter investigates the importance that structural imbalances may have had on Spanish labor markets from 1977-2003. The focus of this chapter is on regional and skill mismatch. We use a Beveridge curve construction to derive mismatch indicators and assess the quantitative importance of regional and skill mismatch. We then evaluate this role in explaining aggregate unemployment. We find that structural unemployment seems to be one important explanation for unemployment, in particular for the period where we observed UV curve shifts.

1. INTRODUCTION

Since 1975 most European economies have been characterized by the persistence of relatively high unemployment rates. The magnitude of the change appears to be related to long run, structural factors rather than purely cyclical forces. Spain experienced the highest increase in aggregate unemployment. However, in contrast to other EU countries, unemployment rates seem to have sharply decreased until 2007 and a new increase till nowadays.[1] In most EU countries, we simultaneously observe a deterioration of the unemployment-vacancy (UV hereafter) relationship (the so-called Beveridge curve) from the mid-seventies until the mid-eighties. It is observed a move backwards of the UV curve after this period. Spain is of course no exception. These two observations for this period suggest

* E-mail address: fonseca.raquel@uqam.ca.
[1] For further evidence about the evolution of Spanish unemployment in the last decade see Bentolila et al. 2010.

the rise in aggregate unemployment might be related to a decrease in the efficient matching of labor supply and demand during this period.

Our analysis focuses on the determinants of Beveridge curve shifts.[2] Why there is deterioration in the efficiency of the matching process? The unemployment-vacancy (UV) relationship is one method employed to separate increases in structural and frictional unemployment from deficient demand unemployment. It is argued that outward shifts in the UV relationship indicate increases in frictional and structural unemployment while increases in deficient demand unemployment results in movements along the UV curve. Different regions may be characterized by different equilibrium levels of unemployment and vacancy rates (different positions along a given UV curve), as well as by different degrees of skill mismatch (different positions of the UV curve itself). The position of the economy-wide UV relationship and the aggregate performance of the economy will depend on both kinds of structural differences.

Labor market institutions, regulations and policies can hamper the adjustment between labor demand and labor supply, OECD Jobs Study (1994). Nickell et al. (2003) found evidence that these movements in the Beveridge Curves may be partly explained by changes in labor market institutions. However, these changes in labor market institutions do not affect equally across skills and regions. This chapter sheds some light on how important the contribution of skill and regional mismatch are to explain these shifts. Differences between skill groups and regions are important for both search and matching efficiency.

Our motivation is to disentangle how structural changes can have asymmetric effects across regions and skill groups. Krugman (1994) emphasizes the adverse effects of a changing skill distribution in the presence of rigid labor markets and relative wages. Different genuine asymmetric changes may be the consequence of relative wage rigidities and bias in the face of asymmetric growth on labor demand (biased technological change, de-industrialisation and/or globalisation and competition from low-wages).

In this chapter, we try to get better insight and understanding of the information contained in the unemployment and vacancy data about the role and importance of structural factors in regions and skill groups. Spain is a country of special interest because both skill and regional mismatch are usually mentioned as factors that may have contributed to the persistence of exceptionally high unemployment rates in that country.[3]

We analyze the UV curve of Spain between 1977 and 2003. Until now there is still controversy surrounding why the aggregate unemployment rates were so high during the period from the mid-seventies until the mid-eighties We then investigate whether an explanation of structural factors, which affect different skill groups and regions, can be realistic (whether the empirical evidence leads to rejection or not).

We first evaluate the role of structural imbalances by looking at structural mismatch indicators. Mismatch is an empirical concept that measures the degree of heterogeneity in the labor market usually across skills, sectors and regions. There is no mismatch in an economy when jobs and workers match in all dimensions. In the literature, we can mainly find different

[2] Even if the subject was more studied in the earlier nineties, there is still an interest issue in the literature for explaining UV shifts, i.e. Shimer, 2005 and 2006, Peracchi and Viviani, 2004, Fonseca and Muñoz, 2003, Nickell et al., 2003, Bentolila and Jimeno , 2006, and Bentolila et al., 2010.

[3] See Bentolila and Blanchard, 1990, Bentolila and Dolado, 1991, Bentolila and Jimeno, 1995, Jimeno and Bentolila, 1997 and more recently de la Fuente, 2001, Peracchi and Viviani, 2004, Bentolila et al., 2010.

indicators such as employment growth, vacancies and unemployment, and the variance of unemployment rates[4].

Measuring mismatch is an important issue in policy advice. The book edited by Padoa-Schioppa (1991) contains numerous examples of estimated mismatch across countries with different matching processes and different mismatch indicators. However, this compact study concludes that there is not a consensus on the measure of mismatch in the literature.[5]

Entorf (1998) tries to shed light on the performance of prominent measures of mismatch. He argues that in situations where the evolution of unemployment rates is determined by non-stationary stochastic processes, mismatch measures based on the variance of relative unemployment rates may be severely biased towards zero. The application of the Jackman, Layard and Savouri (1991), (JLS hereafter), indicator shows the decreasing trend across skills and regions in most of the OECD countries. On the other hand, estimates based on macroeconomic rationing models presented in Drèze and Bean (1990) reveal steadily growing mismatch in Europe. It can be concluded that it is difficult to explain unemployment from the inverse evolution of different mismatch. Vacancies and unemployment simultaneously can occur because of a rigid wage structure (with possible differences in wage levels in the sub - markets) and because of a less flexible distribution of labor (supply and demand) that does not move freely between the sub-markets (Hansen, 1970). Shimer (2004) and Hall (2003a, 2003b) bring to the debate the real wage rigidity in the unemployment and vacancies relationship. In our study, we will assume wages and prices are pre-set and we will focus on the information contained in the unemployment and vacancy data. Our mismatch indicators are obtained through the specification of Beveridge curves that simultaneously take into account regional and skill dimensions. We compare our results to other standard mismatch indicators such as JLS (1991). We examine the relationship of the UV curve for this period with nonlinear regression models and dynamic panel methods of estimation. We then compute our mismatch indicators according to our theoretical framework. Our results assess the quantitative importance of skill and regional mismatch in Spain. Moreover, we evaluate its role in explaining aggregate unemployment in the eighties. Even if institutional factors and business cycles have improved vacancy and unemployment relationship after the eighties, the percentage of mismatch across regions and skills is still important. The chapter is organized as follows. In Section 2 we discuss the data we use and present some descriptive information. Section 3 discusses the methodology of using Beveridge curves in order to derive the mismatch indicators that we apply in Section 4 and Section 5. We conclude in Section 6 with a summary of the most important findings.

2. Spanish Labour Markets Facts

This section analyses some stylized facts in the evolution of unemployment and vacancies in Spain. Our data set contains observations of the unemployment and vacancy rates region by region in Spain, over a period extending approximately from the mid 70's until

[4] See Lilien, 1982, Abraham and Katz, 1986, Jackman and Roper, 1987, Jackman, Layard and Savouri, 1991 and references in these studies.

[5] For further research in this topic, there is also a survey about microfoundations of the matching process; and estimation results of the matching function in Petrongolo and Pissarides, 2001.

the beginning of the 2000s. Our purpose is to analyze the Spanish Beveridge curve in Figure 1 below.

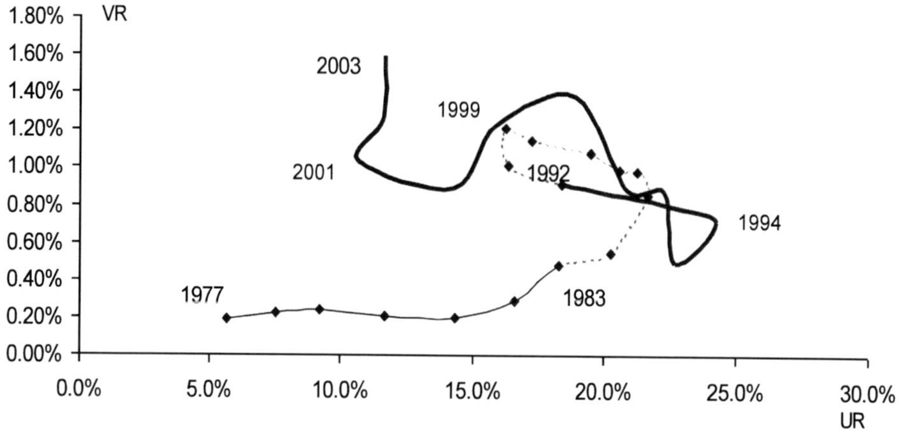

Figure 1. Spanish Beveridge curve (1977-2003).

Employment data are divided by education for 17 regions[6] from the Labor Population Survey (Encuesta de Población Activa, EPA hereafter). This survey collects aggregate data. For our computation and stylized facts we used the definitions of education in the EPA survey. There are five levels of education: illiterate and uneducated people, primary education, low-secondary education, upper-secondary education and superior. We aggregate workers in three categories. The low-skilled workers category is defined as the first and second group, the middle skilled workers category is defined as low-secondary education and the last group - the highly skilled workers category, is defined as upper-secondary and tertiary education. The data for employment are from 1968 to 2003.

Vacancy data are collected from 1977 to 2003 at the regional level. The vacancy rate in our model is calculated as the ratio of job vacancies to the labor force. We used Antolín's vacancy data corrections, Antolín (1994).[7] He corrects data from the National Employment Office (INEM) to take into account privately advertised vacancies. INEM registers unfilled vacancies at the end of the month.

Table 1 presents the average and standard deviations for vacancy rates across regions and unemployment rates across skills and regions during the period 1977-2003. Vacancy rates are very different across regions and we observe larger variance in some regions than others.

---

[6] Andalusia, Extremadura, Canary Islands, Aragon, Baleares, Catalonia, Madrid, Navarra, La Rioja, Asturias, Cantabria, Castilla and Leon, Castilla-La Mancha, Valencian Community, Galicia, Murcia and the Basque Country.

[7] The key equation to correct the official INEM data V_0 is $V=\left(1+k\frac{OUT^n}{OUT^u}\right)V_0$. The ratio $\left(1+k\frac{OUT^n}{OUT^u}\right)$ measures the relative importance of privately advertised vacancies. OUT^n denotes named outflows: named outflows are job-openings where the firm or the employer comes to INEM with the name of the worker who is going to take up the post immediately. OUT^u denotes unnamed outflows: these are job-openings that are registered at the employment office (which the employment office has try to match with a suitable worker), plus job offers removed (withdrawals). The coefficient k measures the relative efficiency of privately advertised vacancies as compared to official vacancies. Antolín (1994) estimates this parameter at 0.25.

Table 1 also shows the difference across regions in unemployment rates by different skill levels. The middle skill unemployed group seems to have the highest unemployment rates and highest variation.

Table 1. Mean and Standard Deviation of Vacancy rates by region and unemployment rates by education and region. 1977- 2003

region	Vacancy rates		high skill unemployed rates		middle skill unemployed rates		low skill unemployed rates	
	mean	sd	mean	sd	mean	sd	mean	sd
Andalucia	0.78%	0.48%	15.18%	3.51%	29.88%	6.84%	25.63%	6.41%
Aragon	0.43%	0.21%	12.81%	4.23%	16.42%	6.64%	8.07%	2.98%
Asturias	0.71%	0.47%	16.50%	5.25%	23.91%	7.12%	10.00%	3.94%
Baleares	0.60%	0.56%	6.97%	2.74%	14.08%	5.01%	9.29%	3.10%
Canarias	0.74%	0.42%	10.20%	2.25%	23.07%	7.06%	18.55%	6.18%
Cantabria	0.41%	0.32%	13.24%	4.04%	21.98%	7.67%	9.56%	3.74%
Cataluna	1.01%	1.01%	8.34%	3.31%	19.28%	7.93%	13.25%	4.87%
ClaMancha	0.55%	0.32%	12.87%	3.36%	19.02%	4.96%	12.22%	3.76%
Cleon	0.44%	0.25%	17.53%	4.38%	20.84%	5.42%	10.41%	3.60%
Cvalenciana	0.55%	0.32%	13.00%	3.58%	20.26%	6.91%	13.63%	4.70%
Extremadura	1.05%	1.19%	15.01%	4.72%	29.00%	7.46%	23.17%	6.36%
Galicia	0.46%	0.31%	13.51%	3.97%	19.31%	5.31%	8.70%	3.91%
La Rioja	0.45%	0.36%	13.50%	4.82%	14.52%	5.41%	7.51%	3.69%
Madrid	0.84%	0.80%	11.48%	3.40%	18.69%	6.04%	12.42%	4.15%
Murcia	0.93%	0.61%	14.48%	3.09%	21.25%	6.48%	13.67%	4.66%
Navarra	0.67%	0.38%	13.09%	4.45%	15.60%	6.82%	7.47%	2.89%
Pais Vasco	0.41%	0.22%	14.64%	4.51%	24.13%	8.50%	12.32%	3.87%
Spain	0.67%	0.35%	12.75%	3.14%	21.46%	6.29%	14.86%	4.36%

The average unemployment rate sharply increases from 1977 to 1985. During this period, most of the increase in unemployment is associated with a huge employment decline, with only slight labor force increases. The unemployment rate decreases significantly during the recovery of the late eighties, despite sustained labor force increases. From 1991 to the mid-nineties, employment falls again and the unemployment rate reaches a record level (about 25%) despite a moderate labor force increase. After 1996 employment increases coinciding with an economic recovery (a similar trend occurred in the eighties). There is a huge decrease in the unemployment rates at the same time as the labor force increases. We analyze the variance of relative vacancy and unemployment rates in Figure 2. Until 1983, vacancy rates seemed to vary a lot across regions. Such wide differences are not observed in unemployment rates. This suggests that the quality of the vacancy data may have remained weak until 1983, which could explain why the observed aggregate UV relationship remained flat during that sub-period (concerning the quality of vacancy data see Antolín (1994) and Dolado and Gómez (1997). After 1995 there is an important variation in vacancies data, but it can be explained by differential changes as we can observe in Figure 1.

Also, in Figure 1, we observe that the shift of the UV relationship clearly takes place from 1977 until 1984-85 and the vacancy rate is stable until 1982. Even if one takes into account the fact that vacancy data do not seem to be reliable before 1983, the shift of the Beveridge curve is worth about 12 percentage points during this period. After 1984, the UV relationship moves in counterclockwise loops. And it begins to shift backwards from the end of the nineties until 2003.

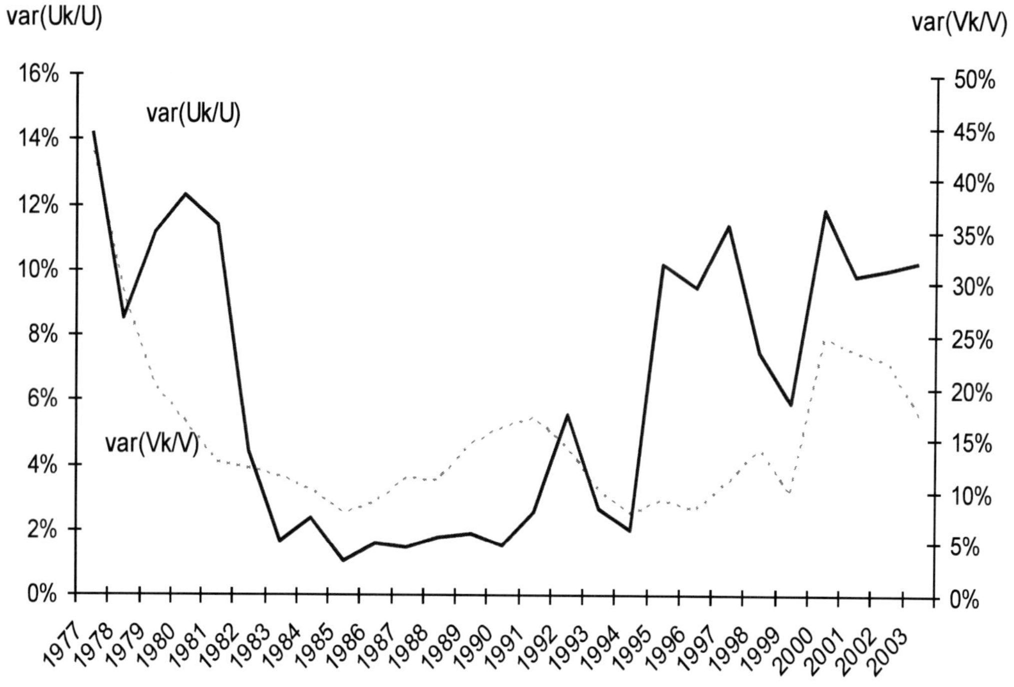

Figure 2. Spanish Variance of relative vacancy and unemployment rates by region.

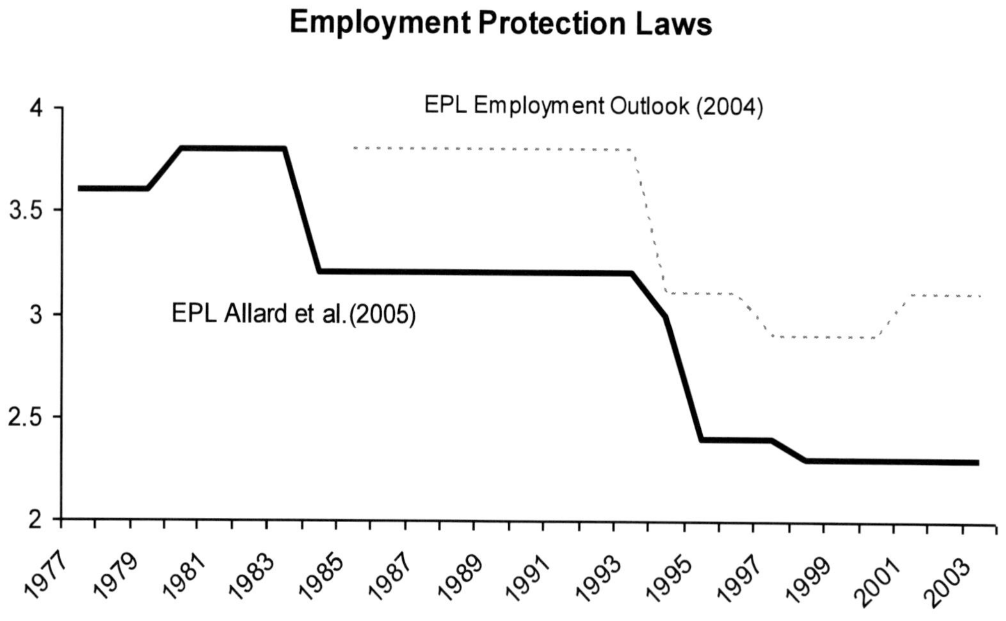

Figure 3. Spanish Employment Protection Laws.

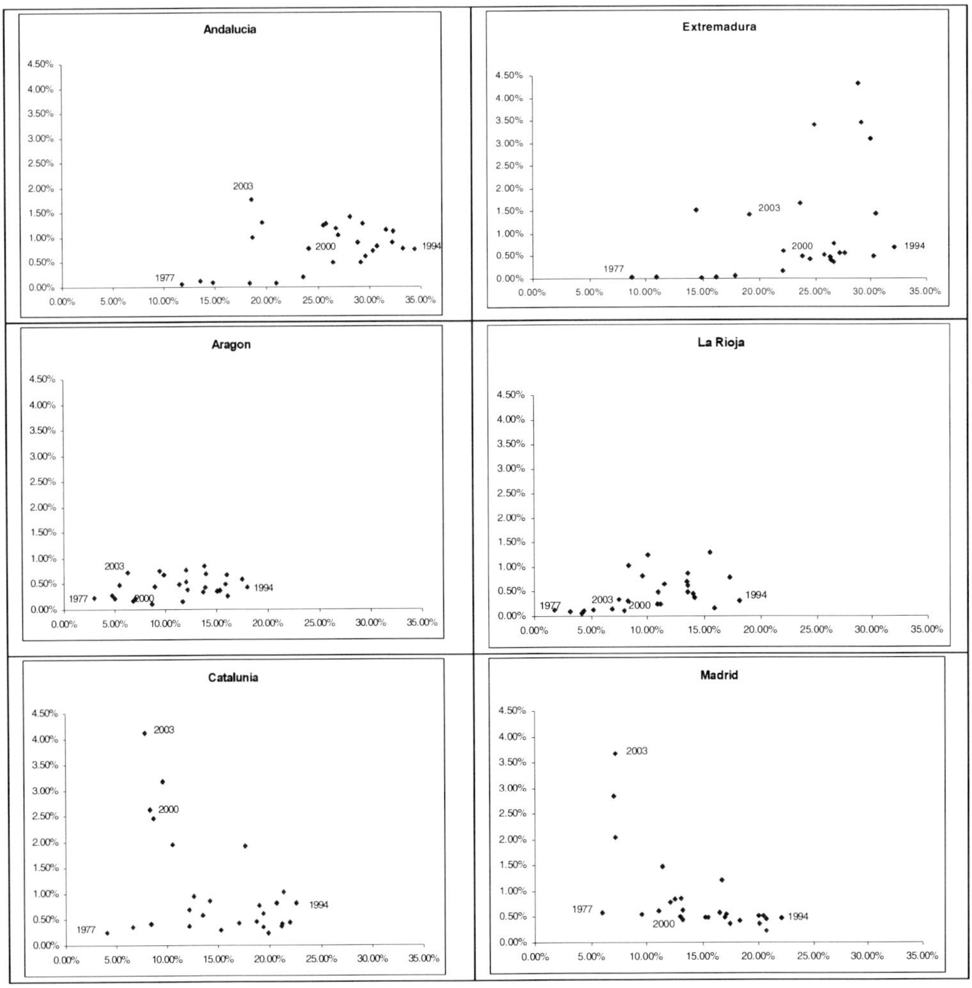

Figure 4. Regional Beveridge curves: Andalucia, Extremadura, Aragon, La Rioja, Catalunia and Madrid.

Spain is one of the countries with a high labour market rigidity index within the OECD.[8] However, recently the situation underwent some changes. Legislation was modified to a large extent with an important deregulation of the labour market (OECD Employment Outlook, 2004). However, this Spanish deregulation (i.e. employment protection laws in Figure 3) can help us to understand part of this aggregate shifts but not differences in regional Beveridge curves and regional disparities in unemployment rates across skills over this period.

As Dolado and Gomez (1997) pointed out, different regional groups of Beveridge curves are observed in Spain. Figure 4 displays an example of three groups of Beveridge curves where their shifts can be motivated by different causes. Aragon and The Rioja Beveridge curves draw different patterns compare to those of Andalucia and Extremadura. An intermediate group as Madrid and Catalonia has different *uv* curves from these other two

[8] i.e. generous unemployment-insurance benefits, restrictive employment protection laws and strong unions as well as homeowners house-market policies.

groups. Reallocation changes and business changes are pointed out as explanations to these differences. Fonseca and Muñoz (2003) show that reallocation changes reproduce better the Spanish labour market features than business changes for the period 1977-1994.

Spain has important unemployment disparities across skills. In Spain, the labor force across skills increases except in the unskilled labor force, which decreases during the studied period. Table 1 shows that these disparities across skills are very unlikely from one region to other. Moreover, after 1998 regional unemployment rates tend to converge towards the average; however, regional disparities persist until now. The unemployment rate decreased, but it is still around 10%.

We will try to disentangle regional and skill disparities and how the ways in which structural factors can explain these patterns. We first present the theoretical framework and then we estimate the UV curves. Third, we apply the mismatch indicators to the Spanish data.

3. Beveridge Curves and Labor Market Segmentation

In our framework, we will not examine the determination of the equilibrium unemployment and vacancies, which can be evaluated with the Beveridge curve and the wage-price setting. We rely on the information contained in unemployment-vacancy data.

We assume imperfect competition in the labor market and in the goods market.[9] The Beveridge curve represents the relationship between unemployment and vacancies in a given segment of the labor market. The position of the aggregate Beveridge curve depends on the dispersion of relative unemployment and vacancy rates across segments as well as on a value of efficiency and an increased dispersion, which shifts the aggregate Beveridge curve outwards.

Structural changes show up as shifts in the aggregate Beveridge curves. Measuring the contribution of unemployment and vacancy variables to observed shifts on the Beveridge curve gives valuable information about how structural difficulties have changed over time, even though it is not a precise measure of their contribution to total equilibrium unemployment changes. The Beveridge curve is obtained by explicit aggregation in a model with heterogeneous firms and workers. The heterogeneity is two-dimensional and distinguishes different levels of skills and different regions. Beveridge curves provide a natural basis to construct mismatch indicators. Through them, we can evaluate and compare the relative importance of frictions, regional mismatch and skill mismatch.

3.1. Employment at the Firm Level

Let us assume that there are a large number of firms that all have access to the same technologies. We also assume that adjustment costs prevent the firm from changing its production technology in response to transitory input shortages so that the technical input-

[9] Wages and prices are assumed to be pre-set. The optimal price level does not necessarily imply full-capacity utilisation, i.e. firms may be sales-constrained or may face labor shortages (see Sneessens, 1987)). We could do without the price pre-setting assumption. Provided there are technological adjustment costs, we would keep the same qualitative features possibility of sales constraints or input shortages (see Fagnart et al., 1998)).

output coefficients are not affected by purely cyclical phenomena but are determined by relative cost considerations. We allow for labor shortages, i.e., vacancies. Each firm may be subject to idiosyncratic shocks. In line with the previous discussion we shall not focus here on wage-price formation, but rather on the derivation of the regional and economy-wide Beveridge curves.[10] The analysis although admittedly partial, provides valuable information on the importance of structural disturbances. Our framework also generalizes about previous analyses by simultaneously taking into account both the regional and the skill dimensions.

To this end, we use as simple a framework as possible based on standard equilibrium unemployment models, extended to include regional and skill dimensions. This does not mean that we do ignore sectoral shocks. To the extent that regions are typically specialized in some sectors, and that sectors utilize different skill mixes, sectoral shocks will typically involve a mixture of regional and skill shocks.

As the focus is on long-term changes, we shall not attempt to reproduce short-run dynamics. In terms of the matching process, this means that our main tool of analysis will be the Beveridge curve rather than the matching function- the former being the long run implication of the latter.

3.1.1. Regional Shocks and Aggregate Performance

What we need is to determine the equilibrium unemployment rate in every region and examine the aggregate outcome. The effects of regional shocks depend very much on: (i) relative wage adjustment; (ii) labor mobility (regional migration); (iii) participation rate changes.

It is generally accepted that in European economies and in Spain as well, wage changes are mainly determined at the national level (there may be regional differences, but the latter are very stable over time). It is also accepted that regional mobility is weak and plays little role. In many European countries (different from the US), most of the adjustment comes from changes in participation rates. In Spain, even these facts seem to be weakly responsive to regional shocks. For more on these issues see Decressin-Fatas (1995) and Jimeno-Bentolila (1997).

To keep as simple a representation as possible of the effects of regional shocks on the aggregate performance of the economy, we thus proceed as if regional shocks had no effects on relative wages and labor forces. In region k:

$$y_k = \gamma (N_k)^{\alpha} \varepsilon_k \qquad \text{with} \qquad \alpha < 1 \tag{1}$$

$$D_k = \omega^{-\eta_1} \varepsilon_k \qquad \text{with} \qquad \omega = w/\alpha\gamma \tag{2}$$

$$N_k = \{ (D_k)^{-\rho} + (L_k)^{-\rho} \}^{-1/\rho} \tag{3}$$

[10] Lambert (1988), derived an approach of the Beveridge curve from microfounded rationing models. First used by Hansen (1970), to derive the Beveridge curve. Each micromarket consists of two components for instance demand-determined employment and supply- determined employment (see Sneessens and Drèze, 1986, for the theoretical analysis of a complete macroeconomic model and Drèze and Bean, 1990, for the estimation of the main European countries and the US).

Let y_k the production function that depends on labor with decreasing returns scale, $\alpha < 1$, γ the aggregate factor and ε_k the regional factor. D_k is the demand of labor in the region k, where w is the wage. The last equation stands for the regional Beveridge curve. By starting from a matching function, one can see that the position of the Beveridge curve in the UV space depends on the efficiency of the matching process and the quit rate. The effects of the latter are represented by parameter ρ. A lower value of ρ corresponds to an outward shift of the Beveridge curve. We will assume throughout that ρ is constant both over time and across regions. There is little indication that the efficiency of the matching process has decreased over time (except through composition effects) and that the quit rate has changed permanently. In any case, we want to check how far we can go in explaining shifts in the aggregate Beveridge curve without introducing permanent changes in matching efficiency and job destruction rates.

The specification of the Beveridge curve adopted here departs from the usual Cobb-Douglas representation. As we shall see later, choosing a Cobb-Douglas rather than a Constant Elasticity Substitution (CES hereafter) representation can have a dramatic impact on "regional mismatch" indicators. The CES representation can be justified by aggregating over "micromarkets" (see Lambert, 1988), at least as long as one is not interested in dynamics. The main motivation for a Cobb-Douglas representation is its tractability, especially in dynamic models. Here we focus on long term changes rather than dynamics and can thus afford more complex representations.

3.1.2. The High Skilled Employment

Firm level will be indexed by i. We assume that there are only two types of skills (high and low-skilled labor). Skills and regions will be indexed by h,l and k respectively. To keep the presentation as simple as possible, we suppose a Cobb-Douglas production function

$$y = \gamma \left(N^h\right)^{\alpha^h} \left(N^l\right)^{\alpha^l} K^{\beta} \varepsilon \text{ , with } \quad \alpha^h + \alpha^l + \beta = 1 \tag{4}$$

N^h and N^ℓ are the high-skilled employment and low-skilled employment respectively. K is capital value. And the different elasticity parameters sum 1, as constant returns to scale. We also assume: $\alpha \equiv \alpha^h + \alpha^l = 1 - \beta$.

Without going much further in a price-wage setting, the optimal relative employment is determined by the minimising of costs on the firm‘s side. The relative employment of low-skilled workers decreases until their relative cost, w^ℓ / w^h increases more than their relative productivity, α^l / α^h .

If we represent by $\overline{\omega}$, the evolution of the relationship between relative costs and productivity, we can express the optimal relative employment as following:

$$\frac{N^\ell}{N^h} = \left(\frac{1}{\overline{\omega}}\right)^{\sigma} \text{ , with } \overline{\omega} \equiv \frac{w^\ell / w^h}{\alpha^\ell / \alpha^h} \tag{5}$$

In the case of the Cobb-Douglas production function, the elasticity of substitution is equal to 1. The high-skilled labor demand D^h can be recast by the maximization of the firm profits. Using (5), we get:

$$D^h = \left(\omega^h\right)^{-\eta_1} \left(\bar{\omega}\right)^{-\eta_2} K \text{ ,with } \omega^h \equiv \frac{w^h}{\gamma\, \alpha^h}\text{ , } \eta_1 \equiv 1/\beta \text{ and } \eta_2 \equiv \alpha^l / \beta < \eta_1 \tag{6}$$

The high-skilled employment can be expressed as:

$$N^h = \text{Min } \left(D^h, L^h\right) \text{ and } \qquad N^l = \left(\frac{1}{\bar{\omega}}\right)^{\sigma} N^h \tag{7}$$

Where L^h is the high-skilled labor supply.

3.2. Regional Employment and Beveridge Curves

Employment can be inferred from the equation 7, and then regional employment will be given by:

$$N_k = \sum_i N_{ki} \tag{8}$$

If we aggregate over individuals firms in a given region k and then, after some rearrangement, we obtain:

$$N_k = \left\{\left(D_k\right)^{-\rho} + \left(\mu_k L_k\right)^{-\rho}\right\}^{-\frac{1}{\rho}} \text{ with } 0 \le \rho \le \infty. \tag{9}$$

Where μ_k is defined as follows:

$$\mu_k = \left\{\sum_s \left(\mu_{sk}\right)^{-\psi}\right\}^{-\frac{1}{\psi}} \text{ with } \mu_{sk} = \frac{1-u_k}{1-u_{sk}} \text{ for s } \in (l,\, h) \tag{10}$$

where s is the index for skills groups. Values of parameters ρ and ψ are non-negative and related to the characteristics of the variance-covariance matrix of the joint distribution (see

Bierings and Muysken (1988) and Entorf and Sneessens (2000)). Intuitively, the inverse of ρ and ψ provides a measure of the dispersion of the idiosyncratic shocks.[11]

In a given region k, μ is a weighted average of the μ_s's , which can be interpreted as measures of the skill composition of the total labor force relative to the skill composition of total employment. Let π_{sk} represent the proportion of workers of type s in the labor force of region k, it is easily checked that the definitions of the μ's must satisfy the following constraint:

$$\sum_s \pi_{sk}\left(\frac{1}{\mu_{sl}}\right) = 1$$

In general, this in turn implies that the unweighted sum of the (inverse of the) μ's will not be equal to 1 except if they both have the same value. Moreover, when the two values are not equal, one will be larger than 1 and the other smaller than 1. If there are structural imbalances [$\mu_{lk} \neq \mu_{hk}$], one of the two terms within the curly brackets in equation 10 will be smaller than 1, and the other larger. With ψ large enough, the value of μ_k will be close to the minimum of (μ_{lk} , μ_{hk}) and smaller than 1.[12]

The value of $1/\rho$ measures the importance of frictions. We normalize by the labor supply and we get:

$$n_k = \left\{(D_k)^{-\rho} + (\mu_k)^{-\rho}\right\}^{-\frac{1}{\rho}} \tag{11}$$

Simply rearranging the terms of equation 11[13] allows one to recast the (regional) employment function as a (regional) Beveridge curve so that we can also obtain the equation from a matching function:

$$\left\{(1-v_k)^{\rho} + \left(\frac{1}{\mu_k}\right)^{\rho}(1-u_k)^{\rho}\right\}^{-\frac{1}{\rho}} = 1 \tag{12}$$

[11] For instance, when ψ goes to infinity, the second term between the curly brackets corresponds to the minimum of the two labour supplies (low- and high skilled, weighted by the technological coefficients), so that one type of labour shortage only can be observed. The values of parameters ρ and ψ are non-negative and related to the characteristics of the distribution of demands and supplies across firms.

[12] The two sides of equation 11 must be raised to the power - ρ . One nest introduces (1-v) and (1-u)/ μ in the first and second left-hand side terms respectively, and takes the weighted sum over all regions.

[13] Where n is equal to 1 minus the unemployment rate ($n_k \equiv 1-u_k$). The relation n/D is equal to 1 minus the vacancy rates ($n_k / D_k \equiv 1-v_k$).

where v_k and u_k stand respectively for the vacancy and the unemployment rate in region k. Equation 12 shows that the position of the regional Beveridge curve depends on the two parameters ρ and μ_k. The inverse of μ_k measures the importance of skill mismatch; the inverse of ρ measures the importance of structural imbalances between goods demand and the availability of labor. These two values may of course change over time. A decrease in the value of μ_k implies an outward shift of the Beveridge curve; similar to ρ, at least as long as μ_k is not too small and ρ not too large.

3.3. Aggregate Beveridge Curves

Different regions may be characterized by different equilibrium levels of unemployment and vacancy rates (different positions along a given UV curve), as well as by different degrees of skill mismatch (different positions of the UV curve itself, reflecting different values of the skill mismatch indicator μ_k). The position of the economy-wide UV relationship and the aggregate performance of the economy will depend on both kinds of structural differences.

$$\left\{(\xi_v)^{\rho}(1-v)^{\rho}+(\xi_u)^{\rho}(1/\mu)^{\rho}(1-u)^{\rho}\right\}^{-\frac{1}{\rho}}=1, \tag{13}$$

where μ is the aggregate equivalent of μ_k (equation 10), defined as[14]:

$$\mu=\left\{\sum_s(\mu_s)^{-\psi}\right\}^{-\frac{1}{\psi}} \text{ with } \mu_s=\frac{1-u}{1-u_s}\cong 1+u_s-u \text{ for s } \in (l,\ h) \tag{14}$$

When ψ goes to infinity, only one type of labor can be binding and the value of μ is then equal to the minimum of the μ_s's. ξ_v and ξ_u are two shift variables related to cross-regional disparities (regional mismatch) defined by:

$$\xi_v\equiv\left\{\sum_k \pi_k\left[\frac{1-v_k}{1-v}\right]^{\rho}\right\}^{1/\rho},$$

$$\xi_u\equiv\left\{\sum_k \pi_k\left(\frac{1/\mu_k}{1/\mu}\right)^{\rho}\left[\frac{1-u_k}{1-u}\right]^{\rho}\right\}^{1/\rho}$$

[14] $m\equiv\frac{1+\bar{\omega}}{\bar{\omega}}$ l. Where l is the proportion between high-skilled workers and low-skilled workers. For unemployment rate, we have: (1-u) = m (1-uh), for vacancy rates: (1-v) = n/D = nh/Dh = (1-vh).

In other words, ξ_v measures cross-regional differences in vacancy rates, while ξ_u measures cross-regional differences in unemployment rates correcting for skill mismatch. Altogether, ξ_v and ξ_u measure two things: first, cross-regional differences in the unemployment and vacancy rates at given, identical regional UV curves.[15] Second, cross-regional skill mismatch differences leading to different positions of the regional UV curves. In sum, if the labor demand function moves to the right in markets with excess demand and shifts to the left in markets with excess supply the location of unemployment and vacancies moves towards higher levels of both *UR* and *VR*; structural mismatch between the submarkets increases.

3.4. Mismatch Indicators

These indicators measure how the many observed shifts in the aggregate UV relationship are due to increased dispersion across "segments" (regions and skills).

There are, in our set-up, only two sources of mismatch at the regional level. As shown by equation 12, the relationship between unemployment and vacancies at the regional level will change if and only if there are more frictions (measured by $1/\rho$) or more skill mismatch (measured by ($1/\mu_k$). At the aggregate level, regional differences can be a third source of mismatch and produce a change in the aggregate relationship between aggregate unemployment and aggregate vacancies.

Let us define the structural unemployment rate at equality, (denoted by *sure*) as the aggregate unemployment rate that would be obtained on the diagonal u=v. From equation 13 we obtain:

$$sure = 1 - \left\{(\xi_v)^{\rho} + (\xi_u)^{\rho}(1/\mu)^{\rho}\right\}^{-1/\rho}. \qquad (15)$$

This structural unemployment rate measures the position of the aggregate Beveridge curve; its value depends both on frictions and on (skill or regional) mismatch effects. We can evaluate the respective role of each component by using the following decomposition:

(i) Frictional unemployment, (which we shall denote by *fure*, "frictional unemployment rate at equality") measures the contribution of $1/\rho$; it is defined by equation 15 when the effects of regional and skill mismatch are eliminated (i.e., $x_v=x_u=m=1$); this yields

$$fure \equiv 1-2^{-1/\rho} \qquad (16)$$

where *fure* goes to zero when ρ goes to infinity.

(ii) Total mismatch, (*TM*) is then defined as the difference between the structural and the frictional unemployment rates at equality (u=v):

---

[15] It is worth pointing out that one can recast the aggregate Beveridge curve in terms of the aggregate employment function. One obtains for the whole economy: $N = \left\{(\xi_v)^{\rho}(D)^{-\rho} + (\xi_u)^{\rho}(\mu L)^{-\rho}\right\}^{-\frac{1}{\rho}}$, which generalises the aggregate employment function used in the EUP programme (see Drèze and Bean,1990).

TM ≡ sure-fure≅ ((1-fure)/(1-sure))-1,

$$\cong 1 - \left\{\frac{(\xi_v)^{\rho} + (\xi_u)^{\rho}(1/\mu)^{\rho}}{2}\right\}^{-1/\rho} - 1 \cdot \qquad (17)$$

When parameter ρ goes to infinity, *fure* goes to zero, and *TM* is equal to the maximum of ξ_v and ξ_u / μ .

Regional mismatch (*RM*) can be defined as the value that *TM* would take if there were no aggregate skill mismatch (μ=1), i.e.

$$RM = \left\{\frac{(\xi_v)^{\rho} + (\xi_u)^{\rho}}{2}\right\}^{1/\rho} - 1 \qquad (18)$$

When ρ goes to infinity, *RM* becomes equal to Max(ξ_v, ξ_u) minus 1. *RM* is thus, ceteris paribus, increasing in ρ.

Skill mismatch (*SM*) is finally defined as the contribution of skill composition effects to total mismatch; this contribution will be measured by the total mismatch less the regional mismatch, which is approximately

$$SM \equiv TM - RM \cong ((1+TM)/(1-RM))-1$$
$$\cong [\{r_v + (1-r_v)\ (1+\mu)^{\rho}\}^{1/\rho}]-1,$$

where $r_v \equiv (\xi_v)^r/[(\xi_v)^r+(\xi_u)]$. When $1/\mu$ is larger than 1 and ρ sufficiently large, the weight r_v has a negligible impact, and the previous expression can be approximated by[16]:

$$SM = \left\{\frac{1+(1/\mu)^{\rho}}{2}\right\}^{1/\rho} - 1 \qquad (19)$$

With this latter approximation, skill mismatch (*SM*) is defined as the value that *TM* would take if all unemployment and vacancy rates were equal across regions (i.e., $\xi_v = \xi_u = 1$). It is positively related to the inverse of μ. When ρ goes to infinity, *SM* becomes equal to max (0, (1/ μ)-1). Ceteris paribus, *SM* is thus (as *RM* is) increasing in ρ. It can also be seen from the definition of μ (equation 14) that the skill mismatch indicator *SM* is based on unemployment rate differences. This way of decomposing total structural unemployment into its various

[16] The structural unemployment, sure, can be decomposed by the skill part when m=1, that means that SM = [{(xv)r+(xu)r (1+m)r }1/r]/[{(xv)r+(xu)r}1/r]-1= [{rv + (1-rv) (1+m)r }1/r]-1, where rv ≡ (xv)r/[(xv)r+(xu)] < 1. The impact of the weight rv is almost negligible when 1/m is larger that 1 and r large enough (r ≥50). When rv ≡ 1/2 (in absence of regional disparities), we get equation 19.

components seems fairly natural and has the advantage of being approximately additive (($sure \cong fure + RM + SM$).). It is clear however, that there are "cross-effects".[17]

We already pointed out that an increase in ρ (decrease in *fure*) increases, ceteris paribus (i.e. at given discrepancies in regional and skill unemployment rates), the values of both *RM* and *SM*. This is because a change in the value of ρ implies a change in the curvature of the regional Beveridge curves - the larger the value of ρ of the *UV* relationship. At given discrepancies between regional unemployment rates, the Beveridge curve obtained by aggregation over regions moves outwards.

4. Interpreting Spanish Data: Further Insights

In this section, we first rely on the methodology developed in the previous sections to evaluate the role that increased frictions, regional and skill mismatch may have had in the observed deterioration of the relationship between unemployment and vacancies (Beveridge curve shifts). And second, we will compare our estimation results with other empirical strategies.

4.1. Empirical Results

The framework developed in the previous sections gives us the means to obtain more reliable estimates and a better chance to disentangle structural and non-structural influences by rigorously exploiting the information contained in the unemployment and vacancy data, across regions and skill groups. For estimation purposes, equations 10 and 12 will be recast as:

$$\left\{(1-V_{kt})^{\rho_t} + \left(\frac{1}{\mu_k}\right)^{\rho_t} (1-U_{kt})^{\rho_t}\right\}^{-\frac{1}{\rho_t}} = 1 + \eta_0 + \eta_t + \eta_k + \varepsilon_{kt} \qquad (20)$$

$$\mu_{kt} = \left\{\sum_i (\mu_{ikt})^{-\psi_t}\right\}^{-\frac{1}{\psi_t}}, \text{ with } \mu_{ik} \equiv \frac{1-U_{kt}}{1-U_{ikt}} \qquad (21)$$

where η_t and η_k represent a time-specific and a regional-specific residual respectively, whose sum over time or regions is normalized to zero. Three skill categories will be distinguished.

The estimation procedure relies on the nonlinear regression models. We then estimate in equation 20 the parameter of friction ρ[18] in order to analyze our mismatch indicators. The

[17] For cross-effects computations see Appendix 1.

first step in the estimation process will be to check for the constancy of ρ over time. We know from the discussion of the previous sections that changes in the value of parameter ρ may affect the estimated value of the mismatch indicators. This value captures frictions in the labor market. We use a panel data with 17 regions and three skill groups for unemployment and vacancy rates are computed only at regional level. We made the estimations for the period 1977-2003. We assume that ρ has the same value in all regions of a given country at a given moment in time. We can estimate a value of ρ for each period. If the values so obtained are not characterized by a systematic drift, we then impose ρ to remain constant over the whole sample period and estimate the other parameters under this constraint. We do this to avoid capturing purely cyclical effects by variations in the value of a structural parameter.[19] The use of disaggregated data allows a priori the direct estimation of the effects of regional and skill mismatch on the UV relationship, at given ρ. We aimed at uncovering the causes of structural unemployment by regressing the estimated values ρ on a set of explanatory variables. We allowed for cyclical effects on the UV relationship by simply introducing time dummies.[20]

Table 2. NL Estimation results on Spanish data

	Model 1	Model 2	Model 3
	$\rho \neq \psi$	$\rho \neq \psi$	$\rho = \psi$
	Time dummies	Time dummies	Time dummies
η_0	-0.0098	-0.0098	-0.0098
	[0.000218]	[0.000211]	[0.000212]
ρ	95.6	=92.14	92.14
	[275.589]		[47.87]
ψ	39.2	41.38	=
	[381.041]	[80.6]	
Log of likelihood	782.148	782.147	782.116
SER (Std. Err R.)	0.0026	0.0026	0.0026

Note: Sample form 1983 to 1992 for 17 regions and 3 skills groups. Standard errors between brackets.
Sources: EPA, employment data and INEM, vacancy data. Own computations.

---

18 Earlier estimates of parameter ρ were based on aggregate "EUP-type" model (see Drèze and Bean (1990)), without explicit regional and skill dimensions, where parameter ρ was calculated as a residual and interpreted as a "catch-all" variable accounting for all kinds of frictions and mismatches. Estimations of ρ were done by Andrés et al. (1990) for the Spanish case. Their results imply a structural unemployment rate (calculated in the same way as fure) rising from 4.2% in 1977 to 6.8% in 1985. The modelling approach was however, quite different, which makes the results not directly comparable.

19 In order to catch up this type of dynamic cyclical effects, we may either introduce a time-specific disturbance term η_t, or try to correct the observed vacancy and unemployment rates for the effect of labour hoarding. Attempts to introduce a labour-hoarding effect failed to give satisfactory results, probably because skill groups are defined by educational levels rather than occupations, which changes the way cyclical fluctuations can affect relative unemployment rates (via deskilling or "ladder"- effects rather than labour hoarding).

20 It is well known that labour hoarding phenomena and differences in the speed of adjustment of unemployment and vacancies over the cycle may generate loops around the long run Beveridge curve. These dynamic features are not accounted for in our theoretical set up (this framework studies the UV curve in a steady state for the long-term) and should preferably not be measured by variations in the value of ρ .

We focus on the period of 1983-1992. This is the period during which most of the UV curve shifts take place (see Figure 1). Before 1983, vacancy data were shown to be unreliable. After 1992, one mainly observes cyclical effects. We thus re-estimated the model on the sub-sample 1983-1992, and imposed a constant value of ρ over this sub-period (see Table 2). As shown in the fourth column, imposing the same value for the two friction parameters ρ and ψ easily passes the likelihood ratios test. Our final estimate of ρ is ρ =92, implies a frictional unemployment rate FURE equal to 0.75%.

We have shortened the sample for estimations of ρ, claiming this captures different frictions that in the rest of the periods could be not captured.

4.2. Robustness

In order to have robustness in our estimations of ρ for the period 1983-1992, we apply another estimation strategy relying to the UV curve.[21] We can also perform a simple exercise to study the relationship between unemployment and vacancies. We estimate unemployment related to vacancies. However, we must consider a lag in unemployment and that the coefficient of Ordinary Least Square regression can be biased. We then use the Generalised Method Moment (GMM) estimator developed by Arellano and Bond (1991) and Blundell and Bond (1998). We estimate the following expression,

$$lur_{kt} = \beta_1 lur_{kt-1} + \beta_2 lvr_{kt} + \eta_k + \varepsilon_{kt} \tag{22}$$

Unemployment and vacancy rates are in logarithms. The unemployment rates depend on their lags and on the vacancy rates. We consider regional fixed effects, η_k and ε_{kt} are the iid vector of disturbances.[22]

Table 3, Panel A, contains the estimation results for the GMM estimator for equation 22. Furthermore, Table 3 presents the results from a Sargan-Hansen test of over identifying restrictions and a test for first and second order correlation. The absence of second order serial correlation is crucial for the orthogonality conditions of the GMM to be valid. We find for the whole period (Model A), as expected positive and significant parameter for lagged unemployment. We find a negative and significant parameter for the vacancy rate variable. However, if we do not consider the first part of the period 1977-1982, the results are not significant and the coefficient of the vacancies becomes positive (Model B). Finally, we estimate for the period 1983-1992 – the same period for our previous non-linear estimations for the parameter ρ. We get the same results that when we had considered the first years (Model A). We can conclude then, that the negative relationship between the vacancy and unemployment is clear in the first part of the period, until 1992. However, it is not so clear

[21] The theoretical foundations of the Beveridge Curve are substantially twofold: the first, starting from a model of Hansen, derives the matching function from an aggregation over distinct markets in the presence of frictions and of limited mobility of labor. The second refers to a model of matching in a stock-flow framework. For a recent review see Petrongolo and Pissarides, 2001.

[22] We use right hand variables lagged forth times as instruments.

afterwards. It can be due to the counter cycle loops that come after this period. This can be taken by other more business cycle factors.

We have also made different robustness analyses. We obtain the negative correlation with ordinary least squares regressions between unemployment and vacancies. We estimated the same problem with different definitions with vacancy rates, defining vacancy rates over vacancies and employment (v=V/(V+E)) with similar results. In Panel B, we got the same results when we lagged the vacancies, $lur_{kt} = \beta_1 lur_{kt-1} + \beta_2 lvr_{kt-1} + \eta_k + \varepsilon_{kt}$ .We test it in order to avoid the simultaneity problem, including the unemployment and the vacancy rate with one lag. This is reasonable, since the lagged unemployment and the vacancy rate refers to the stock that is available at the beginning of the period. The lagged unemployment and vacancy can be treated as a weak exogenous variable. We show results in the Table 3, Panel B.

Table 3. GMM estimates for Spanish data

	Panel A					
	1977-2003		1983-2003		1983-1992	
	Model A		Model B		Model C	
	Param.	z-value	Param.	z-value	Param.	z-value
lur_{kt-1}	.8329	12.71	1.063	28.35	.9041	7.24
lvr_{kt}	-3.3988		.0002	0.01	-5.197	
Const	-5.3959		.0935	0.51	-5.53	
Num. observations	442		340		153	
Sargen-Hansen test χ^2	12.78 [0.120]		15.03[0.059]		12.18[0.143]	
AR (1)	-2.49 [0.013]		-2.40 [0.016]		-2.30 [0.022]	
AR (2)	-0.31 [0.754]		0.71 [0.475]		-0.77 [0.444]	
	Panel B					
	1977-2003		1983-2003		1983-1992	
	Model A		Model B		Model C	
	Param.	z-value	Param.	z-value	Param.	z-value
lur_{kt-1}	.8065	9.93	1.062	31.06	.8046	9.54
lvr_{kt}	-2.397		.007	0.31	-3.0998	
Const	-4.5272		.1265	0.95	-4.46	
Num. observations	442		340		153	
Sargen-Hansen test χ^2	13.55 [0.094]		15.14 [0.057]		13.28 [0.102]	
AR (1)	-2.20 [0.028]		-2.41 [0.016]		-1.30 [0.193]	
AR (2)	-0.09 [0.927]		0.71 [0.476]		-0.18 [0.857]	

p-values in brackets . GMM are the associated two-step estimates with the corrected asymptotic standard errors as suggested by Windmeijer (2000). Sources: EPA, employement, INEM, vacancy data.

In order to apply the methodology developed in the previous section, we will suppose the value of ρ =92 for the whole period.[23]

5. Spanish Mismatch Indicators

In this section, we describe the contribution of skill and regional mismatch to total structural unemployment (*sure*).

5.1. Skill Mismatch

Skill mismatch (*SM*, Figure 5, left panel) starts from a low 1% value in 1977 and ends at 11% in 1994. After 1995, the values are over 6%. In 1997 and following the decrease in unemployment, the *SM* drops to 2.75% in 2003.

Despite a cyclical effect, SM has a clear upward trend until the end of the nineties. It may be argued that defining skill groups by an educational criterion rather than an occupational one is bound to bias the measurement of structural problems when there are so-called "ladder effects" (highly skilled workers taking the jobs of low-skilled workers). Labor hoarding and ladder effects should correct the cyclical counterpart of the skill mismatch. The last part shows an important drop of unemployment rates, which influences the drop of the skill mismatch indicator. However, Beveridge curve shifts are clearly from the mid-seventies till the mid-eighties (see Figure 1). We observe that the movements of the UV curve both loops and shift of the Beveridge curve increased for the period 1983-1994 and the last years the Beveridge curve is better represented as a movement along of it.

SM is the key component to understand the Spanish unemployment. This corroborates the analysis of Bentolila and Dolado (1991), about the importance and persistence of the skill mismatch in Spain.

We compare our results with the measure based on the variance of relative unemployment rates. We find the same results as we have discussed in the introduction, this indicator is severely decreasing towards zero as Entorf (1998) argues. The JLS indicator (*0.5 var(ui/u)*, where *u* is unemployment rates and *i* skills) has a higher value at the beginning of the period but after 1983 the value decreases very accurate towards zero.

In sum, the positive tendency of the skill mismatch is observed during the period. However, due to the cyclical characteristics of the indicator, two questions arise: (i) The cyclicality of the skill mismatch can be explained by the cyclicality of the employment rate of less-educated workers. Thus, higher-educated workers will be hoarded during recessions and less-educated workers will be laid off or be explained by the ladder effect (see Gautier et al. 2002); the process where less-educated workers are replaced by higher-educated workers; or due to technological change, which will bias against the lower-skilled workers. (ii) In this chapter, we have used skill definition by education. We have remarked that the composition of the skill of workers can affect cyclical fluctuations for example via "ladder" effects (see Collard et al. 2009).

[23] We have done sensibility analyses including other values of ρ , after 1992 and the patterns remains.

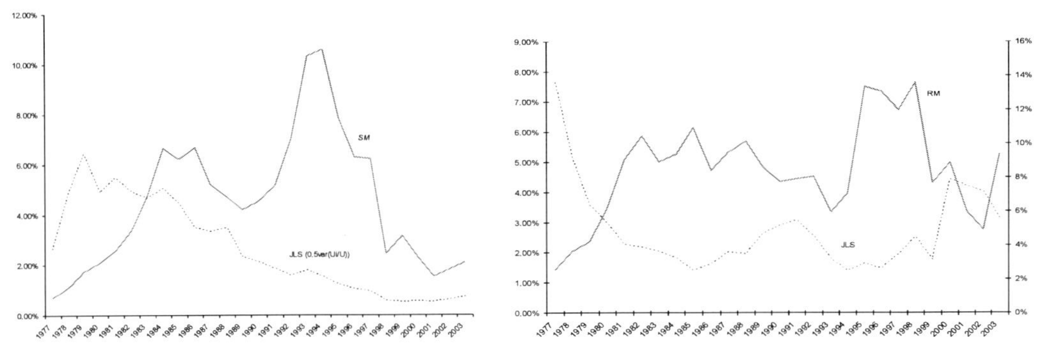

Figure 5. (a) Skill mismatch indicators (left panel) (b) Regional mismatch indicators (right panel).

5.2. Regional Mismatch

Regional mismatch (*RM*, Figure 5, right panel), although relatively less important, is not negligible. The value of *RM* starts from about 1% in 1977 and rises to 6% in the mid eighties, which may be related to the intense industrial restructuring that took place over that period and affected the various regions of Spain differently (see Bentolila and Jimeno (1995)). The importance of regional mismatch slightly decreased after 1985 with values about 4%. However, an increase is observed after 1995 to about 8%, to decrease strongly to 2.7% in 2002, but an increase appears in 2003.

The indicator *RM* also follows the cycle of unemployment very closely. However, it gives us the information of how regional mismatch weight has changed with an increasing tendency as skill mismatch. Jimeno and Bentolila (1997), also point out that relative (regional to national) employment levels have increased in regions with relatively high unemployment rates. We compare our regional mismatch results with JLS (1991), indicator. We find the same decreasing trend in the indicator that Bentolila and Dolado (1991), using the same JLS indicator for Spanish regions. They also conclude that labor mobility is very low in Spain. Jimeno and Bentolila (1997) also show the low inter-regional mobility in Spain, and they conclude that low mobility across regions is important to explain unemployment persistence in Spain.

5.3. Structural versus Actual Unemployment

We have described the skill and regional mismatch, which are two of the most important components to explain structural unemployment in Spain.[24]

In Figure 6, we observe that the structural unemployment rate rises from about 3% in 1977 to 13% in 1985; it slowly decreases during the recovery of the late eighties and next it

[24] The structural unemployment and mismatch indicators discussed in this subsection have all been computed over the entire sample period. We checked that the poor quality of the vacancy data prior to 1983 does not significantly affect the results. We have also checked that after 1993 the value of ρ passes the likelihood ratio test (i.e. given the observed values of the unemployment and vacancy rates, ξ_v has little weight in the formulas developed in previous section).

rises again to about 15% in 1995 then there is a decrease to around 6% in 2002 and an increase in 2003 to 8.24%. Despite the cyclical fluctuations in the estimated structural unemployment, there seems to be a clear upward trend to end of the sample. The cyclical fluctuations probably result from our inability to correct for cyclical characteristics as we discussed in the previous section. We observe how skill mismatch has more weight in the structural unemployment, but regional mismatch explains a large part of the rest of the structural unemployment. We now evaluate the structural unemployment, *sure*, (and the implied outward shift of the Beveridge curve). In Figure 6, we observe that we can evaluate *sure* to be about 12%, which is quite stable after 1984 until mid-nineties. From this point of view, most of the long-term shift in the aggregate Beveridge curve (see Figure 1) could be mainly explained by skill and/or regional mismatch, even though obviously cyclical phenomena may exert a strong impact on relative unemployment rates and on the UV curve shift. Of course, structural factors (frictions plus regional and skill mismatch) are not the single cause of unemployment. Macroeconomic variables and institution changes can also affect to unemployment[25] as we have previously mentioned.

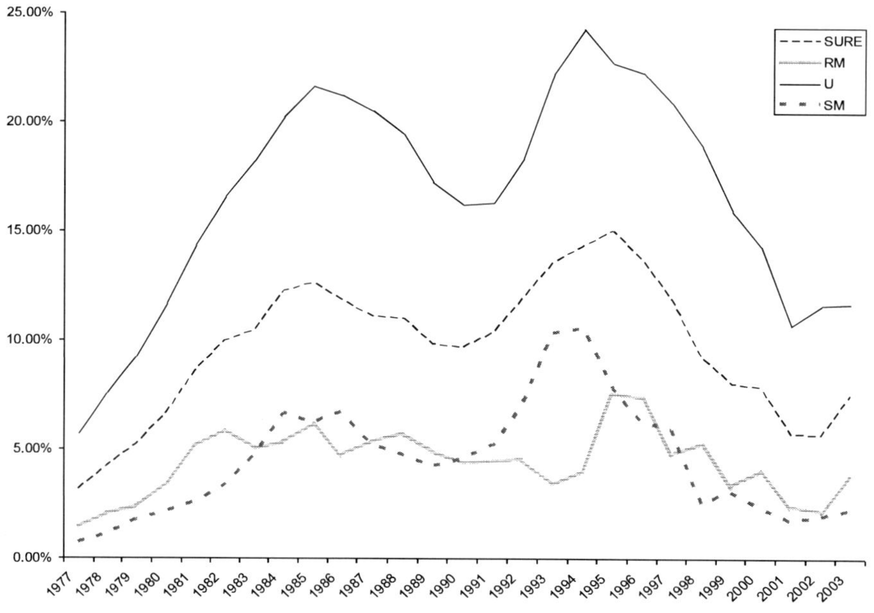

Figure 6. Structural Employment: Unemployment rates, Regional and Skill mismatch composition.

CONCLUSION

This chapter has aimed at contributing to a better understanding of the following structural problems. The relationship between structural imbalances and aggregate equilibrium unemployment cannot be summarized in a simple, universally valid formula. A less ambitious but more realistic approach to start with is to measure the contribution of

[25] Shifts in the wage-price setting schedule and institutions may be associated to outwards shifts of the UV curve as it is suggested in Nickell et al. (2003).

structural imbalances to the observed changes on the unemployment-vacancy relationship. Although such a measure does not definitely provide a measure of all the effects of structural changes on the aggregate equilibrium unemployment rate, it gives us quite important information in order to be able to shed light on the nature of unemployment.

Explicit aggregation over heterogeneous firms using different types of labor allows us to derive Beveridge curves that simultaneously take into account both the regional and the skill dimensions. This result can be used to construct indicators, which measure the contribution of regional and skill mismatch to the observed shifts on the aggregate Beveridge curve. The regional and skill mismatch indicators take different forms.

We used panel data from Spain to evaluate the importance of structural problems in the labour market in this country and provided some stylised facts to describe the pattern of the Spanish Beveridge curve in the last decades.

Our main conclusions suggest that structural changes across regions and skill groups have produced a significant shift in the aggregate Spanish UV curve. We cannot identify the structural factors, but we can quantify in terms of skill and regional mismatch. We can also show that most of the shift took place between the mid-seventies and the mid-eighties where both skill and regional mismatch account for around 6% and 4% in average respectively for the period studied. Moreover, we observe that structural unemployment was increasing until 1985 and that it has been quite stable at about 12% over the period - from the mid-seventies until the mid-eighties.

Therefore structural unemployment, in particular skill mismatch could explain the shift of the UV curve. We have shown how structural unemployment seems to be one explanation for unemployment, in particular for the period where we observed the UV curve shifts. We can also quantify how much is due to skill and regional mismatch. Of course, it is still not the whole picture. Cyclical features and other macroeconomics facts might explain the rest.

APPENDIX 1: SKILL AND REGIONAL CROSS-EFFECTS

There are also cross-effects between skill and regional mismatch. Neglecting skill mismatch may affect the estimate of regional mismatch. This comes from the fact that the regional mismatch indicator takes into account the effect of cross-regional skill-mismatch differences. If there were no such differences (i.e., with $\mu_k = \mu$ for all k's), the regional mismatch indicator would simplify into:

$$RM = \left\{ \frac{(\xi_v)^{\rho} + (\xi_u)^{\rho}}{2} \right\}^{1/\rho} - 1,$$

where $\xi'_u \equiv \left\{ \sum_k \pi_k \left[\frac{1-u_k}{1-u} \right]^{\rho} \right\}^{1/\rho}$. ξ'_u is obtained by setting $\mu_k = \mu$ for all k's in ξ_u (see section 3.3). It is readily shown that the difference between the two mismatch indicators is given by:

$r_v \equiv (\xi_v)^{\rho} / [(\xi_v)^{\rho} + (\xi_u)^{\rho}]$

RM′-RM≅1- ((1+*RM*)/(1+RM′))≅ $1-\left\{r_v^{'}+(1-r_v^{'})\left[\sum_k \alpha_k^{'}\left(\frac{1/\mu_k}{1/\mu}\right)^{\rho}\right]\right\}^{1/\rho}$ where $r_v^{'}=\frac{\xi_v^{\rho}}{\xi_v^{\rho}+\xi_u^{'\rho}}$ and

$\alpha_k^{'}=\frac{\alpha_k(1-u_k)^{\rho}}{\sum_k \alpha_k(1-u_k)^{\rho}}$. The weight $\alpha_k^{'}$ given to each relative skill mismatch term decreases when the regional unemployment rate is above average. If there are no skill mismatch differences across regions, the difference between the two regional-mismatch measures (*RM* and RM′) is of course nil. The difference may otherwise be positive or negative. It is likely to be positive when larger unemployment rates are associated with larger mismatch values, as one would expect. This would certainly be the case if the aggregate skill mismatch indicator $(1/\mu)^{\rho}$ were a simple average of corresponding regional values. In other words, the failure to simultaneously take into account the skill and the regional dimensions will in general lead to biased regional mismatch indicators; the bias is likely to be positive.

REFERENCES

Abraham, K.G., Katz, L. (1986). Cyclical Unemployment, Sectoral Shifts or Aggregate Disturbances?. *Journal of Political Economy, 94(3)*, 507-522.

Allard, G. (2005). Jobs and Labour Market Institutions in the OECD: A New Look of Dynamics, Working Paper Instituto Empresa Madrid.

Andres, J., Dolado, J.J., Molina, C., Sebastian, M, Zabalza, A. (1990). The Influence of Demand and Capital Constraints on Spanish Unemployment", in Drèze, Bean et al. (eds), *Europe's Unemployment Problem* , MIT Press.

Antolín, P. (1994). Unemployment Flows and Vacancies in Spain. IVIE, 94-05.

Arellano, M. Bond, S. (1991). Some Tests of Specification for Panel Data: Monte Carlo Evidence and an Application to Employment Equations. *The Review of Economic Studies, 58(2)*, 277-297.

Bentolila, S., Blanchard, O. (1990). Spanish Unemployment. *Economy Policy, 10*, 233-281.

Bentolila, S., Dolado, J.J. (1991). Mismatch and Internal Migration in Spain: 1962-86, in F.Padoa-Schioppa (ed.) Mismatch and Labour Mobility, Cambridge University Press.

Bentolila, S., .Jimeno, J.F. (1995). Regional Unemployment persistence (Spain, 1976-94), *Labour Economics, 5(1)*, 25-51.

Bentolila, S., .Jimeno, J.F. (2006). Spanish Unemployment: The End of the Wild Ride? in M. Werding (ed.), *Structural Unemployment in Western Europe: Reasons and Remedies*, Cambridge MA, London UK: MIT Press, 2006.

Bentolila, S., Cahuc, P., Dolado, J.J. Le Barbanchon, T. (2010). Two-Tier Labor Markets in the Great Recession: France vs. Spain, IZA Discussion Papers 5340, Institute for the Study of Labor (IZA).

Bierings, H., Muysken, J. (1988). Nested Employment Functions and Structural Unemployment, with an Empirical Application to the Dutch and Belgian Economies", unpublished working paper, Faculty of Economics and Business Administration, University of Limburg, Maastricht, The Netherlands.

Blundell, R., Bond, S. (1998). Initial conditions and moment restrictions in dynamic panel data models. *Journal of Econometrics, 87(1)*, 115-143.

Collard, F., Fonseca R., Munoz R. (2009). Spanish Unemployment Persistence and Ladder Effect, in M. C. Fournier and C. S. Mercier (Eds.*) in Economics of Employment and Unemployment,* Nova publishers.

Decressin, J., Fatás, A. (1995). Regional Labor Market Dynamics in Europe. *European Economic Review, 39*, 1627-1655.

Dolado, J.J., R. Gómez. (1997). La relación entre desempleo y vacantes en España: perturbaciones agregadas y de reasignación. *Investigaciones Económicas, 21(3)*, 441-472.

Drèze, J.H, Bean, C.R., Lambert, J.P., Mehta, S., Sneessens, H.R., (eds), (1990). *Europe's Unemployment Problem*, MIT Press, 1990.

Entorf, H. (1998). Mismatch Explanations of European Unemployment. A Critical Evaluation, European and Transatlantic Studies. Berlin: Springer.

Entorf, H., Sneessens, H.R. (2000). Aggregation in QRM models: The CES Aggregate Employment Function. *Empirical Economics, 2000*, 35-59.

Fagnart, J.F., Licandro, O., Sneessens, H.R. (1998). Capacity Utilization and Market Power. *Journal of Economic Dynamics and Control, 22(1)*, 123-140.

Fonseca, R., Munoz, R. (2003). Can the matching model account for Spanish. *Investigaciones Economicas, 27(2)*, 277-308.

de la Fuente, A. (2001). On the Sources of Convergence: A close look at the Spanish Regions, CEPR Discussion Paper n° 1543.

Gautier, P.A., Van den Berg, G.J., Van Ours, J.C., Ridder, G. (2002). Worker turnover at the firm level and crowding out of lower educated workers. *European Economic Review, 46-3*, 523-538.

Hall, R. (2003a). Modern Theory of Unemployment Fluctuations: Empirics and Policy Applications. *American Economic Review Papers and Proceedings, 93(2)*, 145–150.

Hall, R. (2003b). Wage Determination and Employment Fluctuations, NBER Working Paper 9967.

Hansen, B. (1970). Excess Demand, unemployment, vacancies and wages. *Quaterly Journal of Economics, 84*, 1.

Jackman, R., Roper, S. (1987). Structural Unemployment. *Oxford Bulletin of Economic and Statistics, 49(1)*, 9-37, 1987.

Jackman, R., Layard, R., Savouri, S. (1990). Labor Market Mismatch: A Framework for Thought, in Padoa-Schioppa, F. (ed.) , *Mismatch and Labour Mobility*, Cambridge University Press, 1990.

Jimeno, J.F., Bentolila, S. (1997). Regional Unemployment Persistence (Spain, 1976-1994), *Labour Economics 4.*

Krugman, P. (1994). Past and Prospective Causes of High Unemployment, in *Reducing Unemployment: Current Issues and Policy Options.* Symposium, Federal Reserve Bank of Kansas City, Jackson Hole, Wyoming, 49-80.

Lambert, J.-P. (1988). *Disequilibrium Macroeconomic Models*, Cambridge University Press, Cambridge.

Lilien D.M. (1982). Sectoral shocks and Cyclical Unemployment. *Journal of Political Economy, 90*, 777-793.

Nickell, Ochel, S.W., Quintini, G. (2003). The Beveridge Curve, Unemployment and Wages in the OECD, in P. Aghion, R. Frydman, J. Stiglitz and M. Woodford (eds.) *Knowledge, Information and Expectations in Modern Macroeconomics: in Honor of Edmund S. Phelps*, Princeton University Press, 2003

OECD (1994). Jobs Study, Paris.

OECD (2004). Employment Outlook.

Padoa-Schioppa, F. (1991). (ed.). *Mismatch and Labour Mobility*, Cambridge University Press.

Peracchi, F., Viviani, E. (2004). An empirical micro matching model with an application to Italy and Spain, No 538, Temi di discussione (Economic working papers) from Bank of Italy, Economic Research Department, 2004-12

Petrongolo, B., Pissarides, C. (2001). Looking into the Black Box: A Survey of the Matching Function. *Journal of Economic Literature*, *39* (2).

Shimer, R. (2004). The Consequences of Rigid Wages in Search Models, *Journal of the European Economic Association*, *2(2-3)*, 469-479.

Shimer, R., (2005). The Cyclical Behavior of Equilibrium Unemployment and Vacancies. *The American Economic Review*, *95(1)*, 25–49.

Shimer, R. (2006). Mismatch, Proceedings Federal Reserve Bank of San Francisco.

Sneessens, H.R., Drèze, J.H. (1986). A Discussion of Belgian Unemployment, Combining Traditional Concepts and Disequilibrium Econometrics. *Economica*, *53*, S89-S119.

Sneessens, H.R. (1987). Investment and the Inflation-Unemployment Trade-off in a Quantity Rationing Model with Monopolistic Competition. *European Economic Review*, *31*, 781-808.

In: Labor Markets: Dynamics, Trends and Economic Impact ISBN: 978-1-61470-825-4
Editor: Samir Amine

Chapter 6

REGIONAL UNEMPLOYMENT AND SPATIAL INTERACTIONS IN GREECE

Sarantis Lolos[1,*] and Evangelia Papapetrou[2]
[1]Department of Economic and Regional Development,
Panteion University, Greece
[2]Bank of Greece, Economic Research Department
and University of Athens, Greece

ABSTRACT

The purpose of this paper is to bring empirical evidence on the factors responsible for the evolution of regional unemployment. The case of Greece (1981-2006) has been taken as an example. The empirical analysis is carried out via a dynamic model estimated by the GMM methodology that enables us to search for the existence of spatial unemployment interactions together with the other determinants of regional unemployment. The empirical results point to the existence of significant spillover among regional labor markets that are responsible for the asymmetric behavior of regional unemployment in Greece. Our results call for active regional policies for the reduction of unemployment.

INTRODUCTION

The issue of regional unemployment within a country deserves special attention, since the observed wide disparities persisting for long have adverse social repercussions which may impair social cohesion and lead to a regional divide within the country. Besides, persisting regional unemployment differentials may undermine the efficiency of macro policies by reducing output and putting upward pressure on inflation in an asymmetric manner.

---

* Email: sarantislolos@gmail.com. The authors wish to thank Yannis Sakelis and Theodoros Mitrakos for providing them with data and useful insights into the developments of regional unemployment in Greece. The views expressed in this paper are those of the authors and not necessarily those of their respective institutions.

The interest in regional unemployment for European countries started only in the second half of the nineties and many studies set up the basis for the empirical analysis of regional unemployment. A great number of these studies consider the issue as if the regional labor markets behave independently to each other. However, it is only in recent years that the spatial dimension of regional labor markets is explicitly addressed.

The purpose of this paper is to bring fresh evidence of the driving forces of regional unemployment disparities. The case of Greece over the period 1981-2006 serves as an example in our empirical investigation. Contrary to the case of other European countries with substantial regional unemployment disparities, such as Spain and Italy (Jimeno and Bentolila 1998; Lopez-Bazo *et al.* 2002; Bande and Karanassou 2006; Limosani 2004), empirical evidence of the behavior of regional unemployment in Greece is scarce. Even in European regional panel studies Greek regions are heavily underrepresented mainly due to scarcity of quantitative information at regional level.[1] Our study, by bridging the gap between evidence from Greece on the issue and that of other European countries, provides a better understanding of regional unemployment in Europe.

Our empirical model incorporates region specific labor supply and demand factors and offers an explanatory framework for the evolution of regional unemployment disparities. Furthermore, the spatial association of regional labor markets evidenced in our results offers explanations for the asymmetric behavior of regional unemployment. The Generalized Method of Moments (GMM) methodology used in the study enables us to test for the existence of deterministic factors of regional unemployment and examine possible spatial unemployment interactions. It enables us to estimate regional asymmetries and test how unemployment in one region affects and how it is also affected by unemployment in other regions.

The paper proceeds as follows. Section 2 briefly surveys the main determinants of regional unemployment differentials. Section 3 presents the main characteristics of regional unemployment in Greece. Section 4 presents the empirical model and methodological issues. Section 5 presents the empirical findings, while Section 6 summarizes the results.

UNEMPLOYMENT DISPARITIES

The regional variation of the rate of regional unemployment is explained by two conceptually different views: the equilibrium view and the disequilibrium view (Marston, 1985). The disequilibrium view assumes that the unemployment rates will eventually equalize across space, but due to a sluggish adjustment process in the regional labour markets adverse shocks (e.g. a factory closure) have persistent after effects. Alternatively, regional unemployment disparities may be viewed as an equilibrium outcome, sometimes labelled the natural rate of unemployment. Each region tends to its natural unemployment rate determined by demand and supply side factors and institutional variables, which exhibit little variation over time. Thus, full adjustment is never achieved. The persistence of regional unemployment

[1] For instance, in Decressin and Fatás (1995) Greece is considered to be a single region; in Niebuhr (2003), Greece is altogether excluded form the European panel.

disparities in several countries over long periods of time gives credence to the equilibrium unemployment view.

Numerous hypotheses have been proposed for the explanation of regional unemployment differentials: The unemployment-vacancy approach relates inversely unemployment and the vacancy rates (Cheshire, 1973; Jones and Manning, 1992), while the cyclical sensitivity models explain the rate of regional unemployment by the national rate (Thirlwall, 1966; Brechling 1967) and also by other variables (Gordon, 1985; Taylor and Bradley, 1997; Baddeley *et al.* 1998). In other models, a compensating differential for the higher probability of unemployment is considered to be either regional amenities (Marston 1985, Montgomery 1993) or higher wages (Pissarides and McMaster, 1990; Layard *et al.* 1991; Groenewold, 1997). Other approaches emphasize the wage setting mechanisms and obtain regional NAIRU curves (Blackley, 1989; Payne 1995) or "wage curves" (Blanchflower and Oswald, 1994; Card, 1995), while the "accounting identity" approach relates regional unemployment with the main determining factors of labor supply and labor demand (Gordon, 1988).

However, these models offer partial explanations of regional unemployment since they give emphasis on some factors and ignore others. A more complete approach of the issue for empirical and theoretical analysis relates to the influential work of Blanchard and Katz (1992) which links together labor demand, labor supply and wage setting factors.

Current empirical models view regional unemployment as eventually depending on factors of labor supply (a collection of factors affecting natural change in the labor force, labor force participation, migration and commuting), labor demand and wage setting mechanisms (Elhorst, 2003). A common characteristic of most of these studies is that they consider the issue of regional labor market adjustment without accounting explicitly for its spatial dimension. Regional labor markets are essentially treated as isolated entities.[2]

In recent years there is a growing interest in the spatial association of regional unemployment and spatial factors are explicitly accounted for in regional unemployment studies. It is considered that various types of spatial interactions relating to factors such as migration, commuting, interregional trade, the location decision of firms link regions together. Spatial interactions which are exposed to the frictional effects of distance lead to a spatial dependence of regional labor market developments.

Empirical evidence shows that the probability of migration diminishes with the increase of geographical distance between origin and destination. Furthermore, the direct costs of moving rise with distance while the benefits from migration become increasingly unknown (Tassinopoulos and Werner, 1999; Helliwell, 1998). Also, frictions relating to distance have a significant impact in the determination of the labor matching approach. Burda and Profit (1996) and Burgess and Profit (2001) analyse the significance of distance in relation to job searching behavior of workers and recruiting behavior of firms across regions and they provide evidence for the existence of spatial interactions in job matching in the cases of Britain and the Czech Republic.

Burridge and Gordon (1981) discuss spatial effects of regional labor markets in the case of Britain. They show that migration, induced by variations of regional employment growth, has an equilibrating impact on regional unemployment differentials. Evidence for spatial

[2] However, as observed by Nierbuhr (2003), spatial aspects are in some respect considered through the analysis of factors such as migration, although migration takes place in a non-spatial world, since the location of origin and destination of migration is unimportant.

interaction between regional labor markets in Britain is also provided by Mohlo (1995) where local unemployment is affected not only from local employment growth but also by unemployment in neighbouring areas. The significance of spatial spillover effects in local unemployment adjustment to local shocks for the case of US is reported by Bronars and Jansen (1987).

Lopez-Bazo *et al.* (2002) investigate the determinants of regional unemployment in Spain and their results point to increasing spatial dependence in the distribution of regional unemployment rates. Also, Badinger and Url (2002) find that spatial effects account for about one-fifth of the variation in the unemployment rate in Austria. Aragon et al. (2003), using a spatially autocorrelated error model for the Midi-Pyrénées region of France, show that unemployment differences largely reflect variations in amenities. Trendle (2003) employs spatial econometric techniques to determine the significance of economic and demographic factors affecting differences in regional unemployment in Queensland.

Overman and Puga (2002) show that a polarization process of European regional unemployment rates has been the result of changes in relative labor demand which have been similar across geographical neighbours. Idiosyncratic characteristics, national or regional, can only partly explain this neighbour effect which is strong both within and across national borders. Further empirical evidence for a significant degree of spatial dependence among regional labor markets in EU is provided by Niebuhr (2003).

THE GREEK LABOUR MARKET

The rate of unemployment in Greece increased sharply after the second energy crisis till the first years of the 1980s (1979: 2 per cent; 1981 4 per cent; 1983: 8 per cent) but over the rest of the 1980s it remained at the level of 7-8 per cent. Over the 1990s, the rate of unemployment increased again gradually reaching the highest level of about 12 per cent in 1999. Since 2000 the rate of unemployment has been on a descending trend reaching around 9 per cent in 2006.

However, the evolution of unemployment has not been uniform across regions. Table 1 provides summary statistics on regional unemployment in Greece over the period 1981-2006. Some regions, such as Crete, are very close to full employment (with unemployment not exceeding 5 percent), while other regions, such as Western Macedonia, and register high and persisting rates of unemployment (around 15 percent). Also, the increased difference between the highest (maximum) and the lowest (minimum) rates of regional unemployment reflects the increased probability and therefore difficulty of finding a job across regions.

On the other hand, differences in regional unemployment, as depicted by the standard deviation broadly follow the pattern of the country's unemployment rates. However, another measure of dispersion, the coefficient of variation (standard deviation divided by the average) of regional rates of unemployment follows a descending path which shows that unemployment disparities are diminishing over time. Thus, irrespectively of the movement of the rates of unemployment there is a convergence process of the regional rates of unemployment over the whole 1981-2006 period.

An important characteristic of unemployment in Greece is its duration. In the recent period, the long-term unemployed (unemployed for over a year) exceed 50 percent of the total number of unemployed, being roughly 4 percentage units higher for women. Long-term unemployment is particularly high in four regions (Epirus, Western Greece, Western Macedonia, Peloponnesus) and relatively small in three Regions (Southern Aegean, Crete, Ionian Islands). Also, over 40 percent of the unemployed are first-time entrants in the labor market. Higher percentages of newcomers are observed in four regions (Epirus, Western and Central Greece, Peloponnesus) and lower percentages exist in three regions (Southern Aegean, Eastern Macedonia-Thrace, Ionian Islands).

Table 1. Regional unemployment in Greece

Region	1981	1983	1990	1999	2003	2006
Greece	4,0	7,8	7,0	11,9	9,3	8,8
East Macedonia-Thrace	1,6	4,6	5,6	13,0	10,2	11,3
Central Macedonia	4,5	7,8	6,3	11,8	10,0	9,5
Western Macedonia	4,5	7,8	10,0	14,4	16,0	14,8
Thessaly	2,8	5,9	7,8	13,1	10,6	7,8
Epirus	2,8	6,0	3,2	14,2	11,5	9,2
Ionian Islands	1,9	4,0	3,4	5,8	10,3	11,8
Western Greece	2,6	5,7	7,6	12,0	9,5	9,4
Central Greece	4,1	7,7	6,5	15,2	9,5	8,8
Attica	6,0	11,1	8,8	12,6	8,7	7,8
Peloponnesus	2,1	4,5	5,8	7,9	8,5	8,1
Northern Aegean	4,1	6,6	4,7	11,7	7,6	9,8
Southern Aegean	3,0	4,8	4,5	7,6	10,9	7,5
Crete	1,6	4,6	2,4	7,6	5,2	5,8
Minimum	1,6	4,0	2,4	5,8	5,2	5,8
Maximum	6,0	11,1	10,0	15,2	16,0	14,8
Max-Min Difference	4,5	7,0	7,6	9,4	10,8	9,0
Standard Deviation (*)	0,56	1,02	0,80	1,17	0,82	0,70
Coefficient of Variation (*)	0,14	0,13	0,11	0,10	0,09	0,08

Source: National Statistical Service of Greece; (*) weighted by population.

The Greek labor market is characterized by low employment and low participation rates. Although employment in Greece has risen over the last two decades, the employment rate remains at low level (about 55 percent) being well below the EU average. The overall low employment rate is due to women, since that for men is at about the EU average. Note that the expansion of the labor force exceeded that economic activity resulting in an increase in unemployment. Another particularity of the Greek labor market is the high level of self-employment. In recent years self-employment amounts to almost 25 percent of total employment while the share of salary and wage earners do not exceed 60 percent. Value added in Greece is mainly produced by services, with the contribution of the tertiary sector exceeding 70 percent of the country's GDP. The share of the secondary sector is around 20 per cent, while that of the primary sector has been reduced roughly to less than 10 percent of GDP. The primary sector has more intense presence (10-18 percent) in roughly half of the regions (Thessaly, Eastern Macedonia-Thrace, Peloponnesus, Northern Aegean, Western

Greece, Western Macedonia and Crete). Relatively important is the industrial sector (above 30 percent) in only two regions (Central Greece and Western Macedonia), while services have the higher share (about 80 percent) in the Greek islands and in Attica.

Most Greek regions have a high proportion of employment in the primary sectors of the economy. Employment in agriculture represents more than 25 percent of the total in five regions (Peloponnesus, East Macedonia and Thrace, Thessaly, Western Greece and Crete) but its share is decreasing. Industrial employment represents around 15 percent of total employment (from 22 percent in 1981) across regions, with the exception of Western Macedonia and Central Greece where the industrial employment share exceeds 30 percent. In 2003 employment in services represents around 55 percent of total employment in Greece but it exceeds 70 percent in regions with a strong tourist presence (Attica, Crete, Aegean and Ionian Islands). Greece has strict employment protection legislation (EPL). Strict employment protection legislation, such as restrictive lay-off procedures, is related to lower short-term unemployment and greater long-term unemployment. Moreover, strict EPL rules tend to shift employment into the informal sector, intensifying labor market segmentation in Greece (OECD, 1999). Hours and conditions of employment are subject to extensive government legislation. The unemployment compensation system is rather poor and assistance to those seeking entrance to the labor market is limited. Part-time employment remains low and recently legislation was passed permitting it in the public sector (Law 3230/2004).

Greece's labor market institutions have undergone broad changes in recent years. In the beginning of the 1990s a new institutional framework for collective bargaining was introduced by Law 1876/1990. The law of 1990 freed collective bargaining from direct government control by abolishing compulsory arbitration. The collective bargaining system in Greece was decentralized and broadened. It provided for national general agreements, national agreements in a single industry or occupation, regional agreements in a single industry or occupation and enterprise agreements. National general collective agreements set minimum wages and salaries for private sector employees and for those working in the public sector under private law contracts that act as effective floors for subsequent sectoral and enterprise agreements. National general collective agreements are concluded between the main union confederation of private sector employees and the largest and most representative nation-wide employers association.[3]

THE EMPIRICAL MODEL AND METHODOLOGICAL ISSUES

The empirical analysis is based on an extended model similar to Blanchard and Katz (1992). It is a dynamic model incorporating region specific variables as well as spatial interactions as follows:

$$u_{i,t} = f(u_{i,t-1,} X_{i,t}, S * u_{i,t}) \qquad (1)$$

[3] For an extensive discussion on various features of the Greek labor market, see among other Papapetrou (2006).

where $u_{i,t}$ is the unemployment rate of region i in period t; $X_{i,t}$ is the array of explanatory variables of regional unemployment; $S*u_{i,t}$ is the spillover effect on regional unemployment. Thus, the regional unemployment rate equation is estimated using annual data for the 13 regions of Greece over the 26 year period 1981-2006, as follows:[4]

$$u_{it} = \beta_0 + \beta_1(u_{it-1}) + \beta_2(prod_{it}) + \beta_3(lempl_{it}) + \beta_4(dpartic_{it-1}) + \beta_5(esagr_{it}) +$$
$$+\beta_6(escon_{it}) + \beta_7(esman_{it}) + \beta_8(esserv_{it}) + \beta_9(uD_{it}) + \varepsilon_{it};$$
$$for\ t = 1981, 1982, 1983, ..., 2006; i = 1, 2, ..., 13 \qquad (2)$$

The dependent variable u_{it} is the regional rate of unemployment of region i at time t. It is calculated as the ratio of the number of unemployed persons over the sum of employed and unemployed persons. The first regressor u_{it-1} is the lagged dependent variable. It accounts for possible autocorrelation and gives an estimate of the degree of regional unemployment persistence.

The next seven regressors, $lempl_{it}$, $prod_{it}$, $dpartic_{it-1}$, $esagr_{it}$, $escon_{it}$, $esman_{it}$, and $esserv_{it}$ are the region specific variables. The variable $lempl_{it}$ is total employment and it is measured by the log of employment, while $prod_{it}$ is labour productivity of region i at year t, measured by the ratio of real gross value added over total employment. The variable $dpartic_{it-1}$ is the change in the participation rate of the previous year, where the participation rate in region i is defined as the ratio of the economically active to total population. The economically active population is the sum of employed and unemployed people. The variables $esagr_{it}$, $escon_{it}$, $esman_{it}$, and $esserv_{it}$ are the employment shares of the i-th region in the sectors of agriculture, construction, manufacturing and services respectively. Each share in region i is defined as the ratio of employment in the particular sector over total employment.[5]

The last regressor uD_{it} captures spillover effects with respect to distance between regions. Spillover effects leading to spatial dependence are usually captured by the spatially lagged dependent variable. This specification implies that, starting from a steady state pattern of regional unemployment, region-specific shocks do not only affect the respective labor market, but instead they spillover to neighbouring regions. The induced unemployment changes in neighbouring regions spillover to adjacent labor markets including the location where the shock originated. The process of spatial adjustments continues until a new steady-state pattern of regional unemployment is achieved.

Also, ε_{it} is an error term which it is assumed to have a mean of zero, to be independently distributed over all i and t, and, in order to account for size and other differences between the regions, to be heteroskedastic over i, namely $\text{var}(\varepsilon_{it}) = \sigma_i^2, i = 1, ..., 13$.

---

[4] The selection of the particular explanatory variables is based on the availability of reliable data. The 13 regions of Greece are the following: Eastern Macedonia-Thrace, Central Macedonia, Western Macedonia, Thessaly, Epirus, Ionian Islands, Western Greece, Central Greece, Attica, Peloponnesus, Northern Aegean, Southern Aegean and Crete.

[5] The source of data for employment and unemployment is the National Statistical Service of Greece. Data on real gross value added, sectoral employment shares and working population is obtained from the database of Cambridge Econometrics. Employment variables refer to the age bracket 15-64.

The distance-weighting matrix is meant to account for the spillover effects with respect to distance. We construct two distance matrices (D), namely $D1$ and $D2$, which are used alternatively in our empirical study (Models 2a and 2b).[6]

In the first distance weight matrix ($D1$), the i, j element is $w^{D1}_{ij} = d1^{-1}_{ij}$ where $d1_{ij}$ is the arc geographical distance between two regions i and j. In the second distance weight matrix (D2), the i, j element is $w^{D2}_{ij} = d2^{-1}_{ij}$ where d_{ij} is defined by travel time distance between two regions i and j.[7] Given the definition of w^{D1}_{ij} and w^{D2}_{ij} the distance spillover variables of unemployment $uD1_{it}$ and $uD2_{it}$ which are used alternatively in equation (2) are given by:

$$uD1_{it} = \sum_{j=1}^{13} w^{D1}_{ij} u_{jt}$$

$$uD2_{it} = \sum_{j=1}^{13} w^{D2}_{ij} u_{jt}, \quad \text{for all i = 1,..., 25,} \tag{3}$$

where u_{jt} is the dependent variable in equation (2).

The specification of the spillover variables in equation (3) implies, via equation (2), that the spillover effect is disseminated among regions. Therefore, high unemployment in a region, perhaps due to a region-specific shock, can potentially, via uD_{it}, affect unemployment in all regions. As an illustration, high unemployment in region j could affect unemployment in region i if they are close to each other in terms of geographical distance. The unemployment in region i, in turn, could then affect unemployment in region k if they are close to each other, etc. Thus, a change in unemployment in region j could, in this manner, affect unemployment in all related regions, which could then feedback to region j. Therefore, since inverse distance is used in our formulation we expect that $\beta_9 > 0$.

Panel data estimation is used for the estimation of equation (2). Panel data have the advantage of increasing the sample size; they are better suited to examine the dynamics of change and are able to handle complicated behavioural models. However, panel data estimation faces several estimation and inference problems since the estimation method should combine cross section and time series dimensions. The Generalized Method of Moments (GMM) is used since the estimation our model raises several issues. First, endogeneity is likely to be present. The endogeneity problem can arise because of the existence of reverse causality. It might be the case that all explanatory variables may be jointly determined with the rate of unemployment. This means that the error term of equation (2) in period t is correlated with the explanatory variables and earlier shocks, but uncorrelated with the error term in period $t+1$ and subsequent shocks. Second, some independent variables may be predetermined in the sense that they are uncorrelated with the error term in period t but they are correlated with the error term in period $t-1$. Finally, unobserved hetererogeneity may arise across regions.

[6] See Tables A and B, in the Appendix.

[7] The spatial weight matrix used is a symmetric inverse travel time distance matrix, where travel time depends on kilometre distance and the convenience of access.

To address successfully the above issues the orthogonal deviations generalized method of moments (GMM) estimator is used, since it tackles successfully all these problems obtaining asymptotically efficient and consistent estimators (Bond 2002). The Arellano and Bond (1991) estimators are used to estimate the extended equation (2) with lagged dependent and lagged independent variables acting as instruments. The GMM estimator makes use of the orthogonality conditions to allow for efficient estimation in the presence of heteroskedasticity of unknown form. Arellano and Bover (1995) and also Blundell and Bond (1998) suggest that this type of estimator is efficient for panels with large time dimension (T). Since there are more instruments than right-hand side variables the estimated regression equations are over-identified. To assess the validity of the different specifications we compute the Sargan (1964) test for over-identifying restrictions, which amounts to a test of the exogeneity of the explanatory variables, and AR1 and AR2 tests for autocorrelation.

EMPIRICAL RESULTS

Equation (2) is estimated employing balanced panel data and using the GMM methodology. In the estimation method fixed regional effects are used and it is assumed that none of the explanatory variables is predetermined. Several lags of unemployment and two lags of the explanatory variables are used as instruments.[8] All regressors used in the empirical analysis influence the unemployment rate and vice versa. Our estimation methodology adheres with labor economic theory and the findings of empirical research emphasizing the interdependence of regional variables. Indeed, Elhorst (2003), in his survey of theoretical and empirical explanations of regional unemployment, notes that the general picture emerging from the literature when empirical studies dealing with interactions are gathered is that the regional unemployment rate both affects and is affected by one or more additional regional labor market variables. In the empirical analysis, alternative models of the regional unemployment rate are estimated and the results are shown in Table 2. Model 1 is a traditional model where regions are considered to behave more or less independently to each other. The other two models are extended versions of the first model to capture spatial interdependence, their only difference being the construction of the distance matrix D. In Model 2a, the distance weigh matrix $D1$ is constructed in terms of arc geographical distance, while in Model 2b the distance matrix $D2$ is defined in terms of travel time distance. It should be noted that the sign of the equation variables is mostly an empirical matter since different theories go around on the impact many of the explanatory variables may have on the regional unemployment rate.

In Table 2 are also reported the results of the Arellano and Bond estimator. The diagnostic tests that were carried out show that the empirical results are statistically acceptable (Wald joint test, Wald joint test for the dummy variables, Sargan test of over-identifying restrictions and AR1 and AR2 tests for autocorrelation). The empirical results of Model 1 are as follows:

---

[8] Note that, once fixed effects are included in the model, it makes no difference whether equation (2) is estimated using regional variables in levels or relative to national ones.

(i) *Lagged rate of unemployment.* Many studies have used a lagged dependent variable to explain regional unemployment on the grounds that regional unemployment rates are highly correlated in time and they usually change by small amounts (Blanchard and Katz, 1992; Decressin and Fatás, 1995). The coefficient of lagged dependent variable, reflecting the degree of unemployment persistence, is positive and statistically significant. To test for serial dependence, the unemployment rate $u_{i,t}$ is regressed on its serial lagged value $u_{i,t-1}$. Also, the stationary properties of unemployment are tested, i.e. whether unemployment is a non-trended I(1) process like a standard random walk. Panel unit root tests are employed to examine the order of integration of the variable in this panel data setting. In particular the Levin *et al.* (2002) test which allows for heterogeneity is estimated to test the hypothesis that unemployment has common unit root process. The test rejects the null hypothesis of the presence of a unit root.

Table 2. Panel estimation using GMM methods (Arellano and Bond estimator) Dependent Variable: Unemployment rate (u_{it})

Variables	Model 1	Model 2a	Model 2b
u_{it-1}	0.426*** [5.76]	0.396*** [5.24]	0.381*** [5.11]
$prod_{it}$	-0.178*** [-2.89]	-0.120* [-1.83]	-0.101 [-1.52]
$lempl_{it}$	-4.967** [-2.53]	-3.590** [-2.08]	-3.235* [-1.92]
$dpartic_{it-1}$	10.460** [2.44]	9.782** [2.40]	9.874** [2.51]
$esagr_{it}$	-22.645** [-2.22]	-22.530** [-2.30]	-21.365** [-2.19]
$escon_{it}$	-32.407** [-2.51]	-32.854*** [-2.68]	-35.415*** [-2.92]
$esman_{it}$	-3.596 [-0.33]	-3.005 [-0.32]	-1.260 [-0.14]
$esserv_{it}$	-15.284 [-1.35]	-19.207* [-1.66]	-18.958 [-1.59]
uD_{it}		0.301** [2.11]	0.132*** [3.21]
Wald joint test	77.31***	87.06***	117.4***
Wald joint test for dummy variables	173.2***	2058.0***	608.2***
Sargan test (p-value)	0.997	0.997	0.998
AR (1) test (p-value)	0.003	0.003	0.003
AR (2) test (p-value)	0.475	0.373	0.302
S. E. of regression	2.121	2.095	2.085

Notes: Figures in brackets are t-statistics. The signs (***), (**) and (*) indicate significance at 1%, 5% and 10% level respectively. First differences are used in the estimation of the panel models.

(ii) *Employment.* The effect of employment on the unemployment rate is negative, almost by definition. Considering the accounting identity, the unemployment rate decreases as a result of one extra job, whether it is filled by an unemployed, a non-participant or a job migrant. However, the effect of employment growth needs not to be necessarily negative since the effort to create more jobs may come about through induced migration, thus leading to higher instead to lower unemployment rates (Harris and Todaro, 1970). The effect of employment on the rate of regional unemployment is negative and statistically significant, a result in line with that of the majority of empirical studies.

(iii) *Labor productivity*. In the long run the level of productivity does not affect the natural rate of unemployment. In the short run, however, labor productivity affects the rate of unemployment but its impact can be either negative or positive. According to Mortensen and Pissarides (1994) structural changes associated with technological advances may affect unemployment positively. However, Basile and De Benedictis (2004) and Limosani (2004) provide empirical evidence of a negative relationship between labor productivity and regional employment. Our results show that an upward shock in labor productivity leads to a lower rate of regional unemployment, the estimated coefficient being negative and statistically significant.

(iv) *Participation rate*. The participation rate incorporates the labor supply side effect on regional unemployment. A negative effect can is explained by the association of the level of participation rates with the level of skills and commitment to working life of the population (Fleisher and Rhodes, 1976). However, the effect of the participation rate on unemployment rate can be positive (Layard, 1997) since the participation rate increases along with the number of unemployed. Our results show that an upward change participation rate increases the unemployment rate, since the estimated coefficient is positive and significant.

(v) *Industry mix*. Regional industrial specialization seems to affect regional unemployment (Summers, 1986). Declining industries show generally low employment rates and growing industries high rates. Therefore, regions specializing in declining industries (e.g. agriculture) are expected to exhibit higher unemployment rates compared to those specializing in growing industries (e.g. services). Thus, the spatial industry mix in terms of employment can give an account of the variation in unemployment rates between regions. The employment shares of different industries/sectors are used as explanatory variables of regional unemployment by many empirical studies, but their results are mixed. Regarding the industry mix variables in our study, the effect of employment shares of the various sectors on the regional rate of employment is negative, but with varying strength across industrial sectors.

(vi) The empirical results of Models 2a and 2b are also shown in Table 2. The same diagnostic tests are carried out and the empirical results appear similar, but as will be discussed below, they have a different interpretation. The estimated coefficients retain their signs although the level of statistical significance in some of them is altered. The addition of the spillover variable improves the standard error of regression in both models.

(vii) The estimated sign of the *spatial effect* in Models 2a and 2b is positive and statistically significant. The coefficient of the spatially lagged dependent variable points to significant spillover effects. In order to gain further insight into the mechanisms that may cause spatial dependence of regional unemployment, we experimented with alternative types of spatial lag models in the estimation procedure, such as dependent variable spatial lag models, with no particular success though. Apart from the relevant fundamentals incorporated in Model 1, spillover effects seem to be a considerable explanatory factor of the variation in the rate of regional unemployment in Greece.[9] Thus, the unemployment rate of a specific region is also affected by developments in unemployment rates of neighbouring regions and vice versa. This effect fades out with the increase in geographical distance of the neighbouring regions.

The existence of the spillover explanatory variable gives a different meaning to the estimated coefficients of our model. In particular the solution of equation (2) for u_{it} is:

$$u_{it} = \Theta^{-1}\beta_0 + \Theta^{-1}\beta_1(u_{it-1}) + \Theta^{-1}(\beta_2(prod_{it}) + \beta_3(lempl_{it}) + \beta_4(dpartic_{it-1}) + \beta_5(esagr_{it}) + +\beta_6(escon_{it}) + \beta_7(esman_{it}) + \beta_8(esserv_{it})) + \Theta^{-1}\varepsilon_{it}; \quad (4)$$

where $\Theta = [I - \beta_9 uD]$

Equation (4) is a reduced form equation in levels. Hence it should be clear that once the spillover variable uD_{it} is added in the regression equation, the dependent vector u_{it} not only depends on the spillover variable but each one of the estimated coefficient of the explanatory variable is a function of the spillover variable.

Thus, the unemployment level in each region, u_{it} depends not only upon the "within region" values of the regressors but also upon the values of the regressors in all neighbouring regions. In more detail, let ϑ_{ij} be the i,j-th element of Θ^{-1}.

Then, the change in the expected value of the unemployment level in the j-th region with respect to a change in an explanatory variable, e.g. real productivity in the i-th region, namely, $prod_{it}$ is, via (4):

$$\frac{\partial E(u_{jt})}{\partial prod_{it}} = \vartheta_{ji}\beta_2, \; j = 1,....,13 \quad (5)$$

Similar expressions could be presented for the lagged dependent variable and for the other explanatory variables. In general, ϑ_{ji} will not be zero unless $\beta_9 = 0$, indicating that there is no spillover effect. Alternatively, in the absence of spillover effects the dependent variable in each region will only respond to a change in one of its own explanatory variables.

Clearly, the magnitude of the cross derivative in equation (5) depends upon the direct within region effect of productivity upon the unemployment level of that region, which is β_2, and an indirect spillover effect, which is ϑ_{ji}.

Generalizing, it should be clear that unemployment in a given region would be affected by the values of all significant variables in (4) in all related neighbouring regions because of the existence of spillovers effects due to issues related to distance.

[9] This variable may also catch the effect of missing variables.

Thus, the existence of spatial unemployment spillover [Models 2a and 2b] gives rise to a regionally asymmetric impact (effectiveness) of the factors that affect the rate of unemployment, since the value of the coefficients in the equation varies from one region to another.

CONCLUSION

This paper attempts to bring empirical evidence on the driving forces of regional unemployment disparities in Greece. We estimated a dynamic model for the regional rate of unemployment, using balanced panel data for the 13 Greek regions over the period 1981-2006. The empirical model incorporates region specific variables and spatial interactions in order to test for regional unemployment spillover effects. The GMM estimation methodology used in the study allows us to investigate the existence of deterministic factors of regional unemployment along with the examination of spatial unemployment associations. To investigate the determinants of regional unemployment, the model was estimated without the inclusion of unemployment spillover effects and under the assumption that regions are independent to each other. The empirical analysis shows that regional unemployment variations are related to labor supply and demand factors, such as labor productivity, participation rate, the industry mix and employment. Furthermore, spatial unemployment interactions appear to be important determinants of the rate of regional unemployment in Greece.

APPENDIX

Table A. For the construction of matrix D1

	Geographic coordinates of Greek regions' capital cities			
	Region	Latitude	Longitude	Capital city of Region
1	Eastern Macedonia-Thrace	40,850	25,867	Alexadroupoli
2	Central Macedonia	40,633	22,933	Thessaloniki
3	Western Macedonia	40,300	21,783	Kozani
4	Thessaly	39,633	22,417	Larissa
5	Epirus	39,667	20,833	Ioannina
6	Ionian Islands	39,620	19,920	Kerkyra
7	Western Greece	38,250	21,733	Patra
8	Central Greece	38,900	22,433	Lamia
9	Attica	37,983	23,733	Athens
10	Peloponnesus	37,517	22,367	Tripoli
11	Northern Aegean	39,103	26,553	Mytilini
12	Southern Aegean	37,450	24,933	Ermoupoli
13	Crete	35,333	25,133	Iraklio

Source: www.Astrovox.gr/coordinates-geo.html.

Note: In constructing the row-standardized matrix D1 the following procedure is used. First, the co-ordinates for the capital city of each region are selected. Next, the two co-ordinates (latitude X and longitude Y) are transformed into decimal employing the following formula: decimal = degrees + minutes times 0.01666667 + seconds times 0.00027778. Then, the arc distance d_{ij} between two regions i and j is calculated.

Table B. For the construction of matrix D2

Travel time distances between Greek regions' capital cities (Km equivalent)														
	Capital city of Region	1	2	3	4	5	6	7	8	9	10	11	12	13
1	Alexadroupoli	0												
2	Thessaloniki	349	0											
3	Kozani	490	141	0										
4	Larissa	503	154	145	0									
5	Ioannina	716	367	230	209	0								
6	Kerkyra	1116	767	630	609	400	0							
7	Patra	844	495	486	341	247	481	0						
8	Lamia	651	302	264	150	264	564	193	0					
9	Athens	862	513	506	361	447	481	220	215	0				
10	Tripoli	1000	651	644	499	423	457	176	349	194	0			
11	Mytilini	600	500	850	850	950	900	700	700	500	700	0		
12	Ermoupoli	1650	1100	1100	950	1050	1000	800	800	600	800	500	0	
13	Iraklio	1550	1200	1200	1050	1150	1200	900	900	700	900	700	500	0

When spatial unemployment effects are accounted for, the impact of the explanatory variables varies across regions giving rise to an asymmetric behaviour of regional unemployment in Greece. In other words, the effectiveness of measures for the reduction of unemployment is different from one region to another. Our empirical findings provide an explanation for the fact that the behaviour of unemployment is not uniform across regions. From the policy perspective, a better understanding of the behaviour of regional unemployment disparities allows for the design of suitable cohesion policies at regional level.

REFERENCES

A. Levin, C. F. Lin and C. S. J. Chu, "Unit root tests in panel data: Asymptotic and finite-sample properties", *Journal of Econometrics*, 108, 1-24, (2002).

A. Niebuhr, "Spatial interaction and regional unemployment in Europe", *European Journal of Spatial Development*, 5, October, (2003).

A. P. Thirlwall, "Regional unemployment as a cyclical phenomenon", *Scottish Journal of Political Economy*, 13, 205-219, (1966).

A. Tassinopoulos and H. Werner, "To move or not to move: migration of labour in the European Union", *IAB Labour Market Research Topics 35*, (1999).

B. M. Fleisher and G. Rhodes, "Unemployment and the labor force participation of married man and women: a simultaneous model", *The Review of Economics and Statistics*, 58, 398-406, (1976).

B. McCormick and S. Sheppard, "A model of regional contraction and unemployment", *Economic Journal*, 102, 366-377, (1992).

B. Trendle, *Regional variation in Queensland's unemployment rate*, Working Paper No. 7, May, (2003).

C. A. Pissarides and I. McMaster, "Regional migration, wages and unemployment: Empirical evidence and implications for policy", *Oxford Economic Papers,* 42, 812-831, (1990).

D. Card, "The wage curve: A review", *Journal of Economic Literature* 33, 85-799, (1995).

D. G. Blanchflower and A. J. Oswald, *The Wage Curve,* MIT, Cambridge, (1994).

D. Mortensen and C. Pissarides, "Job creation and job destruction in the theory of unemployment", *Review of Economic Studies*, 61, 3, 397-416, (1994).

D. R. Jones and D. N. Manning, "Long term unemployment, hysteresis and the unemployment-vacancy relationship: A regional analysis", *Regional Studies,* 26, 17-29, (1992).

E. B. Montgomery, *Patterns in regional labour market adjustment: The United States vs. Japan*, NBER, Cambridge, Working Paper No. 4414, (1993).

E. Lopez-Bazo, T. Del Barrio and M. Artis, "The regional distribution of Spanish unemployment", *Papers in Regional Science*, 81, 365-389, (2002).

E. Papapetrou, "The Public-private sector pay differential in Greece", *Public Finance,* 35 *(4)*, 450-473, (2006).

F. Brechling, "Trends and cycles in British regional unemployment", *Oxford Economic Papers* 19, 1-21, (1967).

H. Badinger and T. Url, "Determinants of regional unemployment: Some evidence from Austria", *Regional Studies*, 36, 9, 977-988, (2002).

H. Overman and D. Puga, "Unemployment clusters across Europe's regions and countries", *Economic Policy*, 34, 115-47, (2002).

I. Mohlo, "Spatial autocorrelation in British unemployment", *Journal of Regional Science*, 35, 641-658, (1995).

I. R. Gordon, "Evaluating the effects of employment changes on local unemployment", *Regional Studies,* 22, 135-147, (1988).

I. R. Gordon, "The cyclical sensitivity of regional employment and unemployment differentials", *Regional Studies* 19, 95-110, (1985).

J. Decressin and A. Fatás, "Regional labour market dynamics in Europe", *European Economic Review*, 39, 1627-1655, (1995).

J. E. Payne, "A note on real wage rigidity and State unemployment rates", *Journal of Regional Science,* 35, 319-332, (1995).

J. F. Helliwell, *How Much do national Borders matter?* Brookings Institution Press, Washington, D. C., (1998).

J. F. Jimeno and S. Bentolila, "Regional unemployment persistence (Spain, 1976–1994)", *Labour Economics*, 5, 25-51, (1998).

J. P. Elhorst, "The mystery of regional unemployment differentials: Theoretical and empirical explanations", *Journal of Economic Surveys*, 17(5), 709-749, (2003).

J. R. Harris and M. P. Todaro, "Migration, unemployment, and development: a two sector analysis", *American Economic Review*, 60, 126-42, (1970).

J. Sargan, "Wages and prices in the United Kingdom: a study in econometric methodology", in *Econometric Analysis for National Planning*, 2eds. P.E. Hart, E. Mills and J. K. Whitaker, London: Butterworth, (1964).

J. Taylor and S. Bradley, "Unemployment in Europe: A comparative analysis of regional disparities in Germany, Italy and the UK", *Kyklos,* 50, 221-245, (1997).

L. H. Summers, "Why is the unemployment rate so very high near full employment?", *Brookings Papers on Economic Activity*, 2, 339-383, (1986).

M. Arellano and O. Bover, "Another look of the instrumental variable estimation of the error component model", *Journal of Econometrics* 68, 29-51, (1995).

M. Arellano and S. Bond, "Some tests of specifications for panel data: Monte carlo evidence and an application to employment equations", *Review of Economic Studies,* 58, 277-297, (1991).

M. Baddeley, R. Martin and P. Tyler, "Transitory shock or structural shift? The impact of the early 1980s recession on British regional unemployment", *Applied Economics* 30, 9-30, (1998).

M. C. Burda and S. Profit, "Matching across space: Evidence on mobility in the Czech Republic", *Labour Economics*, 3, 255-278, (1996).

M. D. Partridge and D. S. Rickman, "The dispersion in US state unemployment rates: the role of market and non-market equilibrium factors", *Regional Studies,* 31, 593-606, (1997).

M. J. Greenwood, "Human migration: Theory, models, and empirical studies", *Journal of Regional Science,* 25, 521-544, (1985).

M. Limosani, "Beyond regional institutions: widening unemployment differentials in Italy", Labour, 18 (3), 503-514, (2004).

N. Groenewold, "Does migration equalise regional unemployment rates? Evidence from Australia", *Papers in Regional Science,* 76, 1-20, (1997).

O. J. Blanchard and L. Katz, "Regional evolutions", *Brookings Papers on Economic Activity,* 1: 1992, 1-61, (1992).

OECD, *Employment Outlook*, Organisation for Economic Co-operation and Development, Paris, (1999).

P. Burridge and I. Gordon, "Unemployment in the British Metropolitan labour areas", *Oxford Economic Papers*, 33, 274-297, (1981).

P. C. Cheshire, *Regional unemployment differentials in Great Britain,* Cambridge University Press, National Institute of Economic and Social Research, (1973).

P. Epifani and G. Gancia, "Trade, migration and regional unemployment", *Regional Science and Urban Economics*, 35, 625– 644, (2005).

P. R. Blackley, "The measurement and determination of state equilibrium unemployment rates", *Southern Economic Journal* 56, 440-456, (1989).

R. Bande and M. Karanassou, *Labour market flexibility and regional unemployment rate dynamics: Spain 1980-1995*, Working Paper No. 574, Department of Economics, Queen Mary College, University of London, (2006).

R. Basile and L. De Benedictis, *Regional unemployment productivity in Europe and the US*, European Regional Science Association, Conference Paper, (2004).

R. Blundell and S. Bond, "Initial conditions and moment restriction in dynamic panel data models", *Journal of Econometrics, 87*, 114–144, (1998).

R. Layard, "Preventing long-term unemployment: an economic analysis" in D. J. Snower and G. de la Dehesa (eds.) *Unemployment Policy*, Cambridge University Press, Cambridge, 333-356, (1997).

R. Layard, S. Nickell and R. Jackman, *Unemployment, Macroeconomic Performance and the Labour Market,* University Press, Oxford, (1991).

R. Martin, "Regional unemployment disparities and their dynamics", *Regional Studies*, 31, 237-252, (1997).

S. Burgess and S. Profit, "Externalities in the matching of workers and firms in Britain", *Labour Economics*, 8, 313-333, (2001).

S. G. Bronars and D. W. Jansen, "The geographical distribution of unemployment rates in the US: A spatial time series analysis", *Journal of Econometrics*, 36, 251-279, (1987).

S. Galiani, C. Lamarche, A. Porto and W. Sosa-Escudero, "Persistence and regional disparities in unemployment (Argentina 1980–1997)", *Regional Science and Urban Economics*, 35, 375-394, (2005).

S. T. Marston, "Two vies of the geographic distribution of unemployment", *Quarterly Journal of Economics*, 100, 57-79, (1985).

Y. Aragon, D. Haughton, J. Haughton, E. Leconte, E. Malin, A. Ruiz-Gazen, and C. Thomas-Agnan, "Explaining the pattern of regional unemployment: The case of the Midi-Pyrénées region", *Papers in Regional Science*, 82, 155-174, (2003).

In: Labor Markets: Dynamics, Trends and Economic Impact ISBN: 978-1-61470-825-4
Editor: Samir Amine

Chapter 7

THE RELATIONSHIP AMONG UNEMPLOYMENT, UNEMPLOYMENT DURATION, AND UNEMPLOYMENT BENEFITS REVISITED

Lonnie K. Stevans*
Department of IT/QM, Hofstra University, Hempstead, US

ABSTRACT

Given the voluminous empirical literature that exists on this subject and as far as we can tell, there has not been any research to date that has specifically examined the time series properties and multivariate relationship among unemployment, unemployment duration, and unemployment insurance in the United States. The United States is an example of "free market fundamentalism" and is an exemplar to nations who want to lower unemployment rates by reducing unemployment benefits.Thus, one might expect the U.S. unemployment rate, unemployment duration, and unemployment benefits to be cointegrated with each other, *ceteris paribus*—otherwise, there would be no reason to advocate benefit reduction. In this analysis, we will determine if there are any common stochastic trends among the U.S. aggregate unemployment rate, unemployment compensation, and unemployment duration, *ceteris paribus*--using time series techniques on deseasonalized monthly data from 1959 to 2010.

INTRODUCTION

The assessment of how economic incentives in the unemployment compensation system affect unemployment has received extensive attention in the literature. Surveys of the literature are provided by Danziger et al. (1981), Devine and Kiefer (1991), Atkinson and Micklewright (1991) and Layard et al. (1991) and more recent studies have been done by Holmlund (1998) and Pedersen and Westergard-Nielsen (1998). Lancaster (1979) construed

---

* Email: acslks@hofstra.edu.

that an elasticity of unemployment duration with respect to benefit levels of 0.6 could be considered as confirmed beyond question. Studies from the U.S. and U.K. have tentatively corroborated this result, with point estimates ranging from 0.2 to 0.9 (Moffitt (1985), Narendranathan et al. (1985), Katz and Meyer (1990), and Meyer (1990)). In Europe, the evidence is more tenuous and the typical result is that incentive effects associated with the compensation level cannot be strongly identified (Hujer and Schneider (1989), Groot (1990), Van den Berg (1990), Steiner (1990), and Hernæs and Strom (1996)). However, some authors have indicated significant responses, such as Abbring et al. (1998) and Carling et al. (2001), the latter reporting a compensation elasticity as high as 1.6.

Beginning in the 1970s, the analysis of unemployment insurance has attracted considerable attention in the economics profession--one reason being the emergence of job-search theory as a framework for labor market analysis. This has inspired a considerable amount of empirical research with some of it innovative and cogent for economic policy. The research devoted to unemployment insurance in the past couple of decades is closely entwined with the retreat of traditional Keynesian macroeconomics and the development of theories of the natural (or equilibrium) rate of unemployment. The natural rate framework was suited to incorporate unemployment compensation as a policy instrument. In almost all natural rate models, there is a positive relationship between the equilibrium unemployment rate and the 'generosity' of the unemployment insurance system. In many simple models, the wage replacement rate provided by unemployment insurance is often the only exogenous variable that determines unemployment.[1]

Keynesian macroeconomics maintains that unemployment benefits can be considered an "automatic stabilizer" when the economy slides into a recession. Pre-Keynesian economists had much to say about unemployment compensation which forms the academic basis of the current dialogue on the issue. The British economists A. C. Pigou, John Hicks, Edwin Cannan and Henry Clay, accentuated the *incentive effects* of unemployment compensation that are still the focal point of contemporary discussions about transfer policies. They proposed that unemployment insurance could strengthen the unions' bargaining position and thereby raise wage pressure. In addition, they argued that unemployment benefits would affect job-search behavior, unemployment duration, contracts between firms and workers, and the allocation of labor across industries if the system entails net subsidies to some industries and net taxes on others.[2]

Consistent with the beliefs of the pre-Keynesian economists, the current explanation for persistent high unemployment centers on supply-side inflexibilities generated by protective labor market institutions. Correspondingly, the proposed solution is greater (downward) wage flexibility and stronger work incentives. One explanation for the increase in research regarding cross-country studies of unemployment was the growing gap in employment performance between the U.S. and large European countries after the early 1990s—which has tended to lend support for the orthodox view (Bruno and Sachs (1985), Blanchard and Summers (1986), Lindbeck and Snower (1988)). High unemployment in Europe since the 1980s has given some credence to the idea that the equilibrium unemployment rate has increased along with the actual rate--the consequence of a more generous unemployment

[1] See the survey in Johnson and Layard (1986).
[2] See the review in Casson (1983).

insurance system. As a result, many governments have attempted reforms to make unemployment insurance less generous. Such policies have also been motivated by the need to offset the rise in budget deficits that has been associated with the rise in unemployment. Whatever the origins of high and persistent unemployment might be, unemployment insurance has been brought to the vanguard in the policy discussions about unemployment.

Given the voluminous empirical literature that exists on this subject and as far as we can tell, there has not been any research to date that has specifically examined the time series properties and multivariate relationship among unemployment, unemployment duration, and unemployment insurance in the United States. The United States is an example of "free market fundamentalism" and is an exemplar to nations who want to lower unemployment rates by reducing unemployment benefits. Thus, one might expect the U.S. unemployment rate, unemployment duration, and unemployment benefits to be cointegrated with each other, *ceteris paribus*—otherwise, there would be no reason to advocate benefit reduction. In this analysis, we will determine if there are any common stochastic trends among the U.S. aggregate unemployment rate, unemployment compensation, and unemployment duration, *ceteris paribus*--using time series techniques on deseasonalized monthly data from 1959 to 2010.

UNEMPLOYMENT DURATION, UNEMPLOYMENT COMPENSATION, AND THE UNEMPLOYMENT RATE

Unemployment insurance benefits could be positively correlated with unemployment duration, and *ceteris paribus*, with unemployment rates. We shall refer to this premise as the *incentives* approach that was mentioned previously. However, higher benefit levels may also influence the inflows into both unemployment and employment. Atkinson and Mickelwright (1991) posit that higher benefits can affect only the *composition* and not the level of unemployment. As persons with higher benefits exit unemployment more slowly, this does not necessarily mean that aggregate unemployment would be higher, since the refusal of jobs by one group may lead to the work being offered to others. In other words, it is only the composition of unemployment which is altered.[3]

Higher unemployment benefit generosity can also affect inflows into employment, which could limit or offset the effect of longer unemployment duration on the aggregate unemployment rate. Referred to as the *entitlement* effect, Holmlund (1998) explains that "the rather obvious adverse-incentive effects on job acceptance decisions among those who have just become unemployed are not valid for *all* unemployed; for some workers, in particular those who do not qualify (or have ceased to qualify), higher benefits will make work *more* attractive relative to unemployment."[4] Theoretically, the effect of higher benefits on the duration of unemployment is therefore uncertain, and if work becomes more attractive because it qualifies a worker for more generous benefits should they become unemployed,

[3] Howell, D.R., Baker, D., Glyn, A., and Schmitt, J. (2007). Are Protective Labor Market Institutions at the Root of Unemployment? A Critical Review of the Evidence, Capitalism and Society, vol. 2, no. 1, p. 48.

[4] Holmlund, B. (1998). Unemployment insurance in theory and practice, Scandinavian Journal of Economics, vol. 100, no. 1, p. 116.

this lower duration could also *reduce* the unemployment rate. The possibility of *composition* and *entitlement* effects signifies that there is not necessarily a direct relationship between average unemployment duration and the unemployment rate.[5]

In early research, authors have found that benefit generosity had a strong and positive effect on unemployment duration (Lancaster and Nickell (1980)). However, evidence from the 1970s and 1980s was varied. The evidence from the U.S., U.K. and the rest of the OECD did not suggest that the effects of benefits on transitions out of unemployment were very large (Atkinson and Mickelwright (1991)). Recently, many studies have taken advantage of major policy shifts and these have found evidence for a benefits' effect on unemployment duration, albeit the magnitude of the effects are small (Roed and Zhangs (2003), Lalive and Zweimuller (2004), Jan van Ours and Vodopivec (2005), Pollmann-Schult and Buchel (2005), and Russell and O'Connell (2001)).

The IMF (2003) has concluded that the causes of unemployment can be found in labor market institutions and thus countries with high unemployment have been urged to undertake comprehensive structural reforms to reduce labor market rigidities. IMF researchers have stated that the European adoption of the U.S. model could produce output gains of about five percent and a fall in the unemployment rate of about 3 percentage points.[6] Therefore, it is apparent that the orthodox view of labor market rigidities has become widely accepted with the United States labor market being the archetypal example (Howell, et. al., (2007)).

In the context of the capacious body of knowledge on this subject, we would like to further contribute to the literature by examining the U.S. labor market from a time series perspective. Considering the U.S. model to be the exemplary paradigm and assuming unemployment, unemployment duration, and unemployment benefits in the United States to contain unit roots ($I(1)$) in a multivariate environment, the questions are: (1) is there a single, cointegrating relationship amongst these variables and; (2) what is the magnitude and direction of the effect that unemployment compensation has on aggregate unemployment, *ceteris paribus*? The aforementioned *composition* and *entitlement* effects raise the possibility of no relationship between the aggregate unemployment rate and benefits in the former, and perhaps an inverse relationship between benefits and the unemployment rate in the latter. These situations can be represented as statistical hypotheses and tested within the context of a dynamic and multivariate system.

EMPIRICAL MODEL AND TESTABLE HYPOTHESES

Building on the above research, we begin by modeling only the three variables at issue using a VEC process with monthly, deseasonalized data from 1959 to 2010,

UNR_t - U.S. Aggregate Unemployment Rate,

$UNDUR_t$ - U.S. Mean (Average) Duration of Unemployment,

[5] Ibid.

[6] IMF (2003), p. 129.

$UNBEN_t$ - U.S. Unemployment Insurance Benefits.

All of the above variables are expressed in natural log units. A complete description of all the variables and relevant sources may be found in Appendix A, and the time plot of each variable is in Figure 1. The econometric software EViews 7 was utilized in this analysis.

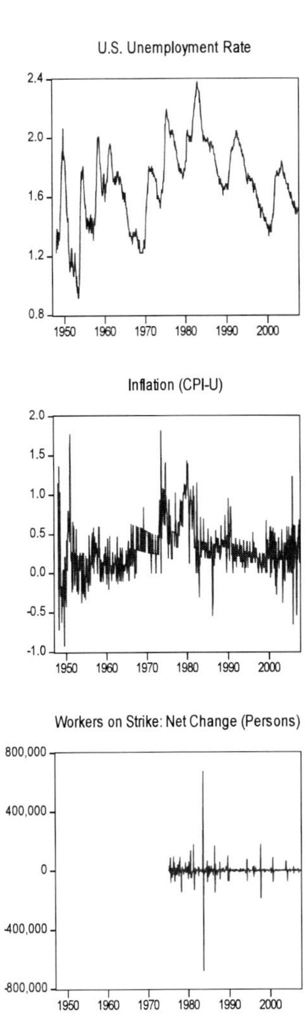

Figure 1.

If all of the above variables have a single unit root, then an error-correction model will necessarily imply cointegration (and vice versa) (Engle and Granger (1987)). The VEC representation for the above variables are,

$$\Delta\vec{X}_t = \vec{\gamma} + \alpha\eta_{t-1} + \sum_{i=1}^{p-1}\pi_i\Delta\vec{X}_{t-i} + \vec{\varepsilon}_t, \tag{1}$$

$$\eta_{t-1} = \beta'\vec{X}_{t-1},$$

where the vector $\vec{X}_t$ contains the variables,

$$\vec{X}_t' = \left(1, UNR_t, UNBEN_t, UNDUR_t\right)'$$

The notion of cointegration, as introduced by Engle and Granger (1987), considers a set of variables in *long-run equilibrium* when,

$$\beta'\vec{X}_{t-1} = \beta_0 + \beta_1 UNR_{t-1} + \beta_2 UNBEN_{t-1} + \beta_3 UNDUR_{t-1} = 0. \qquad (2)$$

The deviation in long-run equilibrium, known as the *equilibrium error*, is η_t in equation (1). If the equilibrium is meaningful, the error process η_t is stationary. It is important to note here that the term "equilibrium" is the econometric definition which makes reference to any *long-run* relationship among non-stationary variables. One of the variables (the unemployment rate) is selected to normalize equation (2) by fixing its coefficient at unity,

$$UNR_{t-1} = \delta_0 + \delta_1 UNBEN_{t-1} + \delta_2 UNDUR_{t-1}, \qquad (3)$$

where,

$$\delta_j = \frac{\beta_j}{\beta_2}.$$

We will refer to equation (3) as the "long-run equilibrium" relationship among the U.S. unemployment rate, unemployment benefits, and the duration of unemployment and our emphasis will be on the estimation and testing of this relationship.

One motivation for the VEC form is to consider the equation, $UNR_{t-1} = \delta_0 + \delta_1 UNBEN_{t-1} + \delta_2 UNDUR_{t-1}$, as defining the underlying economic relations and assume that in the short-run, agents react to the disequilibrium error, $UNR_{t-1} - \delta_0 - \delta_1 UNBEN_{t-1} - \delta_2 UNDUR_{t-1}$, through the adjustment coefficient α in equation (1), to restore equilibrium.

As mentioned previously and according to Atkinson and Mickelwright (1991) and further discussed by Howell, et al. (2007), higher benefits may affect only the composition, not the level of unemployment. As individuals with higher benefits exit unemployment more slowly, aggregate unemployment may not increase, since the refusal of employment by one group of workers may lead to jobs being offered to others—thus, it is the composition, not the level of unemployment that is changed. In addition to the composition effect, Holmlund (1998) and Howell, et. al., (2007) also refer to the entitlement effect which results when higher benefits make work more attractive relative to unemployment. To test the presence/absence of the incentive effect, the null and alternative hypotheses would be,

$$H_0 : \delta_1 = 0$$
$$H_A : \delta_1 > 0. \tag{4}$$

Failure to accept the null would indicate a positive relationship between benefits and the unemployment rate. For the entitlement effect,

$$H_0 : \delta_1 = 0$$
$$H_A : \delta_1 < 0, \tag{5}$$

and we would expect an inverse relationship between benefits and the unemployment rate. Of course, under the null hypothesis in both (4) and (5), unemployment benefits would have no effect on the aggregate unemployment rate, which is the composition effect. Nevertheless, if we failed to accept the null hypothesis then according to Howell, et. al. (2007), we should also expect a tenuous link between unemployment duration and the aggregate unemployment rate—that is,

$$H_0 : \delta_2 = 0. \tag{6}$$

If the entitlement effect is prevalent, then we should fail to accept the null hypothesis in (5) and fail to reject the null hypothesis in (6).

Empirical Results

Before estimating the VEC equation (1), the first task is to test each of the variables for the presence of a unit root, since all must be $I(1)$. Although the results are not included in this paper for the purpose of brevity, the null hypothesis of a unit root has been accepted for each of the three variables using the more powerful Augmented Dickey-Fuller Test with GLS Detrending (DF-GLS) (Elliot, Rothenberg, and Stock (1996)).[7]

Although the VEC (equation (1)) and the cointegrating relation (3), has been specified *a priori*, it is imperative to test whether the variables are indeed cointegrated and the order of cointegration, since more than one linear combination is a possibility. We use the multivariate method developed by Johansen (1988) and the maximum eigenvalue statistic to test the null hypothesis,

$$H_0 : \text{Number of Cointegrating Vectors} = \text{r}$$

versus the alternative,

$$H_A : \text{Number of Cointegrating Vectors} = \text{r} + 1$$

[7] Unit root test results will be made available from the author upon request.

where "r" is the order of cointegration. The results may be found in Table I, Part A. It is important to note that the maximum eigenvalue test indicates there is only *one* common trend among the variables--so we will proceed as if there is only one "long-run," cointegrating relationship amongst the three variables specified in equation (3).

Table I. Johansen Cointegration Test Unemployment Rate, Unemployment Benefits, and Unemployment Duration

Part A				
Sample (adjusted): 1959M09 2010M12				
Trend assumption: Linear deterministic trend				
Lags interval (in first differences): 1 to 7				
Unrestricted Cointegration Rank Test (Maximum Eigenvalue)				
Hypothesized		Max-Eigen	0.05	
No. of CE(s)	Eigenvalue	Statistic	Critical Value	Prob.**
None *	0.040517	23.78257	21.13162	0.0207
At most 1	0.022003	12.79323	14.26460	0.0843
At most 2	6.94E-05	0.039928	3.841466	0.8416

Max-eigenvalue test indicates 1 cointegrating eqn(s) at the 0.05 level.
* denotes rejection of the hypothesis at the 0.05 level.
** MacKinnon-Haug-Michelis (1999) p-values.

Part B				
Unrestricted Cointegration Rank Test (Maximum Eigenvalue)				
Hypothesized		Max-Eigen	0.05	
No. of CE(s)	Eigenvalue	Statistic	Critical Value	Prob.**
None *	0.283450	124.9901	46.23142	0.0000
At most 1	0.100773	39.83247	40.07757	0.0533
At most 2	0.088274	34.65574	35.87687	0.0564
At most 3	0.045707	17.54435	27.58434	0.5334
At most 4	0.036288	13.86108	21.13162	0.3765
At most 5	0.017485	6.614859	14.26460	0.5356
At most 6	0.003473	1.304513	3.841466	0.2534

Max-eigenvalue test indicates 1 cointegrating eqn(s) at the 0.05 level.
* denotes rejection of the hypothesis at the 0.05 level.
** MacKinnon-Haug-Michelis (1999) p-values.

The Johansen (1988) parameter estimates of the cointegrating vector are in Table II, Part A, which we reproduce here in normalized form with the "t" statistics below in parentheses,

$$UNR_{t-1} = 4.94 - 4.59 \cdot UNBEN_{t-1} + 3.41 \cdot UNDUR_{t-1},$$
$$\qquad (-3.883)^{***} \qquad (1.665)^{*} \tag{7}$$

* - statistically significant at $\alpha = .10$ (two-tailed),*** - statistically significant at $\alpha = .01$ (one-tailed).

Table II. Cointegrating Equation Unemployment Rate, Unemployment Benefits, and Unemployment Duration (Natural Log Units)

Part A	
Cointegration Equation Estimates	
Sample (adjusted): 1959M09 2010M12	
Standard errors in ( ) and t-statistics in [ ]	
Variables	Parameter Estimates
Unemployment Rate	1.000000
Real Unemployment Benefits	- 4.593484
	(1.18285)
	[- 3.88341]***
Mean Unemployment Duration	3.413525
	(2.04986)
	[1.66525]*
Intercept	4.939480
Part B	
Cointegration Equation Estimates	
Sample (adjusted): 1975M10 2010M12	
Standard errors in ( ) and t-statistics in [ ]	
Variables	Parameter Estimates
Unemployment Rate	1.000000
Real Unemployment Benefits	-0.004465
	(0.16173)
	[-0.02761]
Mean Unemployment Duration	.574441
	(0.31165)
	[1.84321]**
Capacity Utilization	-1.868182
	(1.10194)
	[-1.69535]**
Output Per Hour	-.970675
	(0.19898)
	[-4.87837]***
Inflation	-0.032134
	(0.19279)
	[- .16668]
Net Change of Workers on Strike	3.82E-05
	(3.4E-05)
	[1.12353]
Intercept	12.90346

* - statistically significant at $\alpha = .10$ ** - statistically significant at $\alpha = .05$. ***-statistically significant at $\alpha = .01$.

Note that these results yield a statistically significant and inverse relationship between unemployment benefits and the aggregate unemployment rate in long-run equilibrium.

However, the effect of unemployment duration is tenuous at best—it is marginally statistically significant (or insignificant) at $\alpha = .10$. These results lend support for the *entitlement* effect, since the null hypothesis (5) is rejected in favor of the alternative and the null hypothesis (6) cannot be rejected at either $\alpha = .01$ or .05.

The above results do not comprise any *ceteris paribus* concerns. For instance, a more valid representation of a model representing the U.S. aggregate unemployment rate should also include measures of labor supply, demand and inflation. Moreover, since unionization is one of the "labor market rigidities" referred to by the orthodox literature, (Howell, et. al. (2007)), some measure of the bargaining power of workers should also be included. Union density has been the most commonly used proxy of workers' bargaining power, but as mentioned in Howell, et. al. (2007), it has its limitations since it really does not gauge unions' ability to influence the market. We use the variable, *U.S. Workers on Strike*, as an overall measure of union power, since a strike could mean disruptions in output and/or instability in other market outcomes. Therefore, equation (3), above, is modified to include the additional variables capacity utilization, productivity, inflation, and the change in the number of workers on strike,

$$\begin{aligned} UNR_{t-1} &= \delta_0 + \delta_1 UNBEN_{t-1} + \delta_2 UNDUR_{t-1} + \delta_3 CAPU_{t-1} \\ &+ \delta_4 OUTPH_{t-1} + \delta_5 INF_{t-1} + \delta_6 STRIKE_{t-1} \end{aligned} \tag{8}$$

Once again, we use the multivariate method developed by Johansen (1988) and the maximum eigenvalue statistic to test the null hypothesis,

H_0 : Number of Cointegrating Vectors = r

versus the alternative,

H_A : Number of Cointegrating Vectors = r + 1

where "r" is the order of cointegration. The results are in Table I, Part B. The maximum eigenvalue test indicates there is only one common trend among the seven variables. Thus, there is empirical support for specifying equation (8) as a single linear relationship among the variables unemployment, unemployment benefits, unemployment duration, capacity utilization, productivity, inflation, and the net change in striking workers over the period 1975 to 2010.[8] The Johansen (1988) parameter estimates of the cointegrating vector may be found in Table II, Part B, which, as before, is reproduced below in normalized form,

[8] Note that the number of observations has decreased in the model just including unemployment, unemployment benefits, and unemployment duration in the model including the six variables due to differences in data availability.

$$UNR_{t-1} = 12.903 - .004 \cdot UNBEN_{t-1} + .574 \cdot UNDUR_{t-1}$$
$$(-.028) \qquad (1.843)^{**}$$
$$- 1.868 \cdot CAPU_{t-1} - .971 \cdot OUTPH_{t-1} \qquad (9)$$
$$(-1.695)^{**} \qquad (-4.878)^{***}$$
$$- .032 \cdot INF_{t-1} + .0000382 \cdot STRIKE_{t-1},$$
$$(-.1667) \qquad (1.124)$$

** - statistically significant at $\alpha = .05$ (two-tailed), *** - statistically significant at $\alpha = .01$ (two-tailed).

When controlling for the influence of other economic variables, the results are different from the simple case of equation (7). Unemployment benefits have a negative, yet *statistically insignificant* effect on the aggregate unemployment rate and therefore the null hypothesis (5) and (6) of the composition effect is accepted. Moreover, an increase in the number of striking workers is found to have no significant influence on the unemployment rate. In a review of research that used union density as an explanatory variable, Howell, et. al. (2007) discovered seven out of eleven studies that found a significant effect for union density. The OECD (2006b) determined that only five of the sixteen studies they analyzed portrayed positive, unemployment-increasing effects and concluded that there is little evidence of an effect of union density on unemployment once other features of the collective bargaining system are taken into account. Our variable, which is a better indicator than density of union influence on the labor market, indicates that this measure of "labor market rigidity" has not impacted the U.S. unemployment rate.

CONCLUSION

Some commentators have argued that extended unemployment insurance (UI) benefits are the key reason for high unemployment in the United States.[9] Using monthly data from 1959 to 2010, we present evidence to the contrary. The results of this study suggest that changes in unemployment benefits have no appreciable effect on the unemployment rate, *ceteris paribus*. In addition, the aforementioned conclusion by the IMF (2003) that the causes of high unemployment can be found in a country's labor market rigidities is certainly not supported by the outcomes of this study. One such measure of a labor market rigidity, the number of striking workers, has had no perceptible impact on U.S. unemployment rates.

Examining equation (9) once again, it is important to note that the only explanatory variables that have a statistically significant impact upon the unemployment rate is duration of unemployment, capacity utilization, and productivity. Thus, given these empirical results, it would appear that the overwhelming share of unemployment is cyclical rather than structural.

[9] http://www.huffingtonpost.com/2010/03/24/jpmorgan-chase-report-say_n_512130.html.

APPENDIX A

Variable Descriptions

UNR_t	U.S. Aggregate Unemployment Rate, %,
$UNDUR_t$	U.S. Mean (Average) Duration of Unemployment, Number of Weeks,
$UNBEN_t$	U.S. Unemployment Insurance Benefits, Bil. $,
INF_t	U.S. Percent Change in CPI-U, %,
$CAPU_t$	U.S. Capacity Utilization, % of Capacity,
$OUTPH_t$	U.S. Output Per Hour, 1992=100,
$STRIKE_t$	U.S. Workers on Strike, Net Change.

Note: All data/variables were downloaded from http://www.haverselect.com/dlx/home.htm.

REFERENCES

Abbring, J., van den Berg, G., van Ours, J. C. (1998). *The effect of unemployment insurance sanctions on the transition rate from unemployment to employment*, Working Paper, Tinbergen Institute, Amsterdam.

Atkinson, A. B., Micklewright, J. (1991). Unemployment compensation and labor market transitions: a critical review. *Journal of Economic Literature, 29*, 1679–727.

Blanchard, Olivier., L. Summers. (1986). *Hysteresis and the European Unemployment Problem*, in S. Fischer (ed.), NBER Macroeconomics Annual 1 (Cambridge: MIT Press), pp. 15-78.

Bruno. M., J. Sachs. (1985). *The Economics of Worldwide Inflation*. (Oxford: Basil Blackwell).

Carling, K., Holmlund, B., Vejsiu, A. (2001). *Do benefit cuts boost job findings? Swedish evidence from the 1990s. Economic Journal, 111, no. 474*, pp. 766–90.

Casson, M. (1983). Economics of Unemployment: An Historical Perspective. MIT Press, Cambridge, MA.

Danziger, S., Haveman, R., Plotnick, R. (1981). How income transfer programs affect work, savings, and the income distribution: a critical review. *Journal of Economic Literature, 19*, 975–1028.

Devine, T., Kiefer, N. (1991). Empirical Labor Economics. The Search Approach, Oxford: Oxford University Press.

Elliot, G., Thomas, J., Rothenberg, J.H., Stock. (1996). Efficient Tests for an Autoregressive Unit Root. *Econometrica, 64*, 813-836.

Engle, R.F., C.W.J., Granger. (1987). Co-Integration and Error Correction: Representation, Estimation, and Testing. *Econometrica, 55*, 251-276.

Groot, W. (1990). The effects of benefits and duration dependence on re-employment probabilities. *Economic Letters, 32, 4*, 371–6.

Hartog, J., Ridder, G., Theeuwes, J. (eds) (1990). *Panel data and labor market studies*, Contributions to Economic Analysis, vol. 192, Amsterdam: North-Holland.

Hernæs, E., Strom, S. (1996). Heterogeneity and unemployment duration. *Labour, 10*, 269–96.

Holmlund, B. (1998). Unemployment insurance in theory and practice. *Scandinavian Journal of Economics, 100, 1*, 113–41.

Howell, D.R., Baker, D., Glyn, A., Schmitt, J. (2007). Are Protective Labor Market Institutions at the Root of Unemployment? A Critical Review of the Evidence. *Capitalism and Society, 2, 1*, 1-71.

Hujer, R., Schneider, H. (1989). The analysis of labour market mobility using panel data. *European Economic Review, 33*, 530–6.

International Monetary Fund (IMF) (2003). *Unemployment and Labor Market Institutions: Why Reforms Pay Off.* Chapter IV in World Economic Outlook (May). Washington, DC: IMF.

Johansen, S. (1988). Statistical Analysis of Cointegration Vectors. *Journal of Economic Dynamics and Control, 12*, 231-254.

Johnson, G., Layard, R. (1986). *The natural rate of unemployment: explanation and policy*, in O. Ashenfelter and R. Layard (eds.), Handbook of Labor Economics, North-Holland, Amsterdam, 1986.

Katz, L. F., Meyer, B. D. (1990). The impact of the potential duration of unemployment benefits on the duration of unemployment. *Journal of Public Economics, 412, 1*, 45–72.

Kennedy, P. (1981). Estimation with Correctly Interpreted Dummy Variables in Semilogarithmic Equations. *American Economic Review, 71*, 801.

Lalive, R., Zweimuller, J. (2003). Benefit entitlement and unemployment duration: The role of policy endogeneity. *Journal of Public Economics, 88*, 2587-2616.

Lancaster, T. (1979). Econometric methods for the duration of unemployment. *Econometrica, 47, 4*, 939–56.

Lancaster, T., Nickell, S. (1980). The analysis of re-employment probabilities for the unemployed. *Journal of the Royal Statistical Society,143*, 141-65.

Layard, R., Nickell, S., Jackman, R. (1991). *Unemployment. Macroeconomic Performance and the Labour Market.* Oxford: Oxford University Press.

Lindbeck, A., D., Snower. (1989). *The Insider Outsider Theory of Employment and Unemployment* (Cambridge: MIT press).

Meyer, B. D. (1990). Unemployment insurance and unemployment spells. *Econometrica, 58, 4*, 757–82.

Moffitt, R. (1985). Unemployment insurance and the distribution of unemployment spells. *Journal of Econometrics, 28, 1*, 85–101.

Narendranathan, W., Nickell, S., Stern, J. (1985). Unemployment benefits revisited. *Economic Journal, 95*, 307–29.

OECD. (1999). *Implementing the OECD Jobs Strategy: Assessing Performance and Policy*, Paris: OECD.

OECD. (2006a). *Political Economy of Structural Reform*, Working Paper No. 1 in Macroeconomic and Structural Policy Analysis, Paris: OECD.

OECD. (2006b). *OECD Employment Outlook*, Paris: OECD.

Pedersen, P.J., Westergard-Nielsen, N. (1998). *Unemployment: what do we know from longitudinal data?*, Chapter 4 in (T. Lange, ed.) Unemployment in Theory and Practice, Cheltenham: Edward Elgar, pp. 67–99.

Pollmann-Schult, M., F., Buchel. (2005). Unemployment Benefits, Unemployment Duration, and Subsequent Job Quality. *Acta Sociologica 48 (1)*, 21-39.

Roed, K., T., Zhang. (2003). Does Unemployment Compensation Affect Unemployment Duration?. *Economic Journal 113*, 190-206.

Russell, H., Phillip J., O'Connell. (2001). Getting a Job in Europe: The Transition from Unemployment to Work among Young People in Nine European Countries. *Work, Employment and Society, 15, 1*, 1-24.

Steiner, V. (1990). Long-term unemployment, heterogeneity, and state dependence. *Empirica, 17, 1*, pp. 41–59.

Van den Berg, G.J. (1990). Search behaviour, transitions to non-participation and the duration of unemployment. *Economic Journal, 100*, 842–65.

Van Ours, J.C., M., Vodopivec. (2005). *How Changes in Benefits Entitlement Affect the Duration of Unemployment*, CEPR Discussion Paper No. 2005-30, Tilberg University, Feb.

In: Labor Markets: Dynamics, Trends and Economic Impact ISBN: 978-1-61470-825-4
Editor: Samir Amine

Chapter 8

REGIONAL LABOR MARKET DYNAMICS IN TAIWAN

Shu-hen Chiang[1,*] ***and Jen-te Hwang***[2]
[1]Department of Finance, Chung-Yuan Christian University
[2]Department of Banking and Finance, Kaikan University

ABSTRACT

Strong international economic competition and regional specialization makes the research of regional labor markets extraordinarily important. Through the channels of employment, unemployment, not in labor force and migration, a dynamic regional labor market model is set to analyze how regional labor market adjusts to regional labor demand shocks. Regressing regional labor market on national economy by employment, unemployment rate and labor participation rate, region-specific variables are obtained from the residuals of the above regression. Next, the structural vector autoregression model is estimated by pooling monthly data of 23 counties between 1981 and 2004 and it is found that interregional migration plays an absolutely critical role in the regional labor market. However, during the economic slump since 2001, labor participation rate is more important than migration. In addition, unemployment rate continues to play very small role and this reflects the presence of natural unemployment rates at the regional level.

INTRODUCTION

The pride of Taiwan's so-called 'economic miracle' has been very low, however, coinciding with a global recession in 2001 and a growing trend for Taiwan manufacturers to relocate to mainland China, Taiwan's unemployment rate and broadly-defined unemployment rate more than tripled from 1.36% and 2.55%, respectively, in 1981 to record highs of more

* E-mail: shchiang@cycu.edu.tw

than 5.5% and 8%, respectively, in 2002.[1] At the same time, the duration of unemployment is more than 31 months, and worse, the first negative economic growth since 1949 occurred in 2001. In addition, real wage is lower than that of ten years ago. Undeniably, the Taiwan economy is facing very serious labor problems and this has already begun to adversely affect the society at large. Thus, regional labor market analysis has triggered a great deal of interest in Taiwan over the past few years.

In addition, although Taiwan is a small open economy, regional differences in labor characteristics, employment condition and living standard are substantial. For example, Hwang and Chiang (1998) discussed regional effects of national minimum wage on regional employment due to significant regional variants. Furthermore, the purpose of the Regional Planning Act in Taiwan is to reduce the problems of regional gaps. For reasons mentioned above, it is worthwhile examining regional labor market dynamics in Taiwan more closely and deeply.

This paper is organized as follows. Section 2 briefly reviews the regional labor market researches. Section 3 provides the theoretical framework of regional labor market dynamics and the description of the data. Section 4 describes the results in common labor market disturbances, and Section 5 applies structural vector autoregression to estimate regional labor market disturbances. Section 6 draws the general conclusions of the paper.

REVIEW OF REGIONAL LABOR MARKET RESEARCHES

With the pace of globalization progressing faster and faster and increasing international competitive pressure, most regions may depend on a greater degree of specialization to maintain or even increase their competitive edge, especially for a small open economy, such as Taiwan. This leads to greater heterogeneity in regional economies, and this may, at least to some extent, account for a renewal of interest in studies on regional labor markets in recent years. Barro and Sala-i-Martin (1991), for example, applied data of 50 U.S. states to test the convergence across states. Krugman (1991), called new economic geography introduced location theory to analyze many economic phenomenon. Card and Krueger (1995) found regional effects of national minimum wage on employment is positive, opposite to traditional view of labor economics and their studies are called new minimum wage theory.

Regional labor market dynamics stemmed from an excellent work of Blanchard and Katz (1992). They provided a dynamic model of regional labor markets to evaluate how a region adjusts and responds to demand shocks through the channels of employment, unemployment, labor force participation and interregional migration simultaneously. Decressin and Fatas (1995) estimated regional labor markets in Europe and compared them with those in the U. S. Clark (1998) extended regional labor markets to include industry-specific shocks using a structural vector autoregression method. Debelle and Vickery (1999), Pekkala and Kangasharju (2002) and Broersma and van Dijk (2002) extended the dynamic model of Blanchard and Katz (1992) to analyze the regional labor markets in different countries. [2]

[1] Compared with unemployment rate, broadly-defined unemployment rate includes non-searching unemployed workers in both the numerator and denominator.

[2] A comparison of cross-country studies is summarized in Gacs and Huber (2005).

Pekkala and Kangasharju (2002) divided labor demand shocks into regional and national types. Broersma and van Dijk (2002) provided an additional research in regional adjustment processes within different regions. It is important to note that most of these studies have shown that interregional migration plays a vital role in the adjustment of regional labor markets; at the same time, the importance of regional dynamics should be emphasized.

Only few attempts have so far been made at the regional market research in Taiwan, except that Hwang and Chiang (1998) used regional data to estimate regional effects of minimum wages and Jiang and Liu (2005) applied panel data analysis to search the causes of regional unemployment. In addition, Chiang (2009a) found that regional diversity can reduce national unemployment through interregional migration. Moreover, Chiang (2009b) quoted the portfolio theory to explain high unemployment since 2000. The purpose of this paper is to scrutinize data on Taiwan's 23 regions during 1981-2004 to investigate interregional interactions among different channels, and to provide some useful recommendations for solving high unemployment issues in Taiwan.

DATA DESCRIPTION AND THEORETICAL FRAMEWORK

Data Description

The database is pooling 23 regions during 1981-2004 monthly for a total of 6,624 observations. These data are adjusted by X12 seasonal-adjustment method. The source of data comes from *Manpower Survey Statistics* by Directorate-General of Budget, Accounting and Statistics, Taiwan.

For the definitions of labor indices, first, unemployment rate is a ratio between the number of unemployed and the labor force. The labor force consists of employed and unemployed. The labor force participation rate is a ratio, which compares the labor force with population between 15 and 64 years of age and this index can reflect the situation of not in labor force. These indices are summarized as Table 1.

Table 1 shows that higher unemployment rise in Illan and Hualien of eastern region and three cities (Chiayi, Tainan, and Kaohsiung respectively) while employment is concentrated in Taipei metropolitan area (includes Taipei city and Taipei county) and neighboring Taoyuang county. In addition, labor force participation rates are mostly more than 60% except Kaohsiung city and the highest labor force participation rates lie in the poorest county: Yunlin and Chiayi counties.

Three variables: employment change, unemployment rate and labor force participation rate are often applied in analysis of regional labor market dynamics, and these variables must be stationary. On the other hand, the data belong to the nature of panel data and the panel unit root tests have higher power than unit root tests based on individual time series. Thus, we conduct panel unit root tests to assess whether these variables are indeed stationary. We will compute five kinds of panel unit root tests, where two tests (LLC and Breitung tests) based on common unit root process and others (IPS test; two Fisher-type tests using ADF and PP tests) based on individual unit root process. Results of five panel unit root tests are listed in Table 2 and it is revealed that employment change, unemployment rate and labor force participation rate are all treated as stationary variables.

Table 1. Basic Statistics of Labor Indices in Regions

	Employment (persons)		Unemployment rate (%)		Labor force participation rate (%)	
	mean	std. dev.	Mean	std. dev.	mean	std. dev.
Taipei County	1,216,215	283,395	2.62	0.013	62.23	0.021
Ilan County	178,032	33,797	3.03	0.013	64.51	0.023
Taoyuan County	584,797	116,858	2.14	0.012	63.17	0.019
Hsinchu County	167,405	33,673	1.84	0.013	66.90	0.035
Miaoli County	236,201	33,302	2.17	0.013	68.33	0.031
Taichung county	542,310	95,013	2.36	0.015	64.27	0.017
Changhua County	498,111	53,193	1.95	0.013	63.19	0.019
Nantou county	232,613	36,996	2.41	0.015	66.93	0.025
Yunlin County	378,925	59,781	2.07	0.013	70.91	0.032
Chiayi County	263,071	36,462	2.09	0.015	71.25	0.034
Tainan County	455,124	58,355	2.39	0.013	69.25	0.025
Kaohsiung County	482,887	71,766	2.88	0.013	65.51	0.017
Pingtung County	372,548	44,323	2.25	0.013	65.22	0.024
Taitung County	117,005	20,547	2.62	0.014	68.38	0.032
Hualien County	145,247	28,479	3.04	0.014	64.74	0.026
Penghu County	37,423	11,450	2.45	0.015	61.30	0.054
Keelung City	151,556	24,461	2.16	0.012	63.53	0.016
Hsinchu City	141,053	34,293	2.73	0.014	65.79	0.034
Taichung city	330,319	65,697	2.98	0.012	61.46	0.018
Chiayi City	106,798	21,202	3.20	0.013	61.07	0.029
Tainan City	288,076	52,786	3.23	0.012	64.20	0.027
Taipei City	1045,778	113,580	2.77	0.010	60.66	0.027
Kaohsiung City	523,677	65,875	3.19	0.013	58.30	0.019

Table 2. Panel Unit Root Tests

	Employment change		Unemployment rate		Labor force participation rate	
	(1)	(2)	(1)	(2)	(1)	(2)
LLC	9.51***	-16.66***	-6.83***	-8.29***	-11.77***	-20.53***
Breitung	-1.60***	-0.782	-3.11***	-0.26	-4.72***	-1.82**
IPS	-12.35***	-18.44***	-7.74***	-7.72***	-12.81***	-15.84***
ADF-Fisher	286.92***	453.76***	149.37***	144.72***	297.22***	354.64***
PP-Fisher	696.61***	924.94***	620.51***	810.52***	706.75***	858.75***

Notes: (1) and (2) are random walk with drift and random walk with constant and time trend. "***", "**" and "*" are 1%, 5% and 10% statistically significant based on Maddala and Kim (1998).

Common Labor Market Disturbances

Following Decressin and Fatas (1995), the regional labor market dynamics is obtained through the two-stage process from common and regional labor market disturbances. The effects of common labor market disturbances on regional labor markets are estimated and then the remainder is to show the regional labor market dynamics.[3]

Our concerned in this section is to determine whether labor market disturbances in Taiwan are distributed symmetrically across regions. In other words, effect in regional employment belongs to be common to all regions will be estimated as following:

$$\Delta \ln(N_{it}) = \alpha_{1i} + \beta_i \Delta \ln(N_{ct}) + \eta_{it} \tag{1}$$

$$\frac{U_{it}}{L_{it}} = \alpha_{2i} + \delta_i \left(\frac{U_{ct}}{L_{ct}} \right) + \mu_{it} \tag{2}$$

$$\ln(\frac{L_{it}}{P_{it}}) = \alpha_{1i} + \varsigma_i \ln(\frac{L_{ct}}{P_{ct}}) + \rho_{it} \tag{3}$$

where N_{it} represents the employment in region i and in time t and N_{ct} is national employment. U, L and P stand for unemployment, the labor force and population and hence (U/L) and (L/P) are unemployment rate and labor force participation rate respectively. α_1, α_2 *and* α_3 are the constant terms of employment, unemployment rate and labor force participation rate equations respectively. β_i, δ_i *and* ς_i represent the elasticities of regional variables with respect to the national variables respectively. Finally, η, μ *and* ρ reveal the error terms from three equations.

Regional Labor Market Disturbances

Regional employment fluctuation can be explained from common and regional labor markets respectively and equations (1) – (3) have answered the former effects. The latter can be obtained through the residuals from the above equations using estimated coefficients values in the following way:

$$\eta_{it} = \Delta \ln(N_{it}) - \hat{\alpha}_1 - \hat{\beta}_i \Delta \ln(N_{ct}) \tag{4}$$

$$u_{it} = \frac{U_{it}}{L_{it}} - \hat{\alpha}_2 - \hat{\delta}_i \left(\frac{U_{ct}}{L_{ct}} \right) \tag{5}$$

$$\rho_{it} = \ln(\frac{L_{it}}{P_{it}}) - \hat{\alpha}_3 - \hat{\varsigma}_i \ln(\frac{L_{ct}}{P_{ct}}) \tag{6}$$

---

[3] Blanchard and Katz (1995) were different from Decressin and Fatas (1995) and they used the ratio between regional and national levels to show the regional performance directly.

where η, μ *and* ρ are regarded as the region-specific variables of employment, unemployment rate and labor force participation rate respectively. Moreover, we will introduce employment rate (E), which is employment divided by the labor force to replace unemployment rate since $\ln E_{it} = \ln\left(\frac{N_{it}}{L_{it}}\right) = \ln\left(1 - \frac{U_{it}}{L_{it}}\right) \approx -\frac{U_{it}}{L_{it}}$ and hence region-specific employment rate, e, is computed from:[4]

$$e_{it} = \ln(E_{it}) - \hat{\alpha}_2 - \hat{\delta}_i \ln(E_{ct}) \tag{7}$$

The Adjustment of Regional Labor Markets

The core of this paper is to search the adjustment of regional labor markets when labor demand shocks happen. We analyze the joint behavior of region-specific employment, employment rate and labor force participation rate in response to labor demand shocks. The system we estimate is set out below:

$$\eta_{it} = \lambda_{10} + \lambda_{11}(L)\eta_{it-1} + \lambda_{12}(L)e_{it-1} + \lambda_{13}(L)\rho_{i,t-1} + \varepsilon_{i1,t} \tag{8}$$

$$e_{it} = \lambda_{20} + \lambda_{21}(L)\eta_{it} + \lambda_{22}(L)e_{it-1} + \lambda_{123}(L)\rho_{i,t-1} + \varepsilon_{i2,t} \tag{9}$$

$$\rho_{it} = \lambda_{30} + \lambda_{31}(L)\eta_{it} + \lambda_{32}(L)e_{it-1} + \lambda_{133}(L)\rho_{i,t-1} + \varepsilon_{i3,t} \tag{10}$$

where λ refers to the coefficients and L is the lag operator. The constant terms are region-specific fixed effects. The system in (8) to (10) is the SVAR structure because it is assumed that contemporaneous changes in employment can affect both employment rate and labor force participation rate simultaneously but not vice-versa. This restriction can meet the need of identification from the relationship between structural innovations and forecast errors (υ from reduce-form VAR) as:

$$\begin{aligned} \varepsilon_{i1,t} &= \omega_{11}\upsilon_{i1,t} \\ \varepsilon_{i2,t} &= -\omega_{21}\varepsilon_{i1,t} + \omega_{22}\upsilon_{i2,t} \\ \varepsilon_{i3,t} &= -\omega_{31}\varepsilon_{i1,t} + \omega_{32}\upsilon_{i3,t} \end{aligned} \tag{11}$$

Finally, it suffices to trace the effects of an innovation in region-specific employment to understand the dynamic effects of an innovation in labor demand on employment, employment rate and labor force participation rate.

It is worthwhile to note that there is additional adjustment channel in regional labor markets, compared with national labor market and this is interregional migration. How to

[4] Using employment rate to replace unemployment rate are followed from all past researches for regional labor market dynamics. A possible explanation is to evaluate the magnitude of interregional migration and related statement will be expressed later.

compute the effects of interregional migration on employment can be described as (Debelle and Vickery, 1999):

$$Migration = d\ln P = d\ln N - d\ln(N/L) - d\ln(L/P) \tag{12}$$

Equation (12) shows that the changes in regional population mainly come from interregional migration and therefore the migration can be computed by the changes in employment minus both employment rate and labor force participation rate. In other words, to the extent that a regional labor demand shock is not reflected in employment or labor force participation rates, it must be absorbed by interregional migration.

COMMON LABOR MARKET ADJUSTMENT

Table 3. Common Shocks in Regional Employment, Unemployment and Labor Force Participation

Region	Employment change		Unemployment rate		Labor force participation rate	
	β	R^2	δ	R^2	ς	R^2
Taipei County	1.79	0.03	1.08	0.97	0.82	0.92
Ilan County	-3.37^{**}	0.01	0.99	0.86	1.38^{*}	0.62
Taoyuan County	0.87	0.01	1.01	0.92	0.66	0.59
Hsinchu County	-2.19	0.01	0.96	0.81	1.63	0.71
Miaoli County	1.91	0.01	1.02	0.91	0.55^{*}	0.84
Taichung county	-0.73^{*}	0.00	1.12^{*}	0.94	0.86	0.59
Changhua County	-0.76^{*}	0.00	1.05	0.94	0.88	0.64
Nantou county	2.17	0.01	1.07	0.91	0.64	0.53
Yunlin County	2.09	0.01	1.06	0.94	1.07	0.84
Chiayi County	1.73	0.01	1.13^{**}	0.91	0.74	0.85
Tainan County	2.01	0.01	1.04	0.91	1.39	0.76
Kaohsiung County	2.49	0.02	1.04	0.92	1.20^{*}	0.64
Pingtung County	1.11	0.00	1.03	0.94	0.79	0.80
Taitung County	1.35	0.00	0.94	0.72	0.84	0.44
Hualien County	-2.50	0.00	1.02	0.79	1.07	0.44
Penghu County	2.04	0.00	0.71^{**}	0.50	-0.54^{**}	0.71
Keelung City	3.89^{**}	0.03	0.66^{**}	0.64	0.72^{*}	0.44
Hsinchu City	0.85	0.00	0.91^{*}	0.73	1.49	0.74
Taichung city	-1.19^{*}	0.00	0.92*	0.85	1.03	0.61
Chiayi City	2.58	0.01	0.79^{**}	0.65	0.86	0.55
Tainan City	4.34^{**}	0.03	0.86^{**}	0.84	1.50^{**}	0.82
Taipei City	0.93	0.14	0.80^{***}	0.93	0.76^{*}	0.96
Kaohsiung City	0.93	0.05	1.04	0.91	0.60^{**}	0.84
Average	1.19	1.70%	1.03	84.52%	0.98	69.04%

Note: "*", "**", and "***" are significantly different from 1 at 10%, 5% and 1%, respectively.

We use equations from (1) to (3) to estimate the effects of national labor market on regional labor markets as Table 3. First, null hypothesis: $\beta = 1, \delta = 1\ or\ \varsigma = 1$ implies regional reactions to national changes are not different from employment, unemployment rate or labor force participation rate and there are 6, 9 and 7 regions of 23 regions in Taiwan to be found to reject the null hypothesis. That is to say, there are the different effects of national economy on regional labor markets.

Next, R^2 can express explained power of common labor market disturbances on regional labor markets. Lower R^2 implies national economy has less influence over development of regional labor markets and the regional labor market dynamics is relatively important. It is clear that very low values of R^2 (lower than 2%) for employment change by comparison with unemployment rate (84%) and labor force participation ratc (69%), so only a limited part of the movement in national economy is reflected in regional employment change. All these amount to say that the importance of regional labor market dynamics in Taiwan should be emphasized.

REGIONAL LABOR MARKETS ADJUSTMENT TO REGION-SPECIFIC DEMAND SHOCKS

In this section, we attempt to investigate regional labor market adjustment and hence shift our focus from national economy to regional analysis. More specially, it is generally believed that adjustment mechanism may vary with different business climate. When national economy is booming and some regions are relatively lagged, migration plays an important role in the adjustment of regional labor markets. However, when the nation suffers economic recession, labor force participation becomes more essential (Pekkala and Kangasharju, 2002). Thus, we will separate this research into three decades: the 1980s, the 1990s and post-2000 to investigate regional evolutions and prove the above suggestions.

From the economic data in Taiwan, it is found that the average economic growth rates of Taiwan in the 1980s, the 1990s and the post-2000 are 8.15%, 6.35% and 2.69%, respectively (the average economic growth rate during 1982 to 2004 is 6.42%). This is a process of Taiwan's economy from high growth, stable growth to recession and this provides a natural experiment to examine the different regional dynamics in different economic situations.

Regional Labor Market Adjustment in Different Decades

We will apply the impulse responses to evaluate how to react to region-specific labor demand shocks through employment rate and labor force participation rate. First, there are many criteria (AIC, HQ and BIC) to determine the maximum lag of SVAR and Breimers (1993) suggested that HQ should be preferred among these criteria. Thus, we choose the number of lag mainly from HQ test. Second, we set the restriction like (11) to estimate SVAR. Finally, we can compute and draw the impulse responses of employment, employment rate and labor force participation rate.

It is obvious that employment rate and labor force participation rate both respond to labor demand shock very little; namely, the shock is almost completely absorbed by interregional migration. Based on equation (12), the relative proportions of employment rate, labor force participation rate and interregional migration with respect to the shock are 0.80%, 5.57% and 93.63% respectively.[5]

The analysis of regional labor market dynamics has been extensively used in many studies and the related results are summarized in Table 4 by comparison with Taiwan. First, it is clear that employment (unemployment) rate mostly is not the main channel when region-specific shock happens while the regional labor market adjustment must depend on another two channels from labor force participation rate and interregional migration. More importantly, it is noteworthy that regional adjustment in Taiwan depends on the interregional migration much more than other nations. Rodgers (1999) suggested that Taiwan is the most flexible labor market in East Asia and Chiang (2008) found that the interregional migration leads to very low unemployment rate in past Taiwan. In addition, the relatively small regions as sample units will create more opportunities in interregional migration. Therefore, the result that interregional migration is regarded as major adjustment for regional dynamics should be reasonable.

During the 1980s and the 1990s periods, the impulse responses are both very similar and the only difference is the increase in the role of labor force participation rate while the importance of interregional migration slide gradually. There is little evidence on the effect of employment rate on region-specific shock.

Table 4. International Comparison of Regional Adjustment to the Shock

			Unit: %
	Employment rate	Labor force participation rate	Net migration
Europe (10 years, 166 regions)	47	32	21
Spain (19 years, 17 regions)	36	23	41
Sweden (28years, 24 regions)	8	26	66
Finland (25years, 11 regions)	27	65	8
Netherlands (7 years, 18 regions)	14	74	12
Belgium (26 years, 3 regions)	-4-22	3-33	45-99
Germany (27 years, 8 regions)	12	93	-5
Italy (27 years, 11 regions)	37	62	1
UK (27 years, 11regions)	12	91	-3
US (13years, 51states)	34	26	40
Australia (20 years, 7 states)	20	40	40
Taiwan (24 years, 23 regions)	0.8	5.6	93.6

Sources: Gacs and Huber (2005), except for Taiwan.

Notes: Except that Netherlands and Taiwan are used by quarterly and monthly data respectively, other studies are used by annual data.

[5] Another tool in VAR is variance decomposition provides information about the relative importance of each innovation in affecting all variables in VAR. However, we only focus that the effects of a shock to one endogenous variable on other variables, so impulse response functions are applied here.

It is surprising that the way of regional labor market adjustment in the post-2000 is totally different from the other periods and the labor force participation-rate channel becomes the most major adjustment mechanism. it is easy to find that the response of labor force participation rate closely mimics the pattern of the impulse in employment and hence_labor force participation rate remains to play a prominent role in absorption of the shock. All these announce that interregional migration is never the critical tool for adjusting the region specific shock.

In sum, the type of adjustment of regional labor market complies with different economic situations like Table 5: interregional migration is relatively important in adjustment of regional labor markets on economic boom while labor force participation rate is more critical to adjust the regional labor markets on economic downturns. When economic development is on the downturn, importance of interregional migration will reduce while the position of labor force participation rate promotes. This conclusion is consistent with Pekkala and Kangasharju (2002). Finally, the employment (unemployment) rate always plays a small role and this is suggested that there is the presence of natural rates of unemployment at the regional level. This investigation is consistent with Deressin and Fatas (1995) and Jiang and Liu (2005).

Table 5. Adjustment Mechanism in the Different Periods

								Unit: %
	1981-2004		1981-1990		1991-2000		2001-2004	
Adjustment Time (months)	1st month	Average of 24 months	1st month	Average of 24 months	1st month	Average of 24 months	1st month	Average of 24 months
Employment	100	100	100	100	100	100	100	100
Employment rate	0.08	0.04	-0.09	0.16	0.29	0.13	3.11	2.20
Labor force participation rate	5.57	7.69	3.21	3.02	11.60	12.07	74.56	73.86
Interregional migration	94.35	92.27	96.89	96.82	88.12	87.80	22.33	23.94

CONCLUSION

Suddenly high unemployment rate in Taiwan since 2000 attracts the interest of studies in regional labor market dynamics and this paper try to analyze the repercussions of the shocks to regional labor markets in Taiwan. Followed the excellent work of Blanchard and Katz (1992) and Decressin and Fatas (1995), we first express the extent to which labor market dynamics are mostly idiosyncratic and hence the importance of regional labor markets cannot be overemphasized.

We apply the SVAR method to evaluate the adjustment mechanism of regional labor markets when the region-specific shock rises. More specially, it is divided into three sub-periods to examine whether regional adjustment may be different on the economic cycle. It is found that interregional migration plays more roles in adjustment mechanism than any other nations and this implies that labor markets in Taiwan is more flexible and hence lead to low unemployment rate. However, when Taiwan suffers the economic recession, interregional migration backslides behind labor force participation rate and labor force participation rate turns into the main channel of regional adjustment. In addition, the very small response of unemployment rate to region-specific shock presents the regional natural rates of unemployment and hence unemployment rates in Taiwan may be difficult to improve.

REFERENCES

Barro, R., X., Sala-I-Martin. (1991). Convergence Across States and Regions. *Brookings Papers on Economic Activity, 1*, 107-182.

Blanchard, O.L., L.F. Katz. (1992). Regional Evolutions. *Brookings Papers on Economic Activity, 1*, 1-75.

Broersma, L., J. van Dijk. (2002). Regional Labour Market Dynamics in the Netherlands. *Papers in Regional Science, 81*, 343-364.

Card, D., A.B. Krueger. (1995). *Myth and Measurement: The New Economics of the Minimum Wage*. New Jersey: Princeton University Press.

Chiang, S. (2009a). The Effects of Regional Diversity on National Unemployment through Interregional Migration: New Evidence from Taiwan. *Applied Economics, 41*, 2401-2406

Chiang, S. (2009b). The Effects of Industrial Diversification on Regional Unemployment: Is the Portfolio Theory Applicable?. *Annals of Regional Science, 43*, 947-962

Debelle, G., J. Vickery. (1999). Labour Market Adjustment: Evidence on Interstate Labour Mobility. *Australian Economic Review, 32*, 249-263.

Decressin, J., A. Fatas. (1995). Regional Labor Market Dynamics in Europe. *European Economic Review, 39*, 1627-1655.

Gacs, V., P. Huber. (2005). Quantity Adjustments in the Regional Labour Markets of EU Candidate Countries. *Papers in Regional Science, 84*, 553-574.

Hwang, J., S. Chiang. (1998). Effects of the Minimum Wage on Teenage Employment in Taiwan. *Taiwan Economic Association Annual Conference Proceedings 1998*, 241-272.

Jiang, F., P.K. Liu. (2003). A Panel Study of Regional Unemployment in Taiwan: 1987-2001. *Journal of Population Studies, 31*, 1-39.

Krugman, P.R. (1995). *Geography and Trade*. Cambridge: MIT Press.

Maddala, G.S., I., Kim. (1998). *Unit Roots, Cointegration and Structural Change*. Cambridge: Cambridge University press.

Mincer, J. (1976). Unemployment Effects of Minimum Wages. *Journal of Political Economy, 84*, 87-105.

Pekkala, S., A., Kangaharju. (2002). Regional Labor Markets in Finland: Adjustment to Total versus Regional-specific Shocks. *Papers in Regional Science, 81*, 329-342.

Reimers, H. E. (1993). Lag Order Determination in Cointegrated VAR systems with Application to small German Macro-models," paper presented at ESEM, Uppsala, August 1993.

In: Labor Markets: Dynamics, Trends and Economic Impact ISBN: 978-1-61470-825-4
Editor: Samir Amine

Chapter 9

STRONG AND WEAK LABOR MARKET REGIONS IN AUSTRALIA: IMPLICATIONS FOR INDIVIDUAL EMPLOYMENT OUTCOMES

Scott Baum,[1,*] William F. Mitchell[2] and Michael Flanagan[2]
[1]Griffith School of Environment, Griffith University, Brisbane Australia
[2]Centre of Full Employment and Equity, University of Newcastle, Newcastle Australia

ABSTRACT

This chapter addresses the question of uneven performance across Australia's labor market regions and asks what impact differential labor market performance has on the job prospects of workers. Taking survey and census data for Australian functional economic regions, the chapter first reviews the dimensions of Australia's labor market performance, prior to applying a broad framework that presents the individual employment outcomes as a function of individual characteristics, personal circumstances, and labor market characteristics. The analysis finds that employment outcomes are associated with individual characteristics and circumstances plus regional labor market differentials. The findings indicate that policy designed to address labor market disadvantage needs to focus on the outcomes of a multilevel framework in order to be effective.

INTRODUCTION

Unemployment remains one of the most apparent forms of social and economic exclusion in our community. Without a job you are dependent on transfers and savings to survive. You are also stigmatised and you are also likely to be located in poverty and you are more likely to be subject to health, family break up and other social problems...The unemployed have few

[*] Email : s.baum@griffith.edu.au.

rights, indeed they are a group who can be easily stereotyped and condemned by anecdote. [1] (p 1).

As the above quote makes clear disadvantage associated with labor market outcomes—not only unemployment but also underemployment—has significant impact on an individual's ability to engage across a whole range of social activities and impacts negatively on quality of life. As the global economy once more recovers from a slowdown, attention turns to understanding the plight of individuals who lost their jobs or become otherwise disadvantaged in labor market terms and who, during the often-long recovery phase, search for meaningful engagement in the paid labor market. Within the public and academic literature questions regarding outcomes for such individuals are often framed with reference to a range of characteristics or assets held by the individual which make them less competitive in a given labor market situation. Although public debate addresses the question of jobs growth following such downturns, once growth occurs employment outcomes are viewed as a supply-side problem where disadvantaged individuals lack the requisite skills and /or motivation to reconnect successfully in the labor market. For policy makers working in this space the appropriate programmatic response is to enact active labor market policies that aim to address this shortfall in an individual's employment skills or assets.

The popularity of such supply side programs have been at their highest across the industrialised world following the OECDs 1994 job study and have certainly held sway even up to the most recent downturn in the economy. Despite the strength of these arguments within the policy realm, an alternative approach exists in parallel that focuses on a broader framework for understanding employment outcomes. Here the key questions are not necessarily how can we increase an individual's *employment assets*, but rather how can we increase an individual's *employability*. While the notion of employability is sometimes contested, [2] a broader employability framework focuses on factors such as job search and labor demand measures as well as characteristics and demographic background of any given individual. Hence it is about the relative ability of any one individual to gain meaningful labor market outcomes given the 'interaction of personal circumstances and the labor market'. [3](p viii) (Canadian Labour Force Development Board, 1994, p. viii).

The academic literature that has followed this line of argument has established the different elements of the employability model focusing on the interplay across a multi-level field of individual characteristics and broader contextual factors [4, 5, 6] (Evans et al. 1999, Kleinman et al. 1998, Hillage and Pollard 1998)(also see figure 1). In this context, an individual's opportunity structure is related to a range of social and demographic factors, information networks and the characteristics, processes and performance of the labor market in which they operate. The characteristics of an individual as they relate to employment opportunities include skills and attributes such as basic education, transferable skills, demographic characteristics and health and well-being as well as a range of personal circumstance attributes such as an individual's social and or family background and their level of social capital and extent of social networks. Empirically, there is a significant body of evidence illustrating that certain groups and individuals are more vulnerable to disadvantaged labor market outcomes. An early Australian study by Wooden [7] identified that the underemployed were more likely to be female, aged less than 25 years of age, un-married and to be from a non-English speaking background (NESB). The likelihood of being underemployed was also higher for those working in less skilled occupations and for those working in the recreation and personal services and construction industries. The more recent work by Wilkins [8] expands these findings illustrating that for males and females part-time underemployment is higher among younger than older respondents, respondents who are single and who have low levels of human capital, although for females part-time underemployment is also high for those aged 35 to 44 years and for respondents in couple families with dependent children. There is also a notable, although insignificant difference between indigenous males and other males. For full-time underutilisation, males aged 25 to 34 years were more likely to be underutilised, while for both males and females there was a higher incidence of full-time underutilisation for those from a non-English speaking background. An early US study by Nord [9] reflects these.

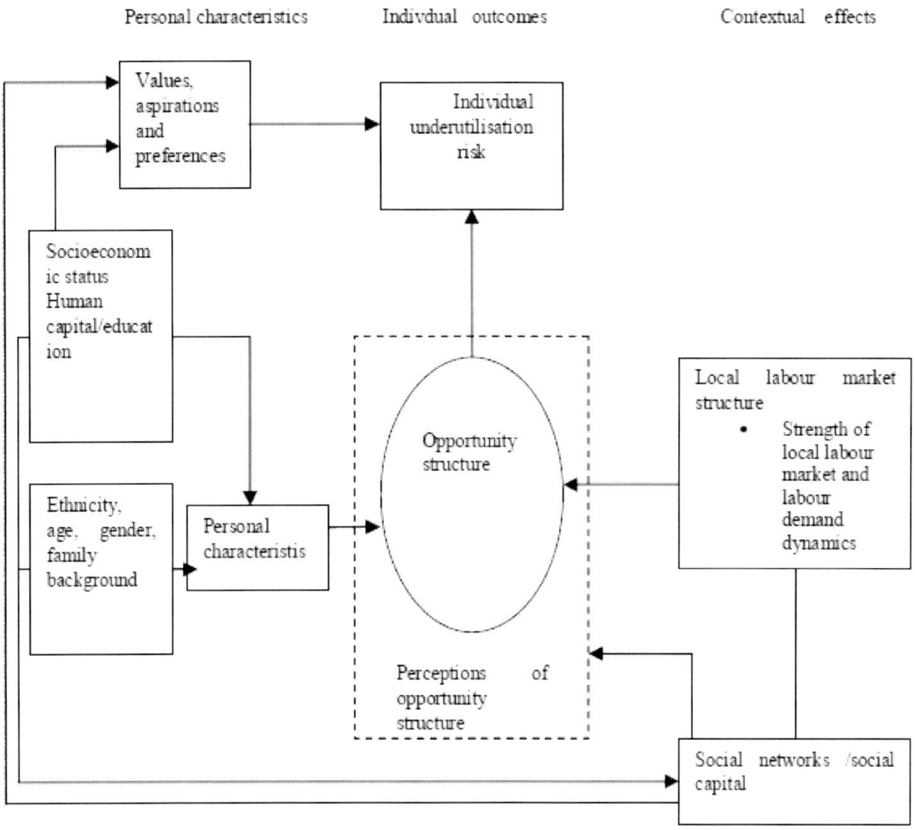

Figure 1. Conceptual Framework.

Australian findings suggesting that human capital and age are among the important factors driving the probability of an individual being underemployed. Jensen and Slack[10] report that the risk of underemployment is strongly related to age, with a u-shaped relationship— those aged 18-24 years having highest risk, with decreases with age, but increasing among those who are nearing retirement age (55–64). The risk is also higher for females, respondents from Hispanic or Native American backgrounds, respondents who were unmarried and those with low education.

These individual level factors only deal with part of the employability equation. The second part of the conceptual framework focuses on the impact of local or regional resources and is most often related to the quality, quantity and diversity of institutions at a neighbourhood or local level. It refers to 'the array of markets and institutions that provide the potential means of social mobility within which an individual may interact, such as labor, housing and financial markets, schools and the social welfare and criminal justice systems'. [11](p.6) McQuaid and Linsday [2] refer to these context effects as a range of external factors that include local labor market demand and enabling support factors such as local jobs policies. In understanding labor market outcomes the spatial organization of regional labor market opportunities is important. Although researchers such as Buck [12] question whether local labor demand can be considered as a source of local or regional contextual effect, others including Green [13], Noble and Smith [14], Gould and Fieldhouse [15] Jargosky [16], Flynn [17] and Sunley [18] all illustrate the necessity of including a regional dimension in an analysis of individual labor market outcomes. As Sunley [18](p 43) argues 'there is no such thing as a national labor market, but rather a complex geographical mosaic of overlapping local and sub-national labor markets' which will have differential effects on individual's opportunity structures and hence on employment outcomes. Early research by Nord [9] specifically considers the importance of broader labor market demand characteristics on underemployment. By including the level of service employment in the local area and the labor force participation rate Nord [9] finds that net of individual characteristics the risk of underemployment is significantly associated with these two demand-side factors. In the more recent paper by Flynn [17], labor market demand variables accounting for the availability of jobs in services and manufacturing were included, with the findings suggesting that net of the range of individual level factors the aggregate labor demand characteristics were important in explaining the risk of marginal employment outcomes. Using regional proxies for labor market demand differences Jensen [10] found that differences in regional labor market performance were significantly related to transitions into and out of underutilization, net of individual level characteristics. The use of regional proxies have been also applied in Australian research with the work by Wilkins [8] finding that the incidence of underemployment is marginally higher in major cities than in other areas. This multi-level framework sets the context for the discussion that follows. Focusing on the particular case of Australian regional labor markets the chapter argues that different human beings, based on their individual capacities (employment assets), can experience the same regional context in profoundly different ways. These differences in turn generate considerable variation in employment outcomes at the individual level. Beginning to understand these processes take up the remainder of this chapter.

Understanding Labor Market Outcomes: Context

When considering the broad conceptual framework described in the previous section it is useful to first discuss the wider regional labor market contexts as they apply to the Australian situation. Like most industrialised countries Australia's economic growth record reflects the peaks and valleys of the combined changes in both the international and national economies. In terms of labor market outcomes the impacts of recession and growth have been obvious and have included significant changes in different forms of joblessness including narrowly defined unemployment and broader measures of underemployment. For Australia, recessions in the early 1980s and 1990s had clear impacts on aggregate unemployment (figure 2) with rates sitting in excess of 10 per cent on both occasions and broader underemployment being significantly higher at more than 16 per cent in the 1980s recession and reaching 19 per cent in the 1990s recession.

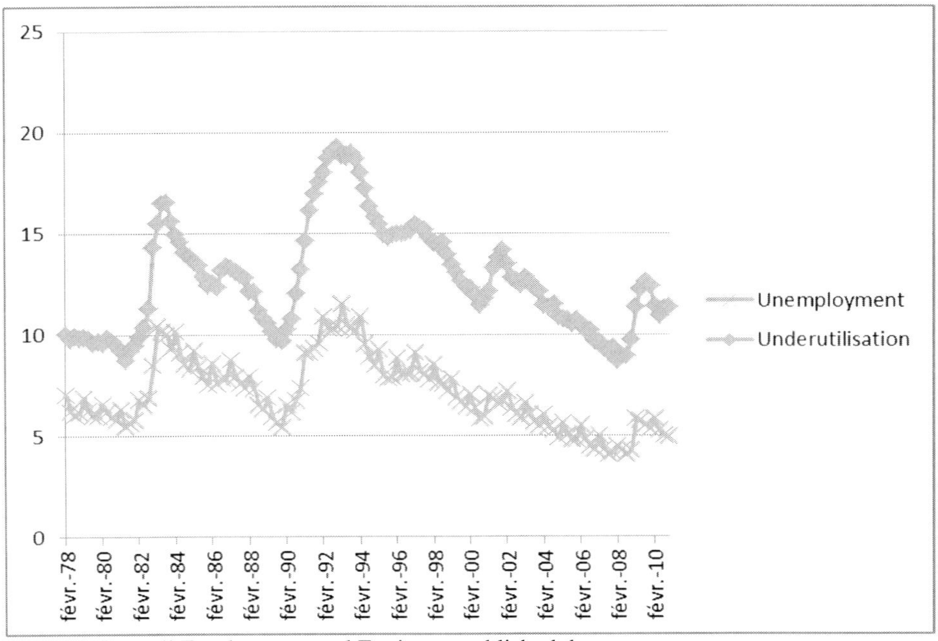

Source: Cente for Full Employment and Equity, unpublished data.

Figure 2. Unemployment and underemployment, Feb 1978 to August 2010, Australia.

Moreover, in each case the time it took for rates to return to pre-recession levels was significant meaning that the labor market impacts of these recessions were long lived. While the rate of unemployment has not risen as high during the most recent economic downturns, it is interesting to note that the broader level of underemployment has risen significantly (most recently in excess of 12 per cent) and that the gap between official unemployment rates and broader underemployment has in fact grown, pointing to the changing nature of labor market disadvantage that has occurred over recent years.

This aggregate level analysis does of course hide significant variations in labor market outcomes across competing groups with higher rates being observed between males and females, between age groups and within different industry sectors. Importantly for the discussion obtained in this chapter there are also significant regional differences in labor market outcomes. While the orthodox view of regional development would suggest that in the absence of any major barriers, labor markets should move towards some equilibrium state over time, the empirical truth is that there exists persistent differentials in labor market performance and hence labor market disadvantage across regional landscapes. Indeed as Sunley [18] (p.43) assert 'there is no such thing as a national labor market, but rather a complex geographical mosaic of overlapping local and sub-national labor markets' and we should therefore expect that there will be significant differentials across these in terms of performance. For the Australian context, much existing research has pointed to the significant disparities in employment growth rates across the country's metropolitan and regional areas, disparities which have resulted in unemployment rate differentials across the same spatial units and accompanying disadvantage. [19]

While details about broader underemployment are harder to obtain, it is possible to gain some understanding of the uneven nature of Australia's regional labor market performance, by considering data taken at the spatial level of labor market regions. The most recently available data (2011) provides an indication of the considerable variations (figure 3). During this period the unemployment rate for Australia as a whole was estimated to be 5.4 per cent, with slight variations between the rates for metropolitan regions (5.2 per cent) and non-metropolitan regions (5.8 per cent). While over half of the labor market regions had unemployment rates lower than the national rate, there was still a significant number which recorded rates higher than the national average. These included labor market regions located in large metropolitan conurbations together with regional and remote labor market regions. Significantly the differences illustrate the inability of regional labor markets act in the way orthodox arguments might assume and also the potential differences in regional labor market performance that might help explain the differential outcomes for individuals that are the focus of this chapter.

DO LABOR MARKET REGIONS MATTER FOR INDIVIDUAL EMPLOYMENT OUTCOMES?

As mentioned the main focus of this chapter is to consider the ways in which individual labor market outcomes are influenced by the uneven nature of regional labor markets. To begin to investigate this issue we can begin by asking what are the reasons that jobless people (unemployed and those classified as hidden unemployed) give for not being able to obtain work.

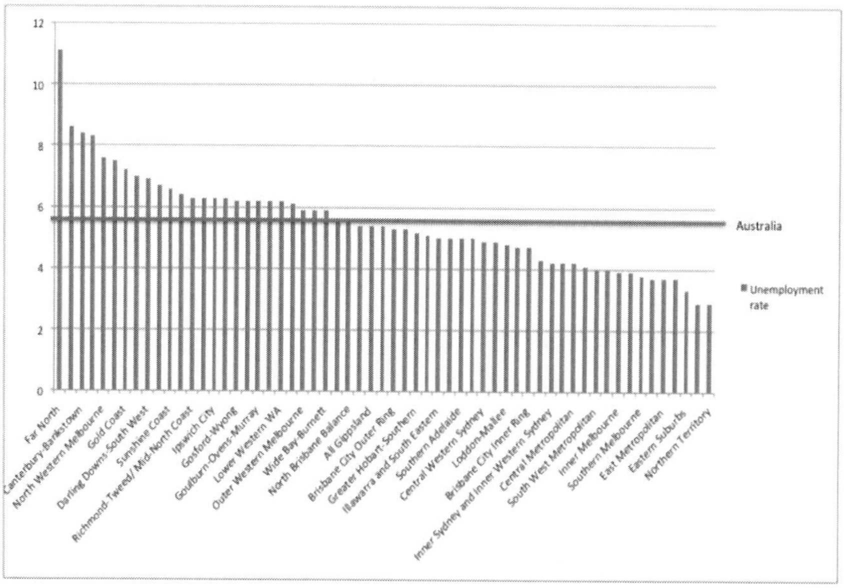

Figure 3. Unemployment rate, ABS labor market regions, 2011.

Australian data from the Household, Income and Labor Dynamics in Australia (HILDA) survey provides information on why the two classes of jobless either cannot find work or are not currently working. For those who are unemployed (table 1) many of the reasons given for not being able to find jobs relate to factors often associated with supply side arguments. The age of the respondent or perceived lack of adequate human capital—either formal qualifications or experience— were important factors as were issues such as having a health problem or disability, which acted against finding a job. Responses for males and females were similar although a higher proportion of females thought that they did not have the required education, training or skills, while slightly more males considered that employers thought the respondent was too young or to old or that the respondent did not have enough work experience. While these individual factors seemed to dominate, a separate set of responses reflected factors that might be a result of problems of demand in a local or regional labor market. Several respondents stated that they were unemployed because there were just no jobs, the jobs were too far away (transport problems / too far to travel), there was too much competition for available jobs or there were no jobs in a chosen sector or line of work. Responses for these reasons were also significant and were high for both males and females.

Table 1. Reasons for not being able to find work, unemployed persons

	Males	Females	Total
Own ill health or disability	9.4	3.4	7.0
Employers thought respondent too young or to old	13.3	11.9	12.1
Hours were unsuitable	1.7	6.8	3.7
Transport problems / too far to travel	8.3	8.5	8.4
Did not have the required education, training or skills	8.8	14.4	11.0
Did not have enough work experience	14.9	10.2	13.0
Language difficulties	3.9	3.4	3.7
No jobs in your line of work	8.8	7.6	8.4
Too many applicants for the available jobs	10.5	11.9	11.0
Just no jobs at all	6.6	5.9	6.4
Discrimination against migrant / ethnic groups	0.6	0.0	0.3
Difficulties in finding childcare	0.0	1.7	0.7
Other family responsibilities	0.0	0.8	0.3
Overqualified	0.0	0.8	0.3
Other difficulties	3.3	2.5	3.0

Source: Household, Income and Labour Dynamics in Australia (HILDA) survey 2001.

Table 2 presents the responses regarding the reason why individuals who are classified as being hidden unemployed or discouraged workers are not working. Clearly in the case of this group of jobless many of the reasons given for not currently having a job relate to a trade-off between working and attending to other personal matters such as the need to provide childcare. Over one quarter of the sample considered in this paper stated that the reason they were not actively searching for jobs was that they preferred to care for children. Other important reasons were that respondents were returning to study or that they had an illness or disability or had to care for someone else with a disability or illness. For males the single most important reason was having a disability or illness, followed by returning to study or having to care for someone else with an illness. For females the single largest reason given for not actively searching for work is the pressures of childcare. Apart from these responses, which would be placed firmly within the supply side, one response in particular—'just no jobs at all'—reflects potential demand side problems.

Table 2. Reasons for not looking for work, hidden unemployed persons

	Male	Female	Total
Have a job to go to	1.9	2.6	2.4
Own illness, injury or disability	13.3	7.8	9.1
Pregnancy/Maternity leave	0.0	2.3	1.8
Studying/returning to studies	8.0	3.4	10.4
Does not need to work	4.8	6.3	6.0
To give others a chance	1.0	0.0	0.2
Welfare payments may be affected	1.0	0.6	0.7
Moved house/holidays	3.8	3.2	3.3
Prefers to look after children	1.0	33.6	26.0
Other childcare reason	1.0	7.5	6.0
Ill health of other than self/other family reason	8.6	5.7	6.4
Too young/too old	3.8	3.2	3.3
Lacks necessary training or qualifications	1.9	2.0	2.0
Lacks necessary experience	0.0	0.3	0.2
Difficulties with language/ethnic background	0.0	1.4	1.1
No jobs available	5.7	1.1	2.2
On a job related training program	1.0	0.0	0.2
Not interested/no time	1.9	0.6	0.9
Taking a break/rest from working	4.8	1.1	2.0
Do voluntary/unpaid work	1.0	0.0	0.2

Source: Household, Income and Labour Dynamics in Australia (HILDA) survey 2001.

These findings relating to the individual reasons non-employed individuals have given for not being able to work or find a job are highly suggestive of the potential impact of labor market performance (i.e. labor demand) in addition to the usual readily identified supply side factors. To test impact of labor market performance further we construct a model that considers an individual's labor market outcome to be a function of a range of factors associated with the individual plus factors that reflate to the performance of the local labor market within which they live. In this approach, which we have applied in various situations, [20,21] we use data from the Household, Income and Labour Dynamics in Australia (HILDA) survey and fit a range of multi-nomial logit regressions with the dependent variable represented by four possible individual level labor market outcomes:

- Employed people;
- Unemployed; Persons not working but actively looking for work;

- Hidden unemployed (also known as discouraged job seekers)- persons not working and not looking for work, who would take a job if one became available.

Against these possible outcomes we consider a range of independent variables covering both individual characteristics:

- AGELS_25 Age less than 25 (1 if aged less than 25, 0 otherwise)
- AGE2544 Age 25 to 44 years (1 if aged 25 to 44, 0 otherwise)
- GENDER (1 if male, 0 if female)
- DEGREE Education at university level (1 if yes, 0 otherwise)
- POST_SECOND Education beyond high school but not university (1 if yes, 0 otherwise)
- MARRIED Marital status (1 if currently married, 0 otherwise)
- HEALTH Self reported disability or long term health issue (1 if have disability or long term health issue, 0 otherwise)
- ENG_PROF Self reported English proficiency (1 if poor or very poor English, 0 otherwise)
- ROLE_MOD measures the impact of parental employment during childhood (1 if no employed adult role model/parent, 0 otherwise);
- ISOLATION, accounting for an individual's social networks and level of social isolation is included to account for the potential impact that social networks may play in labor market outcomes and was developed using responses to questions relating to the extent to which individuals had contact with friends and colleagues.[1]

And characteristics associated with the local labor market region:

- FER_UR; the unemployment rate in the region
- FER_PT; the percentage of part time jobs available in the region
- FER_EMP_SH; the share of national employment in the region
- FER_POP_SH; the share of national population in the region
- FER_EMP_CH; the percentage change in the number of jobs in the region

In this case a labor market region relates to Centre of Full Employment and Equity Functional Economic Regions (FERs), which are similar to commuter zones and work regions used elsewhere. [22]

[1] The social network index was constructed by considering the main components from a PCA of questions coded on a five point Likert scale. The questions included in the index are: People don't come to visit me as often as I would like; I often need help from other people but can't get it; I don't have anyone I can confide in; I have no one to lean on in times of trouble; I often feel very lonely.

Individual and Personal Circumstances Model

The first three columns (2 to 4) of table 3 report the result for the relative risk of being unemployed versus employed. Largely the significant variables reflect the vast amount of research exists which purports to understand supply –side factors that predict unemployment. The two age variables are of the expected direction with only the variable accounting for those aged between 25 and 45 being significant. This age group was significantly less likely than the reference category (aged 45 to 64 years) to be unemployed. Being young (less than 25) increased the relative risk of unemployment, but was, in this case, insignificant. Gender is not significantly associated with the risk of unemployment; however being married reduces the risk of unemployment. Having poor English skills significantly increased the risk of being unemployed as did having a long term health problem or disability. The education coefficients are negatively associated with unemployment illustrating the expected inverse relationship between negative labor market outcomes and increasing levels of education. The variable ROLE_MOD accounts for the presence of positive work role models in a respondent's childhood. The positive coefficient on this variable indicates that the presence of positive role models is important to labor market outcomes and situations where such role models are absent are associated with a higher relative risk of unemployment. In line with an increasing amount of research looking at the role of personal contacts and labor market outcomes the social networks variable is negative. As the social networks measure is constructed so that higher scores indicate stronger networks or more personal contacts, the often hypothesized relationship between having stronger networks and positive job outcomes may be supported in this case. That is, individuals with a higher score on ISOLATION have a lower relative risk of unemployment.

Table 3. Regression results, individual characteristics and personal circumstances and labor market outcomes

	Unemployed			Hidden unemployed		
	Coefficient	Robust z-scores	Exp β	Coefficient	Robust z-scores	Exp β
AGELS_25	0.169	(0.92)	1.18	-0.304	(1.69)+	0.74
AGE2544	-0.207	(2.10)**	0.81	0.023	(0.25)	1.02
GENDER	-0.103	(1.11)	0.90	-0.196	(2.38)**	0.82
MARRIED	-1.340	(9.04)*	0.26	-0.720	(8.21)*	0.49
HEALTH	0.834	(5.29)*	2.30	0.864	(8.08)*	2.37
ENG_PROF	0.466	(2.54)**	1.59	0.704	(5.88)*	2.02
DEGREE	-1.186	(8.93)*	0.31	-1.490	(10.22)*	0.23
POST_SECOND	-0.564	(4.35)*	0.57	-1.182	(10.72)*	0.31
ROLE_MOD	0.667	(3.00)*	1.95	0.509	(3.49)*	1.66
ISOLATION	0.171	(3.56)*	1.19	0.108	(2.18)**	1.11
Constant	-2.357	(19.90)*		-1.807	(22.89)*	

+ significant @ 10%; ** significant @ 5%; * significant @ 1%.

The final three columns of table 3 present the results for the final category; hidden unemployed. Of the two age group variables, only one (AGELS_25) is significant suggesting that younger people are less likely to be characterized as discouraged job seekers. The gender variable has a significant coefficient and indicates that females are more likely to be classified as hidden compared to males and being married also reduces the likelihood of being classified as hidden unemployed. Having a long term health problem or disability significantly increases the risk of being discouraged. Poor English skills have a significant and positive impact on the relative risk of being hidden unemployed. The two variables accounting for education are again significant reflecting the negative association between human capital and the risk of underemployment generally. The positive coefficient on the variable accounting for having parents in paid employment during childhood indicates that the presence of positive role models is also important for understanding the risk of being classified as hidden unemployed. Finally the isolation variable is negative suggesting that the relative risk of being a hidden unemployed person is lower as the score on the ISOLATION variable increases.

Table 4. Regression results, functional economic region characteristics and labor market outcomes

	Unemployed			Hidden unemployed		
	Coefficient	Robust z-scores	Exp β	Coefficient	Robust z-scores	Exp β
FER_UR	0.129	(2.32)**	1.14	0.109	(3.46)*	1.12
FER_PT	0.024	(1.04)	1.02	0.006	(0.47)	1.01
FER_EDU	-0.017	(2.80)*	0.98	-0.013	(2.96)*	0.99
FER_EMP_SH	0.169	(2.51)**	1.18	0.158	(2.89)*	1.17
FER_GWTH_JOBS	-0.150	(1.94)+	0.86	-0.152	(2.30)**	0.86
FER_EMP_CH	-0.005	(0.56)	1.00	-0.016	(2.35)**	0.98
Constant	-4.027	(5.92)*		-2.705	(5.94)*	

+ significant @ 10%; ** significant @ 5% ; * significant @ 1%.

Functional Economic Region Model

To consider the associations between individual level labor market outcomes and the performance and characteristics of broad labor markets, a model containing only the variables associated with the functional economic regions is presented in table 4. As with the previous table columns 2 to 4 present the findings for the category unemployed versus adequately employed. Four of the functional economic region variables are significant. If the strength of the labor market within the region is measured by the overall unemployment rate, then living in a region with a weaker labor market (higher unemployment rate) increases the likelihood that an individual will be unemployed. A positive association is also reported for the national share of employment. As the share of national employment within a region increases so does the likelihood that an individual will be unemployed. Two of the variables have negative associations with unemployment. The variable FER_EDU measures the aggregate level of people with tertiary education. Glaeser and Shapiro [23] have hypothesized that a region with higher levels of aggregate skills (higher formal education) may have more success in attracting firms providing increased regional labor demand. The negative co-efficient on the education variable suggests that as the aggregate level of tertiary education increases in a region the likelihood of being unemployed falls. The final variable accounts for the percentage of jobs found in mining, government administration and defence and construction (the three highest growing industry sectors). As the proportion of jobs found in these sectors increases the likelihood of being unemployed declines.

Results for the final category—hidden unemployed—are presented in columns 5 to 7. Five out of the six functional economic region variables included are significant. As with unemployment, there is a significant positive association between being hidden unemployed and the regional unemployment rate and the share of national employment. In regions where unemployment is high or in regions with larger shares of national employment, the likelihood of being a discouraged job seeker increases. As with unemployment the aggregate level of tertiary education in the region acts to reduce the risk of being classified as hidden. Similarly the proportion of jobs in growth industries found in the region also has an off-setting impact on the likelihood of being hidden. The final significant variable is change in the number of jobs, with the likelihood of being discouraged falling in regions recording higher growth in the number of jobs.

Table 5. Regression results, individual characteristics and personal circumstances, functional economic region characteristics and labor market outcomes

	Unemployed			Hidden unemployed		
	Coefficient	Robust z-scores	Exp β	Coefficient	Robust z-scores	Exp β
AGELS_25	0.185	(0.99)	1.20	-0.292	(1.63)	0.75
AGE2544	-0.204	(2.06)**	0.82	0.031	(0.33)	1.03
GENDER	-0.086	(0.93)	0.92	-0.175	(2.05)**	0.84
MARRIED	-1.378	(9.53)*	0.25	-0.758	(8.43)*	0.47
HEALTH	0.809	(5.16)*	2.25	0.848	(7.68)*	2.33
ENG_PROF	0.497	(2.70)*	1.64	0.713	(5.81)*	2.04
DEGREE	-1.106	(7.92)*	0.33	-1.445	(9.88)*	0.24
POST_SECOND	-0.577	(4.52)*	0.56	-1.184	(10.74)*	0.31
ROLE_MOD	0.596	(2.67)*	1.81	0.443	(3.01)*	1.56
ISOLATION	0.164	(3.41)*	1.18	0.103	(2.10)**	1.11
FER_UR	0.128	(2.39)**	1.14	0.102	(3.39)*	1.11
FER_PT	0.027	(1.16)	1.03	0.013	(0.94)	1.01
FER_EDU	-0.009	(1.29)	0.99	-0.004	(0.92)	1.00
FER_EMP_SH	0.173	(2.29)**	1.19	0.128	(2.31)**	1.14
FER_GWTH_JOBS	-0.173	(2.07)**	0.84	-0.140	(2.29)**	0.87
FER_EMP_CH	-0.005	(0.68)	1.00	-0.017	(2.68)*	0.98
Constant	-3.603	(5.36)*		-2.354	(5.25)*	

+ significant @ 10%; ** significant @ 5% ; * significant @ 1%.

Individual, Personal Circumstances and Functional Economic Region Model

The final multinomial logit model includes factors measured across both individuals and the functional economic region (FER) they reside in. The combination of the two levels of variables results in some changed outcomes across the categories of labor market outcomes. Importantly, the fact that many of regional labor market variables remain significant even after the inclusion of individual level variables, provides support for the potential impact of differential regional labor market performance on individual outcomes. For the category being unemployed— the likelihood increases if an individual has a long term health issue or disability, has poor English skills, lacked an employed role model, lives in a high unemployment functional economic region or in a region with a higher share of national employment. The likelihood decreases if the individual is aged 25-44 years, is married, has a degree or some post-school education, has a lower level of social isolation and lives in a region that has a higher proportion of jobs in the three growth industries. Finally, for the category discouraged job seeker or hidden unemployed the likelihood increases if an individual has a long term health issue or disability, has poor English skills, lacked an employed role model, lives in a high unemployment functional economic region or in a region with a higher share of national employment. These are the same as the unemployed status. The likelihood decreases if the individual is male, is married, has a degree or some post-school education, has a lower level of social isolation and lives in a region that has a higher proportion of jobs in the three growth industries or lives in a region that has experienced an increase in the overall number of jobs.

CONCLUSION

This chapter begins with the premise that in order to understand the shape and functions of labor market disadvantage it is necessary to understand that while individual factors often associated with the supply-side of the labor market are likely to be important it is also important to consider the ways in which characteristics and process associated with unevenly performing spatially distinct regional labor markets will also impact on outcomes. It is certainly not surprising, given the vast amount of existing literature, to find that there was a range of factors associated with an individual's background characteristics or experience that were significantly associated with unemployment and hidden unemployment. Survey results illustrated that individual's often perceived their inability to gain a job or their lack of engagement in the paid labor force as the outcome of individual level factors and the results from a range of regression model supported these arguments. Factors such as an individual's level of human capital or education, level of health or presence or absence of role models all acted to change the relative risk of belonging to a particular labor market outcome group.

However, importantly for the arguments set out in this chapter, the strength of the local or regional labor market was also seen to be important. The background material presented illustrated the ways in which regional labor market performance varied widely across Australia and analysis of survey data illustrated that labor market outcomes at an individual level could be feasibly traced to impacts that were occurring in aggregate at the regional labor market level and reflective of issues of labor demand. When individual's were asked the reasons they were not working many responded by stating that there were no jobs, or they were too far away and the regression models performed as part of the analysis supported the argument that differentials in regional labor market performance are important. Although much existing research tends to ignore the impact of these regional labor market or demand-side factors, focusing only on the narrower supply-side influences, we have illustrated the important impact that aggregate demand variables may have. It is clear that those regional labor markets which have job deficiencies result in an increase in the risk of negative labor market outcomes, in our case labor underutilization, at the individual level net of other characteristics. This is a similar message to that presented by researchers. [13, 18, 24, 25] Deficiencies in jobs may be measured in a number of ways and the variables included in this paper suggested that while the general characteristics of the local labor market is important, it is also important to consider the potential influence of jobs growth. The upshot is that these regional labor market conditions act to ration the supply of adequate employment and interact with individual employability in negative ways.

Identifying the impact that uneven regional labor market impacts have on labor market outcomes for individual workers raises important policy questions, especially as economies attempt to improve employment outcomes across groups in society disadvantaged or left behind in the recent economic downturn. In several industrialized countries the emphasis of neo-Liberal government policy on combating labor market disadvantage is to improve personal employment prospects by introducing schemes which focus on the employment assets of the individual job seeker. However, improving the employability of individuals is, in itself insufficient and to a large extent simply reshuffles the existing queue for the available jobs. A more sustainable and successful approach is likely to include also improving the available job opportunities and considering other contextual effects. This is clearly what the broader employability framework aims to achieve. Within Australia and elsewhere labor market policies which ignore the need for this broader approach remain a significant impediment to ensuring that available workers are employed in the most efficient manner. Until these deficiencies are properly addressed the wasted human resources that are reflected in joblessness and more broadly labor underutilization will remain a significant social problem.

REFERENCES

[1] Mitchell W. and Burgess J. Unemployment should be no longer tolerated: there is an easy solution, On-line opinion, http://www.onlineopinion.com.au/view.asp?article=1380, 1991.

[2] McQuaid R. and Lindsay C. The concept of employability, *Urban Studies*, 2005, 42, 197-219.

[3] Canadian Labour Force Development Board, *Putting the pieces together: towards a coherent transition system for Canada's labour force,* Canadian Labour Force Development Board, Ottawa, 1994.

[4] Evans C. Nathan M. and Simmonds D. *Employability through Work.* Centre for Local Economic Strategies, Manchester, 1998.

[5] Kleinman, M., West, A. and Sparkes, J. Investing in employability: the roles of business and government in the transition to work, *London School of Economics,* London, 1998.

[6] Hillage J. and Pollard E. Employability: Developing a Framework for Policy Analysis, *DfEE,* London, 1998.

[7] Wooden M. 'Underemployment in Australia', *Labour Economics and Productivity* 5, September, 1993, 95-110.

[8] Wilkeins R. The Extent and Consequences of Underemployment in Australia, Melbourne Institute Working Paper no. 16/04, *Melbourne Institute of Applied Economic and Social Research,* Melbourne, 2004.

[9] Nord S. The relationships among labour-force participation, service sector employment and underemployment, *Journal of Regional Science*, 1989, 29, 407-421.

[10] Jensen L. and Slack T. `Underutilisation in America: measurement and evidence', *American Journal of Community Psychology*, 2003, 32(1/2), 21-31.

[11] Galster G. Trans-Atlantic Perspectives on Opportunity, Deprivation and the Housing Nexus, *Housing Studies*, 2002, 17, 1, 5-10.

[12] Buck N. Identifying neighbourhood effects on social exclusion, *Urban Studies*, 2001, 38, 12, 2251-2275.

[13] Green A. and Owen D. Where are the Jobless? *Joseph Rowntree Foundation and Policy Press,* Bristol, 1998.

[14] Noble M. and Smith G. Two nations? Changing patterns of income and wealth in two contrasting areas pp. 292-318 in J. Hills (ed.) *New Inequalities: The Changing Distribution of Income and Wealth in the United Kingdom*, Cambridge University Press, Cambridge, 1996.

[15] Gould M. and Fieldhouse E. Using the 1991 SAR in a multilevel analysis of male unemployment, *Environment and Planning* A, 1997, 29, 4, 611-628.

[16] Jargowsky P. *Poverty and Place: Ghettos, Barrios, and the American City*, Russell Sage Foundation, New York, 1997.

[17] Flynn N. The differential effect of labor market context on marginal employment outcomes, *Sociological Spectrum*, 2003, 23, 305-330.

[18] Sunley P. Martin R. and Nativel C. *Putting Workfare in Place: Local Labour Markets and the New Deal.* Malden, Blackwell Publishing, Massachusetts, 2006.

[19] Mitchell W.F. and Carlson E. *Regional Employment Growth and the Persistence of Regional Unemployment Disparities*, Working Paper No. 03-07, Centre of Full Employment and Equity, The University of Newcastle, Newcastle, 2003.

[20] Baum, S. and Mitchell, W. (2010) Labour underutilisation and gender: unemployment versus hidden unemployment, *Population Research and Policy Review*, 2010, 29, 233-248.

[21] Baum S. Bill A. and Mitchell W. Labour Underutilisation in Metropolitan Labour Markets in Australia: Individual Characteristics, Personal Circumstances and Local Labour Markets, *Urban Studies*, 2008, 45, 1193-1216.

[22] McCulloch A. Local labour markets and individual transitions into and out of poverty: evidence from the British household panel survey study wave 1 to 8, *Environment and Planning* A, 2003, 35, 551-568.

[23] Glaeser E. and Shapiro J. Is There a New Urbanism? The Growth of U.S. Cities in the 1990s, *NBER Working Paper* No 8357, 2001.

[24] Turok, I. and Edge, N. *The jobs gap in Britain's cities*, Policy Press and The Joseph Rowntree Foundation, Bristol, 1999.

[25] Turok, I and Webster, D. The New Deal: Jeopardised by the geography of unemployment, *Local Economy*, 1998, 1-20.

In: Labor Markets: Dynamics, Trends and Economic Impact ISBN: 978-1-61470-825-4
Editor: Samir Amine

Chapter 10

THE VOCATIONAL INTERESTS AND VALUES OF SECONDARY SCHOOL STUDENTS: A THREE-DECADE EVOLUTION IN FRANCE

*Yann Forner**
Université Lille 3, Centre de Recherche sur le Travail
et le Développement, France

ABSTRACT

This paper describes four studies, simple or naive, devoted to the evolution of representations about vocational choice of high-school students in France from the 1970s to the 2000s. These studies indicate that youth internalize very broadly social change in their vocational interests, in the general values that guide them, and in daily activities they want to do. But, more precisely, there are few links between the realities of occupations and the evolution of interests and values of youth. The first career transition (from school to first job) may often be disappointing.

INTRODUCTION

For psychologists, *interests* refer to relatively stable trends, directed to different domains of objects, activities and experiences. *Values* mean *second order* interests, they characterize the aims (like *altruism* or *knowledge*), while interests characterize the means chosen to achieve them (as *nurse* or *teacher*).

The study of these concepts has been particularly developed in counseling psychology, because of their usefullness - for example, in case of indecision. They can help to predict (statistically) career choices that are likely to be made spontaneously at school or at work. They finally allow to structure the self-representation, to keep a realistic and shared with

* Email: yann.forner@univ-lille3.fr.

others discourse about oneself, and to prepare for future career decisions. For this purposes, interests questionnaires have been used collectively in french "Education nationale" in ninth grade (ie the end of compulsory education) during the years 1970-1980 ; then their use became more individualized. Values questionnaires, too, have been used during these years, but less systematically. About these tools some informations are available: calibrations or, at least, means and standard-deviations of scores observed at these years on various groups in secondary school. This paper summarizes several studies comparing the scores on these tests of youth of 70s and youth of today.

INTERESTS AND VALUES IN PSYCHOLOGY

Interests therefore designate patterns or arrangements - relatively stable or lasting - directed to different fields of activities and experiences (Dupont and al.) in a particular cultural setting [1] and a *value* means a persistent belief that a specific mode of conduct or purpose of existence is personally or socially preferable [2] to another (Rokeach).

Studies of interests and, to a lesser extent, of values have been originally conducted to predict the spontaneous behavior of a person and, thus, to provide a basis for guidance advising. These intentions are still there but what is now important is helping the person to develop a self-representation that includes work descriptors and giving her tools for current or future decisions.

Both in theories and in their corresponding tools, direct relationships are rarely established between persons and occupations but intermediate constructs are installed. These constructs (ie the measured characteristics) were initially formulated in *dimensions* [3] of interests or values (Larcebeau, for example.) They are now also formulated in personal and professional *types* under the influence of Holland's proposals [4]. Interests and values fall logically to a psychology of motivation: the study of factors that trigger the activity, direct, maintain it and make it stop. According to Super [5] (see also Tétreau [6]), the basic concept is that of *need*, which means a basic form of relationship with the world, fundamental physiological needs or developed psychological needs.

Roe described the differential effects of family background on tthe preferencie of the child - and therefore also on its future interests of adolescent and adult - such as changes in Maslow's hierarchy of needs [7]. However, because of their relatively stable or sustainable aspect and their interindividual variability, interests and values are in practice considered as a part of personality. Needs cannot, in fact, be usually and directly satisfied in the complex social realities of working life and they must be re-expressed in terms of goals and means. This reformulation needed for a more elaborate motivational functioning is supported by structures within the personality.

Needs reformulation has been analyzed in terms in a psychology of interests initially based on assessments conducted with inventories. The explanations for the success of these tools are: usability, playfulness, low psychological constraints imposed to the person, possible collective evaluations and metrological qualities: according to Prediger, fidelity is usually high [8] as predictive validity, although it may have been overstated [9] (Spokane and al, 2000). Needs reformulation can also be done in terms of values.

In the study of values in psychology, the princeps author has been Spranger (see Helkama [10]). He outlined six major ways to organize his life (*Lebensformen*), that is to say six core values to guide and stimulate self-activity: theoretical, economic, aesthetic, social, political and religious. These values were translated in six persons: - the theoretical man who wants to think and understand - the economic man who thinks in terms of profits and profitability, - the man who seeks the aesthetic beauty and harmony - the social man that values altruism and love of neighbor - the man of power led by the needs of admiration and gratitude, and - the religious man in search of absolute and transcendent. Most authors have been subsequently marked by his designs.

Values - such as interests - were then subjected to a little theorized psychology, affirmed Roe and Ester, values theory has little to offer except a tinkering of structural models [11]. Due to a lack of theoretical research, the origins of differences remain poorly understood and this would also be true for research on value changes over time.

This criticism is unwarranted, in part because values have been variously studied: the differentiel standpoint has been the founding approach because values make sense in psychology since individual differences are assessed. From a cognitive standpoint, values allow the passage of a simple operation (such as meeting a need) to a complex operation (such as constructing a project) and allow decision making by evaluating facts.

From a standpoint of social psychology, values are conceived as internal reflections of reality that allow stabilization and sharing of representations. Worthy and desirable *ways of being*, ideal for action in a particular social group, they could be elements of the Bourdieu's *habitus* [12]. From a developmental standpoint, the formation of a stable system of values contributes to the construction of identity in adolescents and young adults.

They provide general guidelines for action which may be more accessible to representation when they are formulated in terms of persons: it's Holland's approach when he describes both the world of persons and the world of occupations with *types* (realistic, investigative, artistic, social, entrepreneur and conventional) for providing a method of transition from individuals to occupations [4] [13]. Harris-Bowlsbey, Rayman and Bryson said that these types allow the translation of a "psychtalk", a psychological discourse about persons into an "occtalk", a professional speech on occupations [14].

Rokeach took into account a set of 18 terminal values (characterizing goals) and 18 instrumental values (characterizing behaviors) [2]. Other models of the values are more detailed but also less easy to memorize, such as Schwartz who first placed 56 values on a continuum, then summarized them into 10 values organized along two axes: openness to change / conservatism on the one hand, development of self / self-transcendence on the other [15]. The unity of the concept of value has be discussed: values that guide the behavior of the autonomous individual do they cover the same realities as those that are advocated for social organization ? Wojciszke estimates that there are two consistencies: one between skills (or abilities) and individual values, the other between moral and community values [16]. It should be noted that psychologists have been especially interested in personal values.

Determinants of interests and values have been studied. Among these determinants - or variability factors - one can distinguish "personal" factors. Gender, abilities and personality traits are the most studied of these personal factors. Other determinants are "contextual": family, school, leisure experiences, work experiences or friendships. Other determinants, yet more "distant", were considered and their effects described, such as cultural differences. For better describing these distant effects of the environment, should also be considered temporal variations, including effects on the overall development of society.

The links between gender and interests or values are classic, compelling and important. Since Strong, it became necessary to differentiate between genders the intensity of interests and even, sometimes, their nature or structure [17]. Larcebeau opposed scientific, technical and sports interests (where the average for boys is stronger) with artistic, altruistic and business interests (where the average for girls is higher) [18]. Similarly, Botteman and al. opposed relatively more *masculine* interests (mechanics or outdoors), and relatively more *feminine* interests (social service or office work) [19]. Structural differences were considered: Lapan and al. using factor analysis identified a dimension of *care* specific to women [20]. For values, differences seem less marked and are less studied, except for Holland's types. Other psychological studied determinants were mostly personality traits and abilities.

The links between interests (or values) and personality are logically understandable, but they are weak, rarely exceeding .30 (Ackerman and Heggestad [21]; Rolfhus and Ackerman [22]. Interests and values are described as simple concurrent features: Larson and al. note the structural analogy between the model in five personality factors (openness, conscientiousness, extraversion, agreeableness and neuroticism) and the six Holland's types, they also note the logical structure of correlations and their weakness [23].

Values and interests may be conceived as effects of the (causal) organization of personality: thus, the hexagonal or circular organisation of Holland's types would be determined by the importance of two independent psychological factors. Acoording to Prediger and Vansickle, these factors could be opposite attractions: "people / objects" and "ideas / data" [24] ; according to Rounds and Tracey, this could be dimensions of personality "sociability" and "conformism" [25].

Links between interests and skills are, too, logical and weak. In Strong's conception, interest is an effect of success, and success is under the influence of skill [17]. In Bandura's social cognitive theory (see Betz, [26]), relations between interest and performance are reversed: success in a task is possible only if the person has first accepted the task, that is she was interested in. Interest, as others forms of motivation, would depend on the feeling of *competence*, which would explain the variations of interests including differences between genders (Donnay and Borgen [27]). "Value" could be easily substitute to "interest" in these designs (where interests are often assessed by Holland's types).

Among the determinants of interests that have been described, genetic influences seem indisputable for Betsworth and al., but they are perhaps not the most interesting in psychology and, mainly, environmental factors were studied [28]. And the first *proximal* determinants taken in account by Vrignaud and Bernaud [29] are: family, school, leisure experiences, professional or pre-professional experience and friendly relations, that they boil down to using a meta-factor of "cultural resources". The basic process of acquisition would be learning, either direct or through models imitation. There could be more complex processes controlled by a regulator of behaviours: self-concept.

Thus, for Gottfredson, determining the attractiveness of an occupation is computing its proximity to the self-concept, mainly in terms of gender and prestige [30]. Similarly, according to Huteau and Vouillot, the appeal of a specific curriculum (literary or scientific, for example) would result from measuring the difference between self-representation and representation of typical students of the various curricula [31].

In addition to these determinants of the surrounding environment, others were considered remote. Cultural differences have been studied by comparing - groups of people from different countries (Fouad and Dancer [32]) and of - groups within a same country, but which differ in their cultural, social or ethnic origin (Lattimore and Borgen [33]). Often conducted with Holland's typology, they tend to show some differences mainly rather secondary in structures of values essentially identical: Day and Rounds, for example, noted that this structure varies little between *Caucasian*, *African*, *Hispanic* and *Asian* Americans [34].

The question of a general evolution of interests and values doesn't appear to have been asked, unlike the evolution of intelligence which has been well documented since the landmark article of Flynn [35].

Perhaps the answer is too obvious (?) but changes in interests and values of young people seem to be taken into account only when they are problematic. For example, the growing disaffection of sciences and the current enthusiasm for social sciences are deplored (Ourisson, [36]) in many developed countries and the number of scientific students tend to diminish alarmingly.

Explanations are hesitant: scientific teachings are considered "unattractive"... (?). The question of a general evolution of these preferences must be asked (Bréchon [37]). The present study focuses on two potential determinants of values: the major developments in the world of work and the expected weakening of gender differences in workplace representations.

- According to Holland, stereotypes about occupationss are "true" [4]: different jobs require different behaviors, these differences are stable and perceived as such. But are these differences really stable in the long run ? The evolution of the world of work during the past three decades (which could be quickly characterized: minimization of employment in the primary and secondary sectors, development of services, *tertiarization* of all activities, development of various forms of communication, increasing complexity, institutionalization of leisure but also rising unemployment, growing insecurity, etc.) should cause an isomorphic change of interests and values.
- The general evolution of the vocational world could also be marked by a relative erasure of gender as determinant of social roles. According to Gottfredson, occupational preferences vary according to a developing self-representation [30] organized successively on size (3-5 years), gender (6-9), social status (10-13) and finally - identity (from 14 years). So are expected, at the end of high school education: an effect of gender in determining work preferences, and moderate effects of other determinants. Is this effect unchangeable?

  According to Hansen gender differences of interests and values are stable in their organization, but progressively decrease [38]. Observations don't seem consistent, despite the social changes [...] and despite efforts to eliminate gender bias in the items of interests inventories [...], scores obtained by men and women in these inventories continue to highlight patterns [...] of different interests (Tetreau [6]).

These two assumptions, naive but fundamental, guided several researches on interests and values of french high-school students (Forner and al. [39] [40] [41] [42]). These researches are here summarized.

The Evolution of Vocational Interests of High-School Students

Occupations are unstable: consider computers - over time some occupations disappeared (drill-checker), others appeared (home automation), any changed (programmer). One solution would be to study interest in various occupations of the same professional field. Reasoning on groups of occupations is necessary but occupations relevant to the person. This double requirement, stability and interest, leads to study the evolution of the attraction for groups of occupations defined by a common underlying interest.

Survey

200 male and 337 female students of eleventh form completed one or another form of the Questionnaire d'Intérêts pour des Professions (QIP / m for boys and QIP / f for girls), built by Larcebeau [43]. Using Kuder's ipsative or relative approach, the test determines, relatively to the average of the group (same gender, same form and the same type of curriculum), the importance of eight categories of occupational interests: literary, artistic, scientific, sports, altruistic, administrative, technical and business relationships. These categories are common to both genders, and two are specific: nature-type is specific to the male form of the test, and home-type to the female form (!).

The QIP / m has 10 items, each consisting of 9 proposals should be classified by descending order of preference. Example item 1 request to order the following occupations: Archivist (lit), Soloist (art), Biologist (sci), Mountain guide (spo), ... rehabilitation of handicapped children (alt), Horticulturist (nat), Tax collector (adm), Optician (tec) Insurer (bus).

For QIP / f, 9 proposals for item 1 are: Librarian (lit), Modelist in haute couture (art), Botanist (sci), Sports coach (spo), Psychotherapist (alt), Professor of cutting and sewing (hom), Librarian (adm), computer programmer (tec), Representative of a publishing home (bus). Each category of interest being shown 10 times, raw scores range from "10" (maximum interest) to "90" (minimum interest).

The questionnaire has been built for students of eleventh and twelvth grades (final grades of secondary school) and calibrated on groups of students following a literary or economic and social curriculum (A or B in 1970; L or ES in 2005) or a scientific curriculum (C or D in 1970, S in 2005). Data were collected in four public high schools. Results were compared with those obtained in 1970.

Data processing has been performed using SPSS software.

Interests Evolutions

Consider the categories for which sharp variations appear (Table 1). Categories for which there is a decrease: Nature-type occupations (data specific to boys), scientific occupations and, more weakly, technical occupations. Categories for which there is an increase: home-type occupations (data specific to girls) administrative occupations (only among girls) and business relationships.

Table 1. Vocational interests: evolution between 1970 and 2005 according to gender and curriculum: test t, significance and size of effect

Occupational interests	Gender	Curriculum	t-test	Significance	Sizeof effect
"nature"	Boys	Literary	3.04	p< .01	**-.45**
		Scientific	4.20	p< .01	**-.53**
technical	Boys	Literary	1.74	N. S.	+.24
		Scientific	2.93	p< .01	**-.37**
	Girls	Literary	1.29	N. S.	-.12
		Scientific	2.75	p< .01	**-.30**
Scientific	Boys	Literary	1.15	N. S.	-.16
		Scientific	2.18	p< .01	**-.28**
	Girls	Literary	8.42	p< .01	**-.77**
		Scientific	4.35	p< .01	**-.68**
Literary	Boys	Literary	3.36	p< .01	**-.51**
		Scientific	.22	N. S.	-.03
	Girls	Literary	1.43	N. S.	-.15
		Scientific	.25	N. S.	-.03
Altruistic	Boys	Literary	1.87	N. S.	-.26
		Scientific	.00	N. S.	+/-.00
	Girls	Literary	1.10	N. S.	+.11
		Scientific	.77	N. S.	-.09
Sport	Boys	Literary	1.49	N. S.	+.23
		Scientific	.29	N. S.	+.04
	Girls	Literary	3.07	p< .01	**-.28**
		Scientific	1.43	N. S.	-.16
Artistic	Boys	Literary	1.55	N. S.	+.21
		Scientific	2.44	p< .02	+.30
	Girls	Literary	.08	N. S.	+.01
		Scientific	5.33	p< .01	**+.58**
"Home"	Girls	Literary	6.21	p< .01	**+.57**
		Scientific	3.82	p< .01	**+.40**
Administrative	Boys	Literary	2.82	p< .01	**+.40**
		Scientific	2.86	p< .01	**+.35**
	Girls	Literary	.24	N. S.	-.02
		Scientific	.14	N. S.	-.02
Business	Boys	Literary	3.87	p< .01	**+.58**
		Scientific	4.33	p< .01	**+55**
	Girls	Literary	5.82	p< .01	**+.57**
		Scientific	3.19	p< .01	**+.38**

Read, for each category of interests, gender, type of education, value of the Student test, corresponding level of significance and size of effect. The latter is assessed by the difference of average 1970 (m) and 2005 (m ') relative to the standard deviation of 1970 (s) or d = (m' - m) / s, the sign of this size indicates a decrease (-) or an increase (+).

For example, the interest for nature-type occupations, which were presented only to boys (!), fell half a standard-deviation among both among literary (t = 3.04 p <.01, d = -. 45) and among scientific (t = 4.20; p <.01, d = -. 53) students.

Differences between Genders

Boys and girls do not answer strictly to the same items in these questionnaires; comparisons of their mean scores are impossible. Yet it is usually considered that even if the metrics are different, the constructs they use (the categories of interests) are comparable with the exception of interests such as "nature" and "home". If we cannot measure differences in trends, we can compare the effect of changes in girls and in boys: are they concordant (the signs are the same) or discordant (the signs are different)?

Without going into detailed analysis of data and with the notable exception of administrative jobs (for which the interests of boys initially lower are finally in line with those of girls), the last column of Table 1 shows clearly variations of the same direction in both groups. This observation is not decisive but rather calls for a continuation of differences between genders.

Replication

The process was repeated with a sample of 181 boys and 268 girls. The results were compared with those obtained in 1970. The results (Table 2) consistent with the previous ones: - decrease in interest for scientific, technical, and nature-type vocations, - increase of interest for administrative (for males), business, and home-type occupations, plus artistic occupations. Evolution of differences between genders are comparable to previous operation even though the group of "literary" boys seems specific.

Discussion

An adaptive behavior may be seen: evidence for three decades, primary and secondary sectors have lost and are loosing jobs, while business relations have now invaded the whole space of the global village. It should however be noted that adaptation can hardly explain the decline of interest for scientific occupations for which demands are increasing.

Two processes may be seen: on the one hand, a decline in the value of knowledge (disqualified by internet), on the other hand, a rise in the value of power (a consequence of the widespread economic war). Note that the higher interest of girls in home-type occupations is difficult to reconcile with the general evolution of ideas on genders.

Table 2. Replication. Vocational interests: evolution between 1970 and 2005 according to gender and curriculum: test t, significance and size of effect

Occupational interests	Gender	Curriculum	t-test	Significance	Size of effect
"nature"	Boys	Literary	2.53	p< .02	-.40
		Scientific	5.98	p< .01	**-.73**
technical	Boys	Literary	2.26	p< .05	+.34
		Scientific	4.01	p< .01	**-.51**
	Girls	Literary	1.83	N. S.	-.26
		Scientific	2.81	p< .01	**-.33**
Scientific	Boys	Literary	.35	N. S.	-.06
		Scientific	2.03	p< .01	**-.26**
	Girls	Literary	7.12	p< .01	**-.70**
		Scientific	2.52	p< .01	**-.33**
Literary	Boys	Literary	3.86	p< .01	**-.66**
		Scientific	.46	N. S.	+.06
	Girls	Literary	1.61	N. S.	-.18
		Scientific	.27	N. S.	-.07
Altruistic	Boys	Literary	.35	N. S.	+.05
		Scientific	.49	N. S.	+.06
	Girls	Literary	2.97	p< .01	**-.30**
		Scientific	1.08	N. S.	-.13
Sport	Boys	Literary	1.69	N. S.	+.27
		Scientific	.28	N. S.	+.04
	Girls	Literary	1.97	p< .05	-.21
		Scientific	1.17	N. S.	-.15
Artistic	Boys	Literary	2.26	p< .05	-.35
		Scientific	2.40	p< .02	**+.28**
	Girls	Literary	2.86	p< .01	**+.30**
		Scientific	2.65	p< .01	**+.33**
"Home"	Girls	Literary	5.60	p< .01	**+.54**
		Scientific	2.58	p< .01	**+.31**
Administrative	Boys	Literary	2.21	p< .05	**+.33**
		Scientific	3.45	p< .01	**+.43**
	Girls	Literary	2.44	p< .02	-.24
		Scientific	1.65	N. S.	-.20
Business	Boys	Literary	2.71	p< .01	**+.44**
		Scientific	5.74	p< .01	**+1.21**
	Girls	Literary	4.97	p< .01	**+.52**
		Scientific	6.98	p< .01	**+.63**

The Evolution of Values of High-School Students

Survey

Three samples were considered: the current sample (2005) and two previous samples, one observed in 1977 and another in 1981. The 2005 sample had 365 participants: 124 boys (34%) and 241 girls (66%). The ages ranged from 16 to 20 years at an average of 17.59 years with a standard-deviation of 0.77 years. The 1977 sample included 1059 participants: 402 males (38%) and 657 girls (62%). The 1981 sample consisted of 719 participants: 338 boys (47%) and 341 girls (53%). The age distribution is not known for these two samples.

The data have been processed with SPSS.

The *Questionnaire d'Intérêts et de Valeurs*, QIV, has been built by Larcebeau to assess values of high-school students in eleventh grade and higher [43] Using, as the QIP, an ipsative approach, it allows computing 5 scores - relative to the average of the group (same sex, same level, a,d same type of education): - "T (theory): value attributed to objective knowledge and resulting in scientific interests. - "E: aesthetic values expressing the importance given to art and culture and a search of formal perfection, resulting in literary and artistic interests." - "D (dominance): value for power and influence, interest for business and public relations." - "A: altruistic values, concern for the well-being and moral satisfaction of others, resulting in social interests." - "P: practical values resulting in a physical search of profitability, a certain realism and a taste for concrete achievements, most often accompanied by technical interests".

The QIV consists of two parts. The first comprises 40 items which offer choosing one in two values. The second part includes 12 items, each consisting of 5 proposals that should be classified by descending order of preference (a strong interest will be indicated by a low score). For each value, combining the scores of parts 1 and 2 is possible as follows: Total score = 3 (score 1) + 60 - (score 2).

For example, item 1 of the first part offers a choice of an activity 1 corresponding to the aesthetic value and another activity 2 corresponding to the practical value: "You prefer to visit ... a - an exhibition of painting, b - an exhibition of automobiles. Each category of values being presented 16 times, the raw scores of the first part range from "0" (minimum interest) to "16" (maximum interest).

Table 3. Equivalence between modes of categorization: Values (QIV), Holland's types and Interests (QIP)

QIV	Holland	QIP
Theoretical	Investigative	Scientific (Technical)
Aesthetic	Artist	Literary, Artistic
Dominance	Entrepreneur	Administrative, Business
Altruistic	Social	Altruistic
Practical	Realistic, Conventional	Nature, Sport (Techniques)

The item 1 of the second part request to order the proposals respectively corresponding values: theoretical, dominance, aesthetic, practical and altruistic: "You prefer to occupy leisure time: a - reading to enrich your knowledge on a topic that interests you, b - discussing with your classmates to try to make them share your ideas, c - attending a theatrical performance, d - doing odd jobs or any manual labor, d - organizing the leisure of young children ". Each value being presented 12 times, raw scores of this second part range from "12" (maximum interest) to "60" (minimum interest).

Table 3 presents a system of equivalence between modes of categorization: QIV, Holland, QIP.

Comparison of Samples from 1977 and 2005

Read in Table 4 that the boys of literary or economic and social curriculum obtained in the first part of the test in theoretical values stronger scores in 1977 (m= 6.40 s= 2.68) than in 2005 (m= 5.44 s= 1.92), the difference is not significant (t= 1.44, N. S.). The effect (-. 36) would be decreasing (the sign is negative) about one third of the standard deviation.

In the second part of the test (where a low score corresponds to a strong interest in) the boys' theoretical values are higher in 1977 (m = 34.16, s= 5.89) than in 2005 (m= 40.50, s= 4.81), the difference being significant (t= 9.14, p <.01) and the effect of one standard deviation (-1.08).

Table 4. Theoretical values in 1977 and 2005 according to gender, curriculum, and task: mean (standard deviation), size of effect and t-tests

Curriculum	Gender	Part of the test	1977	2005	Size of effect	t - test
Literary and economics	Boys	1	6.40 (2.68)	5.44 (1.92)	-.36	1.44 (n. s.)
		2	34.16 (5.89)	40.50 (4.81)	**-1.08**	9.14 (p< .01)
	Girls	1	6.23 (2.26)	5.84 (2.22)	-.18	1.43 (n. s.)
		2	35.88 (5.87)	40.74 (5.45)	**-.83**	6.95 (p< .01)
Scientific	Boys	1	9.07 (2.93)	7.95 (3.05)	**-.38**	3.10 (p< .01)
		2	29.47 (6.76)	34.75 (8.06)	**-.78**	6.13 (p< .01)
	Girls	1	7.71 (2.53)	6.55 (2.57)	**-.46**	4.02 (p< .01)
		2	32.23 (6.86)	38.75 (6.27)	**-.95**	8.00 (p< .01)

Table 5. Aesthetical values in 1977 and 2005 according to gender, curriculum, and task: mean (standard deviation), size of effect and t-tests

Curriculum	Gender	Part of the test	1977	2005	Size of effect	t - test
Literary and economics	Boys	1	9.45 (3.34)	9.78 (3.44)	+.10	.63 (n. s.)
		2	35.28 (8.79)	33.00 (9.49)	+.26	1.61 (n. s.)
	Girls	1	9.54 (2.71)	10.45 (2.26)	**+.34**	2.87 (p< .01)
		2	33.70 (8.28)	32.27 (6.97)	+.17	1.47 (n. s.)
Scientific	Boys	1	7.24 (2.89)	8.27 (2.39)	**+.36**	3.02 (p< .01)
		2	40.14 (7.99)	38.71 (6.54)	+.18	1.52 (n. s.)
	Girls	1	8.51 (2.74)	9.57 (2.16)	**+.39**	3.57 (p< .01)
		2	36.92 (7.62)	36.32 (6.43)	+.08	.72 (n. s.)

Table 6. Dominance values in 1977 and 2005 according to gender, curriculum, and task: mean (standard deviation), size of effect and t-tests

Curriculum	Gender	Part of the test	1977	2005	Size of effect	t - test
Literary and economics	Boys	1	6.83 (3.13)	6.61 (3.09)	-.07	.27 (n. s.)
		2	36.10 (7.76)	33.56 (8.12)	+.32	1.23 (n. s.)
	Girls	1	5.49 (2.36)	6.02 (2.25)	+.22	1.88 (n. s.)
		2	40.83 (7.14)	38.53 (6.22)	**+.32**	2.73 (p< .01)
Scientific	Boys	1	5.21 (2.54)	6.92 (2.29)	**+.55**	5.63 (p< .01)
		2	40.88 (6.98)	35.74 (6.47)	**+.74**	6.12 (p< .01)
	Girls	1	4.21 (2.21)	5.45 (2.21)	**+.29**	4.93 (p< .01)
		2	43.02 (6.83)	38.41 (6.42)	**+.70**	6.02 (p< .01)

The size of effect was assessed by the difference in means of 1977 and of 2005 reported to the standard deviation of 1977: d = m(2005) - m(1977) / s(1977). The significance of difference was assessed by a t-test. "d" is positive when the difference between means increases and negative when it decreases.

Theoretical values decrease between 1977 and 2005: the 8 measurements, of which 6 are significant, indicate all a decline. The observation is independent of the curriculum, of the gender of participants and the of type of task: choosing (Part 1) or ranking (part 2). The median effect would be large enough, about half or two thirds of the deviation.

Aesthetic values are increasing moderately. All the 8 measurements increase, even if only 3 are significant (see Table 5). The median effect is rather low, about a quarter of the deviation. Dominance values are increasing (see Table 6). 7 of 8 measurements are in this sense (of which 5 are significant). The median effect appears average, about one third of the standard deviation. Altruistic and practical values reveal neither homogeneous nor significant differences.

The Evolution of Differences between Genders

Read (Table 7) that in 1977 the boys in literary or economic curriculum had stronger theoretical values (mg= 6.40 sg= 2.68) in the first part of the test (denoted "theory 1") than girls (mf= 3.23 sf= 2.61). The difference between the means reported a combination of the standard-deviations was +.07 for 1977. Read, then, data for 2005.

For a given year, the size of the difference between the averaged value by gender was assessed by: d = (mf- mg) / swith s = (ng.sg + nf'.sf / (ng + nf).

The difference between the means of boys and girls has been reported to a composition of the standard deviations of these groups, rather than either of their standard deviations, the use report the average difference in standard deviation of the control group did not make sense here. The same procedure was followed for groups observed in 2005.

For each value, the estimated gap in 1977 and the gap in 2005 are interpreted in terms of evolution of this value. Compare the columns "d1" (1977) and "d2" (2005) of Table 7 or read directly the "evolution" column, which gives the difference between the absolute values of differences. A "positive" (ie carrying a sign "+") evolution corresponds to an increase of a difference.

On all 18 measurements, differences appear: 11 increases, 6 decreases and 1 situation is stable. So, it is impossible to conclude to an overall trend of evolution of the differences. More precisely, for a given value, there is no homogeneous evolution: for the theoretical values, for example, there are two increases, one decrease and one lack of progress, while for the aesthetic values are observed two increases and two decreases.

Table 7. Values in 1977 and 2005 according to curriculum, gender: mean (standard deviation), difference between genders and evolution

		1977			2005			
Values	Curriculum	Boys	Girls	d1	Boys	Girls	d2	Evolu-tion
Theoretical 1	L and ES	6.40 (2.68)	6.23 (2.26)	+.07	5.44 (1.92)	5.84 (2.22)	-.18	+.11
	S	9.07 (2.93)	7.71 (2.53)	+.50	7.95 (3.05)	6.55 (2.57)	+.50	+/-.00
Theoretical 2	L and ES	34.16 (5.89)	35.88 (5.87)	+.29	40.50 (4.81)	40.74 (5.45)	+.05	-.24
	S	29.47 (6.76)	32.23 (6.86)	+.41	34.75 (8.06)	38.75 (6.27)	+.56	+.15
Aeshetic 1	L and ES	9.45 (3.34)	9.54 (2.71)	-.03	9.78 (3.44)	10.45 (2.26)	-.23	+.20
	S	7.24 (2.89)	8.51 (2.74)	-.45	8.27 (2.39)	9.57 (2.16)	-.57	+.12
Aesthetic 2	L and ES	35.28 (8.79)	33.70 (8.28)	-.62	33.00 (9.49)	32.27 (6.97)	-.09	-.53
	S	40.14 (7.99)	36.92 (7.62)	-.41	38.71 (6.54)	36.32 (6.4)	-.09	-.32
Dominance 1	L and ES	6.83 (3.13)	5.49 (2.36)	+.53	6.61 (3.09)	6.02 (2.25)	+.22	-.31
	S	5.21 (2.54)	4.21 (2.21)	+.42	6.92 (2.29)	5.45 (2.21)	+.65	+.23
Dominance 2	L and ES	36.10 (7.76)	40.88 (7.14)	+.65	33.56 (8.12)	38.53 (6.22)	+.75	+.10
	S	40.88 (6.98)	43.02 (6.83)	+.31	35.74 (6.47)	38.41 (6.42)	+.41	+.10
Altruistic 1	All	8.41 (3.26)	10.33 (3.20)	-.60	7.71 (2.64)	9.63 (2.64)	-.75	+.15
Altruistic 2	All	34.11 (8.31)	29.09 (8.50)	-.50	33.81 (6.67)	28.36 (7.21)	-.78	+.28
Practical 1	L and ES	8.55 (3.12)	7.99 (2.67)	-.20	10.06 (2.34)	8.88 (2.31)	-.51	+.31
	S	9.58 (2.77)		-.78	9.51 (2.62)		-.26	-.52
Pratical 2	L and ES	39.01 (7.64)	38.35 (7.05)	+.09	39.61 (6.27)	37.99 (5.64)	-.28	+.19
	S	34.47 (7.56)		-.56	35.92 (7.12)		+.34	-.22

Discussion

Observed data are in line with assumptions: changes in career interests may be at least partially explained by a devaluation of knowledge and an overvaluation of power. But what about aesthetic values and interests for an artistic career ? Recent data are consistent, but do not enroll in one or other of the processes taken into account. They could be explained by a third process that is self-fulfillment. Let's caricature: art for women and sport for men ?

GENERAL INTERESTS AT THE END OF NINTH GRADE

Survey

Two samples, one from 1978 and another in 2004, were compared for their scores in QIm4, 3.2. The study participants were 482 students from ninth grade to college: 258 girls (53.5%) and 224 boys (46.5%) enrolled in public schools. The ages of subjects ranged from 13 to 17 years at an average of 15.04 years with a standard deviation of 0.64 years. The *Questionnaire d'Intérêts mixte*, QIm, 4,3,2, has been developed by Larcebeau [44]. This questionnaire is *mixed* in the sense that boys and girls answer the same questions and therefore have comparable scores. The test consists of 12 series each consisting of 9 items or proposals. For each series, the participant must choose the three items that appeal to him - relatively - the most and the 3 items that appeal to him - relatively, too - the least. Each set includes an item corresponding to the categories of interests: 1) literary, 2) artistic, 3) scientific and technical, 4) altruistic, 5) trade, 6) sport, 7) practical, 8) nature, 9) business.

Examples of items of QIm, 4,3,2 (items in the series 1). 1 - Prepare a trip by reading about the remarkable sites, history, art treasures of the country you are visiting (literary). 2 - Create or paint a poster for a party or a show (artistic). 3 - Read a brochure on latest scientific discoveries or technical inventions (scientific and technical). 4 - Help a child with homework and explain lessons (altruistic). 5 - Save and prepare orders for customers in a shop in a period of great commercial activity (trade). 6 - Play tennis and train for competition (sport). 7 - Make minor repairs or installations (Practical, men). 8 - During the holidays, participate in certain activities like picking fruits, etc.. (nature). 9 - Get new members for a club or a movement you belong to (business). NB The item 15 of the B series, "Trying recipes or pastry" is practical (women).

The Evolution of Interests

See Tables 8 (boys) and 9 (girls). - The direction of change of interests in time is inferred from the comparison of means of two distributions of scores (1978 et 2004). - The significance of the difference is appreciated by the normal z test. - The importance of the difference of means is estimated as a percentage of the standard deviation of the initial distribution: d = (m2004 - m1978) / s1978.

Table 8. General interests (activities) of boys in 1977 and 2005: mean (standard deviation), z-test, significance and size of effect

Interests	1978 n = 553	2004 n = 224	z - Test	Significance	Size of effect
Nature	17.08 (4.75)	10.31 (4.84)	9.88	p< .001	**- 1,43**
Scientific	15.21 (4.93)	12.67 (4.87)	6.56	p< .001	**- 0,52**
Pratical M	7.81 (2.47)	7.34 (2.52)	2.37	p< .05	- 0,19
Pratical F	3.75 (2.20)	4.08 (2.12)	1.94	N. S.	+ 0,15
Literary	9.45 (4.12)	8.85 (4.09)	1.85	N. S.	- 0,15
Artistic	10.63 (3.84)	10.36 (3.66)	.92	N. S.	- 0,07
Sport	17.24 (5.77)	18.47 (5.28)	2.86	p< .01	**+ 0,21**
Altruistic	11.67 (4.15)	13.27 (4.14)	4.88	p< .001	**+ 0,39**
Trade	8.55 (4.77)	11.03 (4.69)	6.64	p< .001	**+ 0,52**
Business	9.39 (3.73)	11.64 (3.72)	7.63	p< .001	**+ 0,60**

Table 9. General interests (activities) of girls in 1977 and 2005

Interests	1978 n = 586	2004 n = 258	z - Test	Significance	Size of effect
Nature	13.76 (4.63)	10.40 (4.96)	9.25	p< .001	**- 0,73**
Scientific	10.13 (5.36)	7.35 (4.47)	7.82	p< .001	**- 0,52**
Pratical M	4.26 (2.43)	4.37 (2.44)	.22	N. S.	+ 0,05
Pratical F	5.47 (2.63)	5.36 (2.29)	1.02	N. S.	- 0,04
Literary	10.31 (4.78)	10.30 (5.19)	.03	N. S.	- 0,00
Artistic	12.62 (4.45)	14.80 (4.27)	6.74	p< .001	**+ 0,49**
Sport	12.05 (6.66)	12.68 (6.36)	1.14	N. S.	+ 0,09
Altruistic	17.39 (4.66)	18.22 (4.31)	1.06	N. S.	+ 0,18
Trade	11.03 (5.61)	11.70 (5.20)	1.68	N. S.	+ 0,11
Business	10.73 (4.84)	12.79 (3.79)	6.66	p< .001	**+ 0,43**

Major trends appear similar to previous (taking into account the significant differences at p <.01). Among both boys and girls, there are two cuts. Lower interest for science and technology is important: the order is one half of the standard deviation (for boys as for girls). The decrease in interest for nature is very important: the order is of one standard deviation and a half (boys) and three-quarters of the sd (girls). For both boys and girls, the increase in interest for business is important: about half of the standard deviation. According to the hypothesis about leisure, there are increasing artistic interests (the order is half of the standard deviation) in girls and increasing sport interests (about a quarter of the sd) in boys.

Specific data are added. For boys, there is an increase in interest altruistic (a third of the standard deviation) and commercial (half a standard deviation).

Differences between Genders

The significance of the difference in average interest depending on the types was estimated by d = (mF - moyG) / s with s = (nG.sG nF.sF +) / (nG + nF).

We therefore reported for 1978, the difference between the averages of two groups with a composition of the standard deviations of these two groups, rather than either of their standard deviations, the use of report the average differenc control group did not make sense here. The same procedure was followed for groups observed in 2004.

For each category of interest, compare estimates of differences in 1978 and 2004 and interpret them in terms of evolution of the difference (see Table 10). These differences increase for four categories of interests: literary, artistic, scientific and altruistic. They decrease for five categories: sport, male practical, female practical, nature and business.

Table 10. Interests of boys and girls: mean (standard deviation) difference, data for 1978, 2004 and evolution

	1978				2004				Evo
Interests	Boys (553)	Girls (586)	s	d	Boys (224)	Girls (258)	s	d	
Literary	9.45 (4.12)	10.31 (4.78)	4.46	+ 0.19	8.85 (4.09)	10.30 (5.19)	4.58	+ 0.31	+
Artistic	10.63 (3.84)	12.62 (4.45)	4.15	+ 0.48	10.36 (3.66)	14.80 (4.27)	3.99	+ 1.11	+
Scientific	15.21 (4.93)	10.13 (5.36)	5.15	- 0.99	12.67 (4.87)	7.35 (4.47)	4.66	- 1.14	+
Altruistic	11.67 (4.15)	17.39 (4.66)	4.41	+ 1.30	13.27 (4.14)	18.22 (4.31)	4.23	+ 1.17	+
Trade	8.55 (4.77)	11.03 (5.61)	5.20	+ 0.48	11.03 (4.69)	11.70 (5.20)	4.96	+ 0.13	=
Sport	17.24 (5.77)	12.05 (6.66)	6.23	- 0.83	18.47 (5.28)	12.68 (6.36)	5.86	- 0.99	-
Pratical M	7.81 (2.47)	4.26 (2.43)	2.45	1.45	7.34 (2.52)	4.37 (2.44)	2.48	-1.20	-
Pratical F	3.75 (2.20)	5.47 (2.63)	2.42	+ 0.71	4.08 (2.12)	5.36 (2.29)	2.21	+ 0.58	-
Nature	17.08 (4.75)	13.76 (4.63)	4.69	- 0.71	10.31 (4.84)	10.40 (4.96)	4.90	+ 0.02	-
Business	9.39 (3.73)	10.73 (4.84)	4.30	+ 0.31	11.64 (3.72)	12.79 (3.79)	3.76	+ 0.31	-

THE ISSUE OF RESPONSE BIAS

The observation of a difference between groups must be explained and the explanation can proceed from two main attitudes: one accepting *a priori* the reality of these differences, the other rejecting it, citing *a priori* biases. According to Vrignaud, we are in the presence of a bias when the measure highlights the differences between groups of subjects and that these differences can be correlated with the measured variable or variables [45]. In practical terms, both attitudes lead to evoke different processes to explain the observations.

Construct bias must be invoked "when the instrument does not measure the same latent variable across groups. For example, Vrignaud [45] refers to such a construct bias about "mechanical reasoning" which would imply a verbal encoding in girls and a spatial encoding in boys and thus show its "inconsistency". Such biases are unlikely to intervene, except to question the idea of unity of the process of determining preferences between 1978 and 2004 or between girls and boys. A similar criticism was made about the lack of realism of questionnaire items of interest relating to activities that young people have never practiced and will probably never practice: the question was important for students of low scholastic grade when the interest is measured using prestigious vocational titles. It should be noted that all of the proposed approach is based on the only assumption that the questionnaire, with very different degrees of realism, measures interests.

Bias due to material. "In the age of multimedia and Internet, what can still serve well (item 84)" listen to a radio documentary program on a scientific subject" or (item 39) "Building a transistor radio from drawings and sketches? ". One must answer logically and ask what other type of interests than scientific (and technical) these two activities could assess. Archeology ? One must answer with psychometric arguments: the corrected correlation between item 39 and the total level of scientific interests is + .53, this item is one of the most linked to this total score. As for item 84, its correlation item - total corrected is + .20 and is lower but this item is not linked more strongly to score in any other category of the questionnaire. The scale itself is consistent (alpha = .81). Unless the overall scale would be rejected, these items contribute well to assess scientific and technical interests.

Sampling biases are more important. We can consider two kinds of such biases. The first would include the selection of samples during two sessions: one does not know, for example, the geographical origin of those surveyed in 1978 and it probably differs from that of 2004. One can however recall that the variable (geographic origin) has not shown its importance in the determination of interests. One could argue the same for several other variables.

Other bias would concern the populations of 1978 and 2004. The proportion of young people who were in high-school (and eleventh grade) was low in the 1970s, about 20%, and is currently high, about 80%. Is the change of interests not due to the selection practiced at the end of compulsory school ? Students who had strong business interests could have been those who were not pursuing in high-school. That is why we observe an increase of the interest. The process could ply, but not alone: how to explain the decrease in interest for nature ? whereas, according to this principle, we would have expected the opposite ! You can find some answers by considering seventh grade students. In fact: whether now or thirty years ago, almost all of an age group attends the seventh grade.

Two interests questionnaires, one directed to boys (QIG 7,6,5) and the other to girls (QIF 7,6,5) were presented to students from seventh grade in 2004.

Examples of items. 1) Scientific interests: "Trying to redo at home the experiments made in your classroom during science lessons" (QIG, item 7), 2) literary interests: "Writing for the journal of your school or of a youth group" (QIF, item 17), 3) technical interests (QIG): "Remove an old radio to try to understand how it works" (QIG, item 9) and home interests (QIF): "Make and decorate a birthday cake (QIF, item 9), 4) artistic and manual interests: "Illustrating a book of science or poetry with drawings" (QIG, item 10), 5) social interests:" Being part of a group organizing youth meetings or outings together (QIF, item 10), 6) Trade interests: "Sell raffle tickets for the school party" (QIG, item 24), 7) interests for nature: "Participate in picking fruit for the holidays" (QIF, item 11), 8) sports interests: "Learn to swim or, if you already know, exercise in a pool" (QIG, item 12). The results were compared with those obtained in 1970 and 1976 in comparable studies. It appears (see Table 11), on the one hand, lower interest and scientific in nature and, secondly, an increase of artistic interests, social and business.

Table 11. Evolution (1970 - 2004) of interests of boys and girls in seventh grade: Evolution: increasing (+) or decreasing (-), F - test, size of effect

Interests	Boys			Girls		
	Evolution	F - test significance	Size of effect (η2)	Evolution	F - test significance	Size of effect (η2)
artistical	+	74,54 p < .001	.24	+	156,97 p < .001	.46
social	+	146,12 p < .001	.38	+	169,20 p < .001	.47
trade	+	525,32 p < .001	.69	+	582,27 p < .001	.76
technical	=			=		
sport	=			=		
literary	=			-	188,03 p < .001	.50
scientific	-	246,10 p < .001	.51	-	350,36 p < .001	.65
nature	-	358,03 p < .001	.60	-	111,38 p < .001	.37

Despite the overall adaptation of the interests and values of young people to new social realities, adjustments in the labor market should not be easier than before. In 2007, a report by the DARES entitled "Occupations in 2015" ventured to numerical predictions in the medium term [46]. Three broad areas may be considered.

- This report looks first at the occupational group of "industry technical engineers, computer scientists and researchers. "The needs are still growing" and states that "difficulties in recruiting may arise." It should be noted that young people in high-school are turning away from science (and technology). Although the number of scientific bachelors have increased, they have an increasing share of people (especially girls) who, through science, choose a path of excellence, but show no higher education project in this area. Similarly, by DARES [46] (ibid.) needs of IT professionals were 200,000 in 1985 to 450,000 in 2005 and will be 600 000 in 2015. Clearly the curves of supply and demand diverge.
- We have seen that "trade" and "business" interests are surging. This report explores the same area "of trade and sale" (pp. 137-140). For "management and technical sales," for example, demand should increase from 300 000 (1985) 450 000 (2005) 550 000 (2015). But at the same time, seller jobs should decrease significantly: 950 00 (1985), 750, 000 (2005) 650 000 (2015). In total, employment in this sector should not increase.
- Finally, "altruistic" interests, those activities and occupations where assistance is provided, as well as altruistic values do not mark a clear evolution. The same report

devotes 15 pages to the area of "aid and care for vulnerable people." There is the formula: "The development of these services will be important and represent one quarter of potential new jobs by 2015. And little improvement is expected in the medium term due to evolution of interests.

Aid practices guidance. Given the imbalances between supply and demand, the report offers several recommendations. More modestly, psychologists should continue to modify their practices to help people better adjust. Since Parsons (1909) [47] we gladly recall three pre-requisite to effective decision guidance: - self-representation, - representation of business and the world of work, - decision-making.

- Representation of self. The interests questionnaires were typically used to predict (statistically) the subsequent spontaneous choice, particularly among those expressing a strong indecision, are now used as an "aid to self-knowledge." Holland's typology is often used to encourage people to characterize stably to make informed policy decisions current or future. This usage is common and can be problematic if not accompanied by an effective incentive to overcome these current interests are only one example of development of the self among many other forms of development. We must advocate for open use assessments of interests and values, use that encourages to seek new experiences.
- Representation of businesses and the world of work. In secondary education, teachers and guidance counselors, psychologists struggle against gender stereotypes. Advertise teenagers in school that "occupations do not have sex" is: 1) draw their attention to facts that do not usually interest them, 2) get them to see that the reverse is - currently - true, 3) done at a point of development where they are supposed to build an identity (sexualized). Effects of interventions aimed at reducing gender stereotypes must be assessed because they may only activate stereotypes in this area.
- Process. Formulas as "the advisor must know how to be a dream breaker" or "choosing is renouncing" recall the distance between expectations and realities of labor market. The present observations indicate a recognition of the economic and social development and they also show that the distance does not decrease overall, and in some cases increases. This will require, for unattractive occupations: appeal to groups (national or migrants) who are not in a position to refuse any job ! help people, downstream, to accept activities they are not interest in, or not yet ! encourage persons, upstream, to broaden their conceptions of possible occupations. The first solution requires to compel people and the second to handle them ; so we hope that the third will be the most developped. All call for the development of the psychology of transitions: the first entry into the world of work would be (more than ever?) a difficult one.

REFERENCES

[1] Dupont, J.-B., Gendre, F., Berthoud, S., Descombes, J.-P. (1979). *La psychologie des intérêts*. Paris: P.U.F.

[2] Rokeach, M. (1973). *The nature of human values*. New York: Free Press.
[3] Larcebeau, S. (1967). Psychologie différentielle des intérêts: l'influence du sexe. *B.I.N.O.P.*, 23-3, 165-207.
[4] Holland, J. L. (1985). *Making vocational choices: A theory of vocational personalities and work environments*, 2nd ed. Englewood Cliffs, NJ: Prentice Hall.
[5] Super, D. E. (1964). *La psychologie des intérêts*. Paris: P.U.F.
[6] Tétreau, B. (2005). L'essor d'une psychologie des intérêts professionnels. *Carriérologie*, 10(1), 75-118.
[7] Roe, A. (1956). *The psychology of occupations*. New York: Wiley.
[8] Prediger, D. J. (1998). Is interest profile relevant to career counseling ? *Journal of Counseling Psychology*, 45, 204-211.
[9] Spokane, E. L., Meir, E. I., Catalano, M. (2000). Person-environment congruence and Holland's theory: A review and reconsideration. *Journal of Vocational Behavior*, 57, 137-187.
[10] Helkama, K. (1999). Recherches récentes sur les valeurs. In J. L. Beauvois, N. Dubois and W. Doise (Eds.), La construction sociale de la personne, chap.3. *Grenoble:* P.U.G.
[11] Roe, A., Ester, P. (1999). Values and work: Empirical findings and theoretical perspectives. *Applied Psychology*, 48, 1-21.
[12] Bourdieu, P. (2002). Le bal des célibataires. *Crise de la société paysanne en Béarn*. Paris: Seuil.
[13] Holland, J. L. (1996). Exploring careers with a typology. *American Psychologist*, 51, 397-406.
[14] Harris-Bowlsbey, J. A., Rayman, J. R., Bryson, D. L. (1976). Discover: A computer-based career guidance and counselor-administrative support system. *Fiels Trial Report*. Westminster, MD: Discover Foundation.
[15] Schwartz, S. H. (1994). Are there universal aspects in the structure and contexts of human values ? *Journal of Social Issues*, vol. 50, 19-45.
[16] Wojciske, B. (1997). Parallels between competence - versus morality - related traits and individualistic versus collectivistic values. *European Journal of Social Psychology*, 27, 245-256.
[17] Strong, E.K. (1943). *Vocational interests of men and women*. Stanford, CA: Stanford University Press.
[18] Larcebeau, S. (1982). Intérêts, valeurs et choix professionnels. *L'Orientation Scolaire et Professionnelle*, 11, n°4, 341-354.
[19] Botteman, A., Forner, Y., Sontag, J.-C. (1997). *Manuel du Relevé d'Intérêts Professionnels*. Paris: E.C.P.A.
[20] Lapan, R. T., McGrath, E., Kaplan, (1990). Factor structure of the basic interests scales by gender across time. *Journal of Counseling Psychology*, 37, 216-222.
[21] Ackerman, P.L., Heggestad, E. D. (1997). Intelligence, personality, and interests: Evidence for overlapping traits. *Psychological Bulletin*, 121, 219-245.
[22] Rolfhus, E.L., Ackerman, P. L. (1996). Self-report knowledge: At the crossroads of ability, interest, and personality. *Journal of Educational Psychology*, 88, 174-188.
[23] Larson, L. M., Rottinghaus, P. J., Borgen, F. H. (2002). Meta-analysis of big six interests and big five personality factors. *Journal of Vocational Behavior*, 61, 217-239.
[24] Prediger, D. J., Vansickle, T. R. (1992). Locating occupations on Holland's hexagon: Beyond RIASEC. *Journal of Vocational Behavior*, 40, 111-128.

[25] Rounds, J. B., Tracey, T. J. G. (1993). Prediger's dimensional representation of Holland's RIASEC circumplex. *Journal of Applied Psychology*, 78, 875-890.
[26] Betz, N. E. (2000). Self-efficacy theory as a basis for career assessment. *Journal of Career Assessment,* 8(3), 205-222.
[27] Donnay, D. A.C., Borgen, F. H. (1999). The incremental validity of vocational self-efficay: An examination of interests, self-efficacy, and occupation. *Journal of Counseling Psychology,* 46, 432-447.
[28] Betsworth, D.G., Bouchard, T. J. Jr., Cooper, C. R., Grotevant, H. D., Hansen, J. C., Scarr, S., Weinberg, R. A. (1994). Genetic and environmental influences on vocational interests assessed using biological and adoptive families and twins reared apart and together. *Journal of Vocational Behavior*, 44, 263-278.
[29] Vrignaud, P., Bernaud, J. L. (2005). L'évaluation des intérêts professionnels. *Sprimont:* Mardaga.
[30] Gottfredson, L.S. (1981). Circumscription and compromise: A developmental theory of occupational aspirations. *Journal of Counseling Psychology*, 32, 152-159.
[31] Huteau, M., Vouillot, F. (1988). Représentations et préférences professionnelles. *Bulletin de Psychologie*, 42, 144-153.
[32] Fouad, N. A., Dancer, L. S. (1992). Cross-cultural structure of interests: Mexico and the United States. *Journal of Vocational Behavior*, 40, 129-143.
[33] Lattimore, R. R., Borgen, F. H. (1999). Validity of the 1994 Strong Interest Inventory with racial and ethnic groups in the United States. *Journal of Counseling Psychology,* 46(2), 185-195.
[34] Day, S. X., Rounds, J. (1998). Universality of vocational interest structure among racial and ethnic minorities. *American Psychologist*, 53, 728-736.
[35] Flynn, J. R. (1984). The mean IQ of Americans: Massive gains. 1932 to 1978. *Psychological Bulletin*, 95, 29-51.
[36] Ourisson, G. (2002). Désaffection des étudiants pour les études scientifiques. Rapport de Guy Ourisson. www.education.gouv.fr/rapport/ourisson/ourisson.pdf.
[37] Bréchon, P. (2003). *Les valeurs des Français*. Paris: A. Colin.
[38] Hansen, J. C. (1988). Changing interests of women: Myth or reality. Applied Psychology: *An International Review*, 37(2), 133-150.
[39] Forner, Y., Ferrer, S., Le Veler, C., Thiéry, S. (2006a). Les intérêts professionnels des collégiens: l'évolution sur un quart de siècle. *Psychologie du Travail et des Organisations,* 12, 29-38 .
[40] Forner, Y., Lasne-Cordonnier, A., Mercier, C.-M., Salhi, H. (2006b). L'évolution des intérêts des adolescents à la fin du collège: 1978 - 2004. *L'Orientation Scolaire et Professionnelle*, 35, n°3, 337-362.
[41] Forner, Y., Duvergne, A., Gabet, H., Holl, D., Pollet, C., Willems, M. (2008a). L'évolution des intérêts professionnels des lycéens de classe de première: 1970 - 2005. *Pratiques Psychologiques*, 14, 223-236.
[42] Forner, Y., Jeannerot, A., Lasne, A. (2008b). Les valeurs des lycéens de classe terminale en France: quelle évolution en trois décennies. *Carriérologie,* 11, n° 3-4, 541-565.
[43] Larcebeau, S. (1974). Le choix professionnel d'élèves de classe terminale, Premiers résultats d'une enquête. *L'Orientation Scolaire et Professionnelle, 8,* 215-244.

[44] Larcebeau, S. (1978). Q.I.V. Questionnaire d'intérêts et de valeurs. Paris: C.N.A.M. / I.N.E.T.O.P., Service de Recherches.

[45] Vrignaud, P. (2002). Les biais de mesure: savoir les identifier pour y remédier. *Bulletin de Psychologie*, 56-6, 625-634.

[46] DARES (2007). Les métiers en 2015. Rapport du groupe "Prospective des métiers et qualifications". *Centre d'Analyse Stratégique*, janvier 2007.

[47] Parsons, F. (1909). *Choosing a vocation*. Boston: Houghton Mifflin

INDEX

A

B

C

E

F

G

H

I

J

K

L

M

Q

R

S

T

U

V

W

Y